OPERA

SAYERS

BY STEVE WRAITH

CW00658564

Mojo Risin'
Publishing Ltd

Published in 2020 by Mojo Risin' Publishing Ltd
www.mojorisinpublishing.com

Copyright © 2020 Steve Wraith
All rights reserved

The moral rights of the authors have been asserted

No part of this book may be reproduced or transmitted in any form or by any
means without the prior written permission of both the copyright
owner and the publisher
Unauthorised use of images within this book will result in legal action

British Library Cataloguing in Publication Data:
A catalogue record for this book is available from
the British Library

ISBN-13:
978-1-9163867-3-0

Cover design
David Stanyer

Layout
Neil Jackson, Media Arts
www.media-arts.co.uk

Printed & bound by PrintGuy
Proudly published Up North

This book is dedicated to the memory of Yvonne Sayers, Louise Smith, and Joanne Sayers.

I wish to thank Dave Beaney, John Wraith, Neil Jackson and Richard Haswell for their time taken proof reading, spell checking and legal advice.
I would also like to thank my family for their love and support.
Finally, thanks to The Chronicle photographers for permission to use some of their photographs.

Foreword

There is no better person to write a book about my family than Stevie Wraith. He has known me and my brothers for the best part of 25 years now and we all trust him like a brother. I was over the moon with my first book 'Tried and Tested' and I am sure this book will satisfy the curiosity the reader has about us bad boys.

I gave Stevie access to hundreds of my old files and depositions and he has worked his way through them to produce this book. I just wanted the chance for people to read about these cases from our side of the story instead of what many of you will have seen and read in the media.

The calibre of witnesses used by the police over the years to try and secure a conviction against me and my brothers beggars belief and will certainly open your eyes. This book dispels the lies and myths and highlights those who have used defamatory tactics to smear our good name.

Stephen Sayers May 2020

Stephen and Steve Wraith attending Joanne Sayers Funeral

When I sat down with Stephen Sayers over six years ago now to write his best-selling book 'The Sayers Tried And Tested At The Highest Level', we both knew that we would only be scraping the surface of the life and times of the 'Sayers' family. We felt that we needed to introduce you, the reader, to who Stephen was and give you an insight into what led him on his particular journey. So many lies have been written about Stephen and his brothers over the years that it was time to set the record straight and we certainly did that.

This book, although written from my perspective is the perfect companion for Stephen's book. Using my original notes from book one, transcribed from Rebecca Sayers' interviews and detailed research from original court documents, depositions, statements and audio recordings I guide you through the Sayers life and crimes and the various police operations launched against them such as Operations Camelot, Jester, Mescal, Negano, Plantagenet , Stirling, Erebus and Rockstar which saw Stephen and his brother Michael jailed for Blackmail.

I take a detailed look at the murders of Viv Graham and Freddie Knights and give you access to statements made about those particular cases. I also take a look at the calibre of witnesses used each time to try and secure a conviction.

This book is the most concise and definitive book on the 'The Sayers' brothers to date and will certainly open your eyes to the world in which we live in.

Steve Wraith May 2020

Stephen Sayers and Bez from the Happy Mondays and Steve Wraith

Chapter One: Born A Barrow Boy

Stephen Sayers was born on the 12th August 1965 at 7:30pm at 13 York Street to John Brian Sayers and Yvonne Bulman. He was a house birth and weighed in at a healthy 10lb and he screamed the house down. His Dad arrived to see the birth. He had just been released from prison after spending 9 months inside.

His family on his mother's side were very law abiding. Yvonne was highly intelligent and educated and worked as a civil servant running the Dole office in Swan House Newcastle for a number of years until her retirement. She was multilingual speaking Latin, French and German fluently. One of her personal hobbies and pastimes was to time herself and see how fast she could complete the latest Times crossword. Brought up and raised from a wealthy background, her Father Harry Bulman had owned a large and very successful demolition company and invested in quite a bit of property throughout Newcastle. When Yvonne and John were married, he gifted them a big house on York street that was bought and paid for as a wedding present. The Sayers brothers John, Stephen and Michael were all born here and spent their formative years in and around Elswick. John was born in Newcastle General hospital on 25th September 1963 and was the eldest of the three. Michael was the youngest and born on 30th august 1967.

Stephen had a mixed childhood. There are different shades to it but on the whole, it was interesting and happy. He would hang around the barrows with his Granny Liza and with cousins Philip and Frankie. He would stop at his Grannies overnight and then they would be up sharp for breakfast. It wouldn't be unusual for there to be about 20 people downstairs having a cuppa before the day ahead. Uncle Albert might be there before he did a day's graft on the suitcases selling Gold or watches and the like and there would be another cousin who would be selling scarves or something. Barrows back then were illegal and weren't legalised till the 80's so Stephen used to keep 'toot' for the Police coming. It looked less suspicious if a bairn was up a lamppost looking along the street and he got paid for doing it so he was happy.

During the six weeks summer holidays he would work on his Uncle Alberts barrow in town. Each day he would wake up with the noise of his granny shouting 'do you want a cup of tea son'. He would get washed and ready and would head downstairs where his Uncle Albert would be waiting. He would always ask him if he wanted to go to work with him and he'd say yes. Albert would always head for his stock before picking Stephen up and then they would walk from his Grans on Westgate Road to the Grainger market in Newcastle. There they would meet Stephens' Uncles Thomas and Georgie Kelly who were in the same game. They would compare stock and then they would make their way to the van which was parked in Nunn Street and started unloading the barrows. The 'Uncles' would head off with their stuff then Uncle Albert would put his barrow outside the Clock bar and they would get to work. They would flash the barrow up so it looked presentable to the customers. There was always something going on around that Grainger market. You could guarantee come half past ten in the morning Stephen's cousins Michael and Terry Pattinson would drive past on their way to work. They were like clockwork. They would always arrive but it was always very late. Some say they used to get to the market that late that they were actually arriving early for the following day but they just used to laugh and crack on. They had their own pace and nobody was going to speed them up. Uncle Albert would then put the price labels up and scales out and they would get to work. The good thing about working for his Uncle Albert was that he would always buy him a sandwich and a cup of tea whereas the other barrow boys would tell him to eat the fruit off the barrow. Those holidays were great times. Not a care in the world, working outside with the sun on his face, a full belly, a bit of money in his pocket and no bother with the Police. The only bad things with holidays is that they have to come to an end and he would have to head back to school.

Between the barrows there was a lamppost with a big wooden box leaning against it and Stephen would stand on it looking up and down the street looking for a particular tall skinny bizzy (police officer) whom had taken a personal dislike to all the barrow boys. The lads had to be on their toes when he was about. One of the family would give the word he was about and news spread quickly. This officer was so well known amongst the family because of his arrests that they disregarded whatever his name was or what he represented. He had one name and went by one name only 'the long streak of piss.' Over the previous four weeks he had arrested quite a few of the barrow boys for causing an obstruction while street trading.

On one particular day Stephen was catching the sun and keeping lookout when he suddenly caught glimpse of a reflection of this copper trying to creep up on them alongside a slow-moving van. Stephen shouted to his Uncle. "Hedge up". They couldn't see him so they carried on serving. So, he shouted Nitto (slang for stop), he's there behind the van it's the long streak of piss." Stephen took down the price signs removed the weights as fast as he could and gave them to his Aunty Silvia who had been watching the commotion from a distance. He had also grabbed the money that was in waste band pouches and his Aunty put them in her shopping bag. His uncles picked the barrow up and started moving away so by the time the 'long streak of piss' caught up and stopped them there was no prices up on the barrow and there were no weights so he couldn't prove that they had been trading. The hapless copper had been outsmarted by a 6-year-old child. Stephen felt like hero that day and he was given 10 bob for his troubles when he got back to his Granny Lizas.

The house was always full of family and close friends at the end of the day with money being counted and stories being told. There would be food for everyone, A big bowl of vegetable broth soup and some freshly roasted hot beef sandwiches were her speciality. There was nothing like a bowl of that broth after a cold day on the streets. The stories about various scams and crimes amongst the elders in his family on his Dad's side would fascinate him. The young Stephen was watching and listening and absorbing everything like a sponge.

Chapter Two: Learning The Hard Way

Stephen attended Saint Mary's School. He was not alone with twenty cousins also in the various classes. He wasn't a great scholar but did attend school. His home life was in turmoil and school seemed like the better option to him. His Dad had become involved with another woman and had been quite open about it. He was staying at York Street three days a week, Tuesdays, Thursdays and Sundays and the rest of the time with his other family. Like most men John Brian enjoyed a drink and could be violent depending on his mood.

Stephen would dread his Dad returning home. John ran a haulage business on Skinnerburn Road on the Quayside. He had six wagons that were all working for Scottish and Newcastle breweries and he would drive one himself. In those days the dray men who delivered the beer would have a drink in all the bars they delivered to so you could just imagine the state they got themselves into. Without a drink he was a loving caring Dad but the 'evil' drink changed him and he'd think nothing of laying into Stephen and his brothers and then Yvonne for trying to stop him. It would be the same story week in week out. Yvonne and the kids would be in the house having their tea listening for John to arrive.

On one particular night they heard John's wagon drive up the street and he was shouting out of the window. He was mortal drunk again so Yvonne sent the brothers bed to get away from him. He came in the front door and he was full of himself shouting for his tea. Michael was 4 Stephen was six and John was 8. They all got into the same bed and waited. They could hear him at the bottom of the stairs shouting, 'You little bastards where are youse?' They could hear their Mam pleading with him to leave them alone which would always end up with her getting a good hard slap. John was six foot and seventeen stone and strong as a bull through lifting beer kegs all day none of them stood a chance.They ignored him but could hear his voice getting more and more aggressive. They were all looking at each other and shaking with fear. They could hear Yvonne pleading again with him telling him that he wasn't being himself and that they were just kids. There was a silence then an almighty slap followed by a long scream. Instinctively the three boys jumped out of bed and ran down the stairs and started screaming at their Dad to stop it. He just saw this as sport and lashed out at the three of them catching them on their backs with his heavy hands making them cry. Tears on top of tears. In the melee they climbed onto their Mam who was also in tears and tried to protect her.
John stopped and looked at them all cowering and called them all 'Soft shites'. He walked to the kitchen and cracked open a bottle of Newcastle Brown Ale. It had gained the nicknames 'Mad Dog' and 'Wife Beater' around the doors, very appropriate. They all knew what was coming next. He called the three of them in and then started interrogation. It was always the same he would start off by saying that he would batter them if they went thieving. Then he would ask them, 'What do you say if the police arrest you?' They would just be standing

with their backs still red raw from the heavy-handed slaps of their Dad and tears streaming down their faces saying nothing. If one of them piped up and said 'We say nothing dad' that would be the trigger for the slaps to come raining down on them again.

Yvonne would always try to help her boys but she couldn't because John was just too strong. He would then grab them by the hair and drag them into the back yard screaming and pleading for him to stop. He would leave them in the backyard. It didn't matter if it was freezing cold, he would just leave them all there shivering. They would climb into the dog's kennel one by one and then huddle together for the night ahead. John and Stephen kept Michael in the middle to protect him and they covered themselves in old coats that their dog 'Judy' lay on. They were stinking. 'Judy' seemed to sense the boy's distress and snuggled into them to try and keep them warm. The boys then watched from the kennel through the window as John beat Yvonne. In his mind he thought leaving them to sleep in the dog's kennel would make them better people. There is no doubt that this trauma affected all three brothers deeply and they made a pact that when they grew older that nobody would ever lift their hands to them again.

One thing about Stephen and his two brothers is that they were quick learners. After their first night in the kennel they decided to give it a facelift. It was about 6-feet-long and 4-feet-wide and 3 and half feet tall. They put carpets and blankets in to keep warm for the next time they found themselves in there. Their Dad continued to discipline the boys using the kennel and would drum it into them all that in no circumstances do they say anything to the Police.

On another occasion their Dad made John go out of the room and placed a bottle on the chair and then told him to come back in. Stephen and Michael were just watching silently but were very suspicious. The script never changed it was always about how to conduct yourself when arrested in a police station and some of the tricks the police would do to fit you up. John walked into the room and he just stood there looking at this bottle on the chair and looking at Stephen and Michael for some kind of hint. They couldn't help him because they were none the wiser. John decided not to touch the bottle so his Dad give him a slap with the back of his hand and that was that. Test over. Getting the back of the hand rather than the face of the hand was a result.

Their Dad's training wasn't wasted. Ten years later three men robbed a newsagent in North Shields and the owner got squirted with a toxic substance. They got away with £10k and John and a friend called 'Cabs' were nicked for it. After getting woken in the middle of the night by two detectives John was taken to the interview room and when he walked in there was a bottle on the chair for one purpose and one purpose only and that was for him to pick it up and put his fingerprints on it. John had a flashback as the memory of his dad and his interrogations came flooding back and he knew instantly what was happening so he ignored the bottle much to the annoyance of the Police. The fact that John was wise to this tactic and the evidence for the defence given by a good friend of theirs Paul 'Ashey' Ashton helped to sway the case in the lad's favour and they got a 'not guilty.'

When Stephen turned 11 his Dad abandoned the family altogether and decided to move in with his other family. Even though this put an end to the drunken interrogations and beatings all Stephen wanted was his Dad back home. A few weeks after he had moved out, he saw him in the street and begged him to come home but he just ignored him. On another occasion he passed Stephen in his car with his new family and Stephen waved at him but he blanked him again and drove straight past him. He was devastated and could not stop crying. He felt so unwanted and lonely. So, what did John Brian Sayers unique way of fatherhood produce? I'll tell you. Three hardened criminals who feared nobody and who could tackle any situation. I will leave the final word on his Dad to Stephen.

"Do I hold a grudge against my Dad for the way that he treated us? Do I fuck…I love him. It was just his way of preparing the three of us for a life of crime and his teaching gave us the advantage over all of our rivals."

Chapter Three: The 8-year-old Millionaires

John Brian Sayers was a villain there is no getting away from it, and a bloody good one at that, but he did dabble in legitimate business now and then and he ran a very successful scrap yard in Newcastle. If you go along Skinnerburn Road now the land and the staithes are still there leading onto the vast River Tyne. Stephen started hanging around there and making a few quid from the age of 8 and was aware that his Dad had his fingers in a few pies and that more often than not he would be up to no good. He would always say to the boys that if he ever got nicked that they would need to get rid of anything he left in the house. As he would never leave anything in the house, I guess it was just a precaution but one which would serve the boys well.

One afternoon they got word that their Dad's cousin had been arrested. The boys knew the procedure. They checked the house over from top to bottom, but there was nothing there. 13 York Street was one of those old-style houses where downstairs, two rooms had been knocked into one and had glass doors separating them. Stephen was just going to sit down when he saw an old suitcase on the floor that they all must have missed earlier. He picked it up as John came into the room. He wasn't sure whether to open it or not but curiosity got the better of them and they put it on the table and unclipped the locks and slowly opened it. The suitcase was neatly packed full with money on both sides. Both boys' faces lit up at the find. As they were looking at each other Yvonne walked in and her face was a picture too. They all just stood and stared for what seemed like two or three minutes before the reality hit their mother and she slammed the suitcase shut and said, 'Ah me babies, me babies you can't see this, we'll all be arrested.' She threw herself over the case to protect the boys from it. Even at 8 years old Stephen had learned not to panic and with the help of John they managed to calm her down. They told her that they knew what they had to do because any minute the police could burst into the house. Within moments they had emptied the suit case in to an old army duffle bag and were off with it before the Police turned up and took them all away.

They headed up to the top of the street onto Elswick Road to the Cemetery. To most people it was just a derelict disused, vandalized and over grown cemetery but to the Sayers boys it was their headquarters and their playground and they knew it like the back of their hand. They were known locally as the 'Elswick Mafia Boys', a name given to them by the Police, and they had a reputation for thieving and violence which had been well established generations before. The grass was over four-foot-long in places which made a great hiding place. It is still the same today. Within minutes of them taking up their position in amongst the graves they saw the Police arrive at the house. They were there for a while searching high and low but found nothing. As they were leaving Stephen saw one of them staring straight over to where they were hiding. It was as if he could sense the boys watching him.

John Brian had been arrested along with his cousin and was being questioned about an unrelated crime. So it was down to the boys to look after the case like two little soldiers until there Dad came home. They remained camped in the cemetery but couldn't help themselves. They took another look into the duffle bag. "How much do you think is in there?" asked John. "I'd say a million dollars" Stephen replied. He put his hand in his pocket and pulled out a penny and chucked it on top of the notes. "There's over a million now" he said and they both started laughing. 8 years old and millionaires! They were never going to be 9 till 5ers after that were they?

The mandatory holding time when you were nicked back then was 3 days so they had to work out what to do with the duffle bag. There was one tomb in the cemetery which they could both move and, in the past, had used it to hide in when they were getting chased or playing games. They headed over to it and sure enough there was a gap just big enough for them to slide down into. They had some old rope in the bag and they tied it to the duffle bag and then slowly lowered it into the tomb. By this time, it was getting dark and as they were about to pull the cover back over the tomb, they could hear shouting and screaming and what sounded like somebody being chased into the cemetery. Without thinking they both slid their way down the narrow hole down into the darkness and pulling the grass and stones back over the top of themselves leaving a little gap. Sure enough a young lad was being chased by the Police but had dodged into the cemetery and managed to give the officer the slip. Stephen and John held their breath as they watched the size 12 boots pace up and down past the hiding place. Realising they had lost their suspect they headed off and the brothers breathed out a sense of relief. You might think hiding in an old tomb would scare the shit out of an 8-year-old boy but not Stephen. It was dark and dingy but secure just like the dog kennel in the back yard that their Dad used to make him sleep in.

As the days went by, they stayed in the cemetery and kept watch over the Tomb. It was crazy what you could witness on Elswick Road late at night. There was prostitution on the streets during the seventies and all the pubs were full. There was a lot of drunken violence and domestic violence. The boys armed themselves with a little stick and a kitchen knife each and they had their loyal dog with them too, an Alsatian, called 'Wor Prince' that would attack on their command. They were like little soldiers guarding that duffle bag. Three days and nights passed and then their Dad and his Cousin were released without charge and they handed the money back over. They expected a bit of praise but it didn't come. They did what they were supposed to do so why should they be thanked was their Dad's attitude. He said their true reward was in the experience of it all. About a year later some bloke got nicked in a foreign country trying to pass some of the notes over. Turns out they were forgeries; in fact, they were the best The FBI had ever seen!

Chapter Four: Where There's Muck There's Brass

Working in his dad's scrap yard was a fantastic experience for Stephen in many ways. At the time there was about six or seven people working there, Davey Mares, Derek Bennett and a man called 'Bimbo' to name a few. They all worked on the yard and Davey was in charge of them all. There was also another man living in the yard, he was John Brian Sayers friend called 'Big' Trevor Harrison. Trevor had nothing to do with the yard he just lived there in his trailer and he was a man to avoid when he arrived back to the yard after a full day on the drink.

On one particular occasion Stephen and 'Big' Trevor's son Jimmy Harrison were lying on a car bonnet skiving, with their shirts off and sunbathing with their music turned up. The perks of being the boss's son. They didn't hear the wagon pull up outside. They were rudely awoken by a sudden snap and then another. First Jimmy was in pain and a split second later so was Stephen. 'Big' Trevor was back and full of drink and had a horse whip in his hand. Jimmy and Stephen scarpered but unfortunately for Jimmy he got whipped again all the way down his back. The next day the lads would remind Trevor about what he had done. He simply saw the incident as part of the lad's education. He would say "Let this be a lesson to you two, don't let anyone sneak up on you, and remember that this is a business and people can steal off you, keep your eyes open at all times."

Stephen disliked school with a passion. He didn't see the point of attending lessons when he could learn first-hand about 'business' from his Dad and friends. He had learned how to break into and steal cars and was now an expert. Davey Mares used to drive the wagon to the scrap yard half a dozen times per day and he would always take Stephen with him. One day he pulled over and jumped out from his wagon walked round to the passenger side looked at Stephen and said, "Jump over your driving." Stephen looked at him with a big smile on his face and asked, "Are you sure?" Stephen was nervous. But he moved into the drivers' seat. He put a hat on and put a coat on the seat to boost him up to look bigger. He adjusted the mirrors as if he knew what he was doing then pulled away... and stalled. Davey encouraged the 11-year-old to take his time and concentrate. He started the wagon back up and took his time. He looked in the mirror and he was away. He drove with confidence and was buzzing as five minutes into his maiden journey he was driving over the Tyne Bridge, on his way to another scrap yard in Gateshead to weigh two vehicles in on the back of the wagon. This became a regular job for him and his confidence soared.

He continued to work at the scrapyard instead of going to school, and the young Stephen was more likely to be found dismantling a car radiator or gear box than doing an experiment with a Bunsen burner or learning about the Battle Of Hastings in a classroom. Stephen was more interested in learning how to steal vans and cars, and with a bit of practice he was becoming perfect at that. His Dad caught him on numerous occasions jiggling the locks on cars in the scrapyard and he used to ask him what he was doing. He would come out with a silly excuse but John Brian wasn't daft.

Stephen's good friend Fish Tams would go and see him all the time with bottles of pop and sandwiches. There was a close bond between the Sayers and The Tam's family as the older generation were good friends and all grew up in the same area together. Stephen would regularly lock the yard up and walk up Forth Banks to a pub that is now in the gay triangle which was formally known as the 'Kings head pub.' The pub was owned by an uncle of his Ward Smith. The bar would fill up with different characters. Most would be wearing bibs and braces from Scottish and Newcastle breweries. 90% of these men were from the Tams family. Old Giddy Tams was his favourite amongst them. Stephen always had a lot of time and respect for him and he did for Stephen.

One night his Dad asked Stephen how things were going in the yard and he replied not too good and that they needed some stock. It seemed to Stephen that he had lost interest in the scrap yard with the strain of the double life he was living. This saddened Stephen for a lot of reasons and he was concerned about the yard and was determined to keep it open, but with no stock to sell they had no money and things were not going to change. The scrap yard had been his life for the previous two and a half years and he had loved every minute of it so he was not prepared to let it close down without a fight. Secretly he was praying and hoping that if he got the scrap yard business back on its feet that it would get his Mam and Dad back together. He decided to put his plan into action.

Chapter Five: Learning The Ropes

During the mid-70s the price of potatoes rocketed. They went from being around £1 to £1.50 per bag then up to £10 per bag in a very short space of time. Whatever the reason was behind this, John Brian Sayers and his associates were looking to get a piece of the action. Stephen was spending a lot of time on Skinnerburn Road and his Dad asked his middle son to give him a shout if he saw a boat or ship coming along the river. On this particular day his Dad was in the forklift moving pallets of potatoes back and forth. Stephen was catching 40 winks and catching a bit of sun when he was given the fright of his life by the blasting of a ships horn. There was no need to shout for his Dad as he had already clocked the vessel coming down the Tyne. He drove straight over towards Stephen still on the forklift and parked it up and got off. As he stood next to him, he rubbed his hands together with anticipation of a few quid coming and under his breath he said, "Son I hope we can fit all this in this warehouse". The potatoes were getting loaded out of the cargo part of the ship by the ton. Stephen was just looking on in amazement as John and the lads got to work loading the pallets into the Warehouse. John took a break and told Stephen to head back home. Stephen was disappointed but did what his Dad said and John promised that his son could back the next day. Stephen ran home but decided not to tell his siblings about his adventure as they would want to join him the following day.

Stephen was woken up the next morning by a loud bang outside the house. It was 5:30am. He looked out the window and there was his brother John getting in the wagon with his Dad. Stephen was devastated. He headed back to bed and was woken a couple of hours later by his Mam for his breakfast and then school, but his mind was not on school. To avoid suspicion, he got ready for school, had his breakfast and then walked his Mam to the bus stop to see her onto the bus to take her to work. She gave him a cuddle and a kiss and told him she loved him. He smiled and told her he loved her too then waved at her as the bus went out of sight. He then turned straight around and headed back home. When he got back, he climbed up the lamp post above the front door and along the guttering at the side of the house and climbed though the bedroom window above the front door and he was in. He had no intentions of going back to bed though! He was on a mission. He went in the backyard got on Johns' chopper bike and went peddling down to the Quayside. He knew exactly how to get there. It took him half an hour or so and when he arrived, he was taken aback with the sheer quantity of potatoes in the warehouse. It was full to the brim and they were still unloading them. He could see his Dad from a distance, making arrangements with the man who was in charge of renting the premises. There must have been ten tonnes worth of potatoes in the main part of the warehouse and in the adjacent room it was full of chocolates, pallets and pallets of chocolates and cigarettes. There was a cigarette wagon getting unloaded as Stephen watched on amazed and excited.

This was a Long Firm in full flow and even at a young age he knew the mechanics of it. A Long Firm is when one business gets as much financial credit as they can and they keep doing businesses until it reaches its limits. Then whoever is running the scam puts in a big order and then don't pay. The company gets dissolved, stripped of all its assets and they move on with the procedure. It's a very profitable crime. It fascinated Stephen watching this take place and it all just felt so natural. This was preparing him for the criminal life that lay ahead of him.

The place was a hub of activity there were vans and wagons getting loaded with potatoes all morning. It may seem strange that a Dad would want his young lads with him on a job like this, but it was a way of life to John Brian Sayers. His boys were his little eyes and ears.

John Brian told his sons to count the bags of potatoes that were getting taken out and to make sure they got it right as these people would steal from them given half a chance. He was heading off but would be back in a bit to check on them. It was typical of the boys Dad. He drummed it into the boys that they should never trust anybody. The boys wanted to impress and because they were being so cautious it slowed down the process which caused a huge tailback with 25 vehicles waiting for potatoes and other goods. When their Dad got back, he started laughing he told Stephen lighten up and use his initiative. He pointed towards the length of the queue and he said the delay would cost them money. He got one of his mates to take over the job and then got Stephen and John together and walked them into the warehouse. He led them through the side door where there was a wagon reversing in where they saw one of their dads' cousins jumping out of the wagon.

Now the lads were loading cigarettes from the warehouse back into the wagon. They had to count how many went in. This wagon was due to take fifty cases of cigarettes and fifty cases whiskey. They counted them up, loaded them up, then counted them again. Everything was correct and the wagon was sent out. There was half a dozen of pallets of cigarettes and cigars and about forty or so bottles of spirits left that day and a pallet of Cadburys chocolates. The lads had never worked as hard. Stephen and John headed home with their Dad with the remaining stock. They were rarely rewarded for their help as their Dad would always tell them that the reward was in the experience. On this occasion though they were given the chocolate. They were the large retail boxes you would get from a cash and carry and they were all over the house. The lads couldn't get moved for them. Stephen opened a box and had a couple. Then he had a couple more. Before he knew it, he had eaten a box full. Well at least it was one less to trip over!

They all loved sport in the Sayers household and they were very competitive. Stephen was like all the other young lads his age, bang into football and he supported Newcastle United. As a player he was a left footed striker. The previous year he was the top goal scorer at his school, Saint Mary's and this year he was in the upper class and he was still the top scorer in the season. There were four boys who had been asked to go for trials at the time for Newcastle. There was Stephen and his best friends Bryce Moses, Anthony Cross and an Irish lad John Gibson.

The early trials went quite well for Stephen and the lads and they were called back on more than one occasion. Two lads called Jimmy Moses and another lad called Robert Cross could play a bit too and were also called back. One of the trials was cancelled and the next one was arranged for a few weeks later so Stephen and the lads had a bit of time to kill. The consumption of the chocolates had begun to reach new levels at York Street and Stephen was doing more than his fair share of eating them. When he turned up for his next trial a few weeks later he had put on two stone in weight. He had actually put on three stone since his first trial a few months earlier. He couldn't run or move fast enough and he got substituted after fifteen minutes which he recalls he was glad about as his shorts were cutting right in to him. It was the end of his dream of pulling on the Number 9 shirt and scoring at the Gallowgate End. He had eaten his way out of a goal-den opportunity.

The extra weight made him look older. He was only ten at this time but he looked about 13 or 14. On one particular day he was playing football in the Gem Park which is just off Westgate Hill. Stephen and his pals finished their game and he picked up the ball to head home as he was starving. The ball was a present from his Mam for his Birthday and was his pride and joy. As Stephen was walking along Elswick road bouncing the ball a big blue transit van pulled up on the road alongside him. The back doors and side doors opened and the police came jumping out and pinned him against the wall face first. It was the Special Patrol Group (SPG). It was their job to fight violence with violence wherever violence maybe. They were known for their heavy handedness. To Stephen they were just a group of bullies.

So, they had his face against the wall and they asked him where he had been and why he was sweating and who had been chasing him. Unbeknown to him a house had been burgled and they thought he had done it. Stephen had listened to what his Dad had told him. He gave them his name but would say nothing else. As soon as he gave his name he got punched in his kidneys and they proceeded to pin him down on the floor and put his arms behind his back, and began kneeing and punching him. Remember Stephen was only 10 years of age. Let that sink in. By now they were kneeling with all their weight on his body and the pain was unbearable for the young boy as he started to cry and wet himself. Suddenly they stopped abusing Stephen. One of them asked Stephen how old he was. Through his tears he defiantly replied "Ten".

There was a look of shock on the officers faces as the reality of what they had just done sunk in. They told him to get home. They got back in their van and drove off at speed leaving Stephen, still in pain, crying at the roadside.

15

As the pains started to dull Stephen looked up and saw his ball rolling down the hill. He sat there for a few moments pulled himself together and then went home and got changed. Stephen was more upset that the bastards had made him piss himself. If his Dad hadn't already convinced him that the Police were the enemy then this was a pivotal moment in young Stephens criminal education.

Chapter Six: Thievin' Stephen

It was a Wednesday night and Newcastle United were playing at home which was ideal for Stephen Sayers. The Sayers home on York Street is not far from St James' Park and you can hear the roar of the crowd when they score from the front door. Stephen wasn't going to watch his heroes play though. Instead he had a special bunch of keys from the scrapyard which he had kept in his pocket. He'd had his tea and then made his way along Buckingham Street. He knew where he was going and he knew what he was looking for. He had his mothers' shopping bag with his boiler suit in, a woolly hat and a pillow to sit on, not forgetting his gloves. He was looking for Ford cars to break into.

The scrapyard was short of stock so what he was looking for was the dirtiest scruffiest car that looked like it belonged in a scrap yard as many cars did back in those days. He found what he was looking for and there was a dozen or so in the same street. He walked up and down the street and looked at the cars one at a time. He opened the car boot of one car and removed the spare tyre placing it in the old banger that he was about to steal. He repeated this a few times. He got about ten spares, some hydraulic jacks and then he got in the first car and started it up in seconds. He drove the car down to the scrapyard. There was nobody around as he placed the stolen car in the scrapyard. The match had kicked off but with only 15 minutes played he had plenty of time and he wanted more cars.

As he was driving car number 2 into the yard a man pulled up and asked if he had a tyre for sale. He had driven up for the match and ended up with a puncture. Stephen pocketed £30 for a spare tyre and a jack and got a lift back off the man to his happy hunting ground. The bloke parked up and Stephen was back to graft. He repeated the same theft but in different streets. This time he took six tyres and another ford car. He used the same procedure with the tyres on the next vehicle but this time it was taking him longer to do as the two tyres he had got from out the boot of the car were badly. With the match about to finish he jumped into his latest vehicle and took it down to Skinnerburn Road then he walked home from there with a sense of self achievement.

His dad was spending less time at the scrap yard but it did not bother Stephen in the slightest as he knew the business inside out. As far as he was concerned, he could not wait for the next Newcastle home game. Saturday came round quickly and he was prepared for it. He had his Raleigh Grifter bike with him this time and he meant business. He managed to steal four cars that night all as rough as each other using the same procedure. As soon as he opened the car doors, he would put his peddle bike in the back on the seat and jump in the front of the car, and drive it down to the scrapyard.

Over the course of the next four weeks he stole over twenty cars and business was booming again and he had managed to make £1200 for the business. He used his initiative and spent a few quid on repairs to the wagon and brought in some staff who were getting £4 a day at the time. It had been about 4 weeks since his Dad had been to the yard so it was a surprise to see his him pull in. John Brian could not believe his eyes. He clocked the 'new' cars first and then the five customers waiting to be served. He walked over to Stephen and asked him what was going on? Stephen told him that he had 'been busy' and he handed him a large wedge of money. He took the money and then told Stephen he was closing the yard. Stephen was devastated but put on a brave face but worse was to follow.

After the yard was closed a few weeks later John Brian moved out of York Street and moved in with his new family. Stephen had tried his best to keep the family together but it was just not meant to be.

Chapter Seven: Bonner Night With the Elswick Mafia Boys

Living on Elswick road was one big adventure for the Sayers brothers. At the beginning of October all of the kids from Elswick used to get together and build their own bonfires. During the seventies there were a lot of empty buildings and they would strip them of wood using doors, beds, floorboards and anything else they could get their hands on. They were like worker ants carrying the furniture backwards and forwards. There would be a procession of about thirty people emptying these derelict buildings. But before all this started there was procedure, they had to go through which consisted of a group of the lads going down to Newcastle central station. Not the main entrance where the passengers go in at the front of the building, but at the back of the station where the parcels would get delivered and collected from. This area was always cordoned from the public as it was a hub of activity. The lads knew they had to wait until there was only a skeleton shift before they struck. The prize was a sack barrow. They were about 7-feet-long and 4-feet-wide and ideal for storing and carrying the ill-gotten gains from the houses. They would also take the 'Royal Mail' bikes from the station to siphon petrol from their tanks.

The 'Bonners' the lads built were huge and there was a lot of competition to see who could build the biggest one. In some cases, they would have the circumference of 2 three-bedroom houses and would be made up of 300 doors, a load of settees along with anything else they could find that would burn. It would be built up to the height of a lamp-post.

As bonfire night approached the lads took turn to guard their 'Bonner' as other gangs from Scotswood and Benwell would turn up to try and steal their wood before the big night. The Elswick lads were not daft though and they used the siphoned petrol to set fire to their rival's bonfires and would then escape on the stolen bikes. To John, Stephen and Michael as children witnessing this, it was very impressionable and all very exciting. Like a game of cowboys and Indians with one faction attacking another. With bonfire night getting closer the excitement was building and the boys would ignore Yvonne's cries for them to come home. She would be frantic until her boys eventually trudged home.

On another night the older lads had decided to cut down a disused telegraph pole to use as a centre pole for their bonfire. It was about half twelve at night when Stephen looked out of his bedroom window and heard a noise so he pulled the window up open and popped his head outside to have a look and he could see the older lads at the top of the street and they were going for the telegraph pole. The Sayers brothers were not going to miss out on this. Stephen woke John and they both dressed quickly and then shimmied down the lamp-post from a bedroom window. Michael was too young to accompany them. As they approached Elswick flats they started to see familiar faces, the lads were saying that when they had cut down the tall unused telegraph pole it had accidentally toppled over and hit an overhead electricity cable and this had caused a power cut in the area. Despite this mishap they had decided to all go together

19

along and carry the pole back and were cutting the wires off the telegraph pole to make it portable.

Stephen and John were just standing taking all this in. As they started to walk across Elswick road they saw a police van with its lights on and sirens blaring come screeching around the corner heading in their direction at high speed. They shouted bizzies! Everyone dropped the telegraph pole at the same time and ran. In doing so they left the telegraph pole in the middle of the road and the police van was coming at high speed in the dark towards it. The police van was on its way to another job and unaware of what the lads were up to. The van hit the telegraph pole at high speed and the driver lost control, the van leapt in the air upon impact and when it landed it swerved all over the road until it came to screeching halt as it hit a brick wall. Fortunately for the policemen they were not hurt they were just in shock. The Sayers boys were laughing uncontrollably. Some of the lads started shouting abuse at the police as they were getting out of the van all dazed. They quickly put two and two together and realised that this group were to blame for their mishap and started shouting and running in their direction.

Some of the lads had a head start and while Stephen was only little he knew how to run and he did, as fast as he could. He could hear the policeman behind him. He was about 50 yards away and catching him up. His little heart was beating. The policeman was shouting for them to stop while screaming for assistance on the radio. Stephen thought he was going to catch him until he felt a pull on his coat. It was John who put his hand over his mouth and dragged him into a bush. Four policemen ran straight past them. As the lads stayed still, they could hear the police saying what a beating they were going to give them when they caught them. The boys stayed there for about half an hour or so until the coast was clear and they managed to double back on themselves to get home as quickly as possible. The quickest and safest way for them to get home was to cut through the cemetery which suited them right down to the ground as they knew it like the back of their hands and nobody was going to catch them in there, or so they thought.

They started sneaking through but suddenly a torch shone in their direction temporarily blinding them. Stephen knew it was the police. The copper shouted 'stop' and charged towards them. The chase was on. The boys could see more torches being shone. There were three or four more coppers now shouting "There they are there is a couple over here". The boys kept running, jumping in the air as if they were skipping really high to stop the long grass getting tangled around their feet. They knew that the long grass would slow down the police not to mention the overturned grave stones. The police fell into the Sayers boys trap and the copper leading the chase slipped and then stumbled over a grave stone landing in a muddy puddle which give the boys enough time to jump over the cemetery wall and sprint down their Mams back lane and into the house. They wedged open the kitchen window and could hear the police shouting "I know the little bastards went down here somewhere; they are in one of these yards!" Stephen closed the window and he smiled at his brother John. Another day another getaway. A sign of things to come.

Chapter Eight: Behind Bars

As Stephen entered his teens, he started working with his cousin Joe Reilly and his Uncle Albert Sayers. In the early eighties about six months before the licenses were to be granted for the barrows, he was working just off the entrance of Eldon Square on Northumberland Street in Newcastle city centre. He was too big to shimmy up lamp-posts now so would stand at vantage points on street corners. He'd often keep toot with his other cousin Philip to make a day's pay. There was also a very good family friend named Michael Carr, AKA The Chocolate Mouse who had his lads working for him on Northumberland street selling the, at the time very popular, rubix cubes for £2.99.

The mouse was taking a fortune and he had a hedge of customers surrounding him all day every day taking fists full of money. He had two lads working for him doing the same job. A lad known as 'little legs', little Brian Stewart and his mate 'Tub' Downey. They were all doing the same job and got on well.

As time went by and Stephen got older, he was living more of a double life than ever before. He was thieving around the West end at night time and working the barrows in the day time. The life of crime was pulling him in like a magnet. Over the years he had received one hell of an education and as a child he was clearly influenced by those around him. Some people may try to justify why they fell into a life of crime. As far as the Sayers were concerned, they were prepared and bred for it. Let's not forget they had quite a few fighters and boxers in the family who not only taught them how to box and fight but they taught them how to fight with bad intentions.

One-night Stephen was hanging around outside the famous Dolce Vita nightclub in Newcastle. It was closing time and he could see a lot of the older Westenders having trouble with some people. A few fights broke out and there were men and women fighting at the same time. The very heavy-handed door men threw them out of the exit doors where the fight continued and grew much bigger until there was a free for all going on with over 20 people. At first Stephen just stood back and watched. He saw a certain Westender knock half a dozen people out with a hammer that he had found in a back lane and that seemed to have sealed the victory.

With the trouble over people started to head home. Stephen jumped in a car with four lads he knew including Tom Brayson and Joseph Ramsey. As they were driving though Newcastle, they saw a group of five or six of the people who were fighting earlier who were now armed with sticks. The lads pulled over and got out of the car. A few words were exchanged and an incident occurred where a man was hit in the face with a steel wheel brace. The police were alerted by somebody and arrived on the scene as the lads were leaving leading to a high-speed police chase through the city centre. They skidded off the road at high speed in this big ford granada car and drove straight into a big street lamp. Two young girls stood petrified on the other side of the lamp which had undoubtedly saved their lives. The crash had taken its toll on the lads too. Stephen had seriously sprained his two ankles so much that he couldn't put pressure on his feet. He tried to get out of the car but as he did a big copper slammed the door against his ankles. The driver (who was never caught) managed to get away.

The police took Stephen and his friends to hospital in an ambulance and for some strange reason took them to the RVI instead of the hospital in the West End. When they were ushered into A and E there was a man sitting with a big bandage on his eye obviously in a lot of pain waiting to be seen. The two girls from earlier were there too still in shock. They had waited for an hour to be seen when they could hear loads of noise and shouting from a group of people being brought in. Talk about bad luck! It was the people who they had run into earlier with the sticks. It then clicked! The lad with the bandage on his head was the guy who had fallen out with the wheel brace. The noisy group wanted to set about Stephen and his mates but they were in no fit state to walk never mind fight. The nurses saw what was happening and screamed for the police. They were about to take Stephen to the X-ray department when the police came running in at first thinking Stephen and co were victims. They were very heavy handed with them which is very amusing when you consider who the victims really were! Stephen, Tommy and Joe were all lying on stretchers. Stephen was convinced his ankles were broken, and there was a lot of blood coming from Tom's feet. Once the police assessed the situation, they placed them all under arrest. They spent a few more hours in A and E. Tom went in for an operation. Stephen came out of X-ray and they gave him some crutches. They were then taken to Pilgrim Street police station.

Stephen was struggling to walk and kept falling over. The coppers weren't helpful at all and would laugh as he struggled to get back up. One copper was barking orders. Stephen managed to reach the top of the stairs with this copper being really heavy handed. When he was at the charge desk in reception, he was using his crutches as support as he could put no weight on his feet. The copper made it quite clear that he was not a fan of the Sayers family. Back in those days his Dad and his uncle's reputation was bigger than Stephen, John and Michael's but that was all about to change.

As Stephen began emptying his pockets out with great difficulty the copper decided to kick his crutches away from him. He slipped and banged his head really hard off the counter. For a split second he went dizzy then he fell to the ground in agony. He thought he was going to fall unconscious. He heard the police laughing at him so he refused to stand up. He wouldn't give his name or date of birth to sign in to say he had been arrested. The Sergeant told the copper to help him up and put him on his crutches which he did. He also asked Stephen if he wanted a Doctor, but he declined.

Stephen would still not reply or give his name or address. He told the copper to take him downstairs and let him sleep it off. As Stephen was hobbling towards the stairs leading to the cells, he felt a hand on his back and he lost his balance and tumbled down the stairs. As Stephen reached the bottom the copper started screaming for assistance claiming that Stephen had attacked him. As his back up arrived Stephen heard one of the senior officers tell the bully 'Enough is enough you've had your fun.' After a few hours in the cells the three lads were charged with GBH with intent and were going to be up in court on the Monday. They were remanded for a week. After 5-6 weeks Stephen got judge in chambers and then 6 months later the trial started at Kenton Bar crown court.

There was no doubt that Stephen was going to the detention centre. He was 15 years of age. Joe and Tom 'brass neck' Brayson received two years imprisonment and Stephen received three months in a detention centre. On the bus on the way back to prison after being sentenced Stephen knew all the lads on the bus. His reputation was growing even back then. While he was getting off the bus all the older lads found it funny as they had done detention centres in their youth and they were yelling things like bob and weave with bursts of laughter.

As Stephen walked into the detention centre, he hadn't been in the building ten seconds and a screw spoke to him in a very disrespectful way so he replied in the same tone of voice. There was a screw hiding behind a mesh curtain and he hit him with the back of his hand right across his face. It hurt Stephen but he did not show it and turned and told the screw "Do that again and I will fuck you up in front of your friends," at which point the one of them approached Stephen and went to slap him again so Stephen blocked his arm and then grabbed it and bent it up his back turning him around and pushed him over a desk. There was nothing he could do. The other screw pressed the bell and then more screws ran in and pulled Stephen off. The Governor walked past and asked what was going and what had happened to Stephen's face and why was it red raw. Stephen told him that he had fallen over. Even though it was Stephen against the screws he would still never grass on anybody. The Governor moved on to his next meeting and the situation got resolved and Stephen did not get put on report. The screw seemed to respect him after that.

The purpose of a detention centre was a sharp short shock based on the first 8 weeks of basic training in the army but with plenty of sadistic brutality mixed in by the screws. Being brought up fighting on Elswick Road though Stephen fancied his chances with every single screw in there. There was no way in the world he was going to let these bullies intimidate him and there was not one of them that could have been half as bad as his father when he was drunk. These men just did not put fear into him at all

Chapter Nine: Big Brother's Not Watching You

Stephen was a free man again. It was 1984 and he was drinking in the Greyhound bar in Pitt Street in Newcastle. This was a bar his Dad would buy years later. The same bar where Stephen's cousin Frankie Donnelly tried to shoot his other cousin Frankie Slater. Stephen was working with a very good friend of his at the time a man called Michael 'Pie' Curtly. He was a diamond of a geezer and as game as a pebble. They worked well as a team. At the time thieving out of motor vehicles was a very common practice. People were far from security conscious and let's not forget technology in those days was way behind what it is today. Thieving was rife in the West End of Newcastle. There were a lot of people who would specialise in breaking into vehicles whether it be wagons, vans or cars. Most people used a piece of tungsten steel that had been drilled out in the centre, with a leather lace knotted in the hole. They would wrap the end of the lace around their fingers and swing it towards the car window which would shatter instantly, this device was called a popper and it originated on Tyneside. It was simple and very effective. You would always hear in the Greyhound of either someone having a good tickle, (good financial result) or comments along the lines of, 'I've got myself a good bookie or a florist'. This meant a villain somewhere had stumbled across some bookie (betting shop) which would be privately owned, probably in a discreet district of a different city. The bookie unknowingly would be getting some unwanted attention from a firm of bad lads whom had one sole objective, to get away with stealing his money. So, this man would unknowingly be educating a firm of bad lads on his every movement. A quiet eye would be kept on this creature of habit until Grand National day when the takings could quadruple if not more.

The day of the Grand National would come and everybody would be in place. The lads would be watching him leave, follow him to his destination which would probably be the pub. Once they entered the bar it was on. They would always leave their brief case with the prize in inside of the vehicle whether it be in the boot or under a seat and the lock would be jiggled or the window would be smashed.

The firm would normally consist of two or three people depending on the graft, one would drive, one would burgle the car and one would put a bicycle lock on the bar doors just in case he did come back out. The goodies would be discreetly removed from the vehicle and they would leave. The same technique worked with florists on occasions like Valentine's Day or Mother's Day as the takes would be considerably higher. They were all full with cash in those days as credit cards were not nearly as popular as they are today. What would also happen to the florists would be that a very large order of flowers would be made for delivery where there was a little walk to the house door. If there was two people delivering you would put an order in up to £100 as in the 80s that got you armfuls of flowers and at least two people had to carry them and that left the vehicle unattended. That was when the gang would pounce and grab the cash, and that's how it worked. There was also quite a few ramraids going off at the same time around the City. Cigarettes were always a favourite. Anything else didn't come near, yes there were videos to be had but they would normally get broken in the crash.

There was a warehouse in Gateshead full to the rafters of cigarettes. The fire exit doors naturally led onto the street. The lads stole a little escort van and reversed it down a little narrow path and rammed the fire exit door. The door smashed off the hinges and fell to the floor inside of the premises, but the alarms did not go off. The lads did not waste a second and they immediately proceeded to load these cartons of cigarettes that were holding 6000 cigarettes at a time to the back of the vans. There were no alarms ringing but the lads were still going against the clock and they had to leave.

They got back to the slaughter (safe house, distribution point) where one of the lads kept repeating that the bells didn't go off and nobody had seen any flashing lights inside which was strange as it is usually the procedure.

When the lads where leaving the warehouse, they pulled out quickly and the back door was open causing two large boxes of cigarettes to fall out of the back door. A man was driving up the road and he knew these people and he knew exactly what they were doing. Stephen spoke to this man much later on and he told him "Stephen I couldn't believe it. I didn't have a penny to my name and I came across two boxes of cigarettes. 6000 cigarettes in each box in the middle of the street. The roads were dead it was a Sunday and not a sinner on the roads, so I picked them up and put them in my car. I could see the warehouse was open and there were no alarms going off, not even a light, so I thought I'll have a bit of that!" Three or four firms turned up at that warehouse that night and took over 5 million cigarettes.

It was common practice in the Greyhound bar to hear criminal stories like that. There was a good community spirit in the bar and everybody was anti-police. Stephen and his pals would constantly get up to mischief and humour always played its part. Stephen was 18 years old by now and on this particular occasion he was with Fish Tams, Pie Curtly and Charlie Huggins. It was sunny and far too hot to go thieving. But not too hot for frisk (fun). They had just spent their last few quid on a packet of cigarettes, some tab papers and matches, fuel, pop and sweets. They came out of the shop at the petrol station, and walked straight behind the building where they found an automatic car washing machine. One of the lads pulled out the spare boxes of poppers that were still in the tray. They opened them up and shared them out and started tying them on the threads on the wheel of the giant buffers that washed the sides and top of the vehicles. They even super glued them on with the super glue that they had bought in the garage and melted them with a lighter so they didn't come off. Now they just had to wait and see who was going to turn up.

They sat at the side of the petrol station, parked up next to other cars so they didn't look out of place and had a good view of the shop and desk but could not see the carwash. A couple of hours went past and they were still sat with the windows closed with the car full of clouds of marijuana smoke. Then in pulled a big man in a suit driving a new, but dirty jaguar car. The lad's toes started to curl as they realised, he was not there for fuel. He got out of the car and bought a token for the carwash then got back in his car correcting his sun glasses in his pinstriped suit. The lads were stoned as they watched the man start to drive though the carwash.

At this point the lads couldn't see properly as the car had filled with smoke so Fish opened the windows and it started billowing outside. No sooner had he opened the windows then the lads could hear the noises of the poppers hitting the Jag, BANG, BANG!! Over and over again, non-stop. They all looked at each other and started laughing uncontrollably. The poppers had kicked in and some, but they didn't expect it to go as far as this. As the buffers touched the car windows, they shattered instantly sending the glass into the car. Every window front back and the sides of the Jag were shattered, scratching the car to bits. The horn of the car was going off and the man was revving the car trying to get out but there was no way out. With the size of the giant car buffers surrounding the car and the fact they were moving quite fast it made it impossible. Followed by high powered jets of water and bubbles.

Next there was a loud sharp grinding of metal scraping against metal which was really loud, but not nearly as loud as the man himself who was screaming "STOP THE FUCKING THING". As the last buffer raised up, he drove out screeching his back wheels spinning to the front of the garage. He didn't have one window left in the car, it was scratched to bits and the inside of the car was flooded and completely full of foam. The lads could not see the man until he got out and he got out very quickly and started screaming to the high heavens. There was an awful lot of steam coming from the man as he ripped his jacket off and slammed it to the ground. He was in pain and beetroot red and soaking wet. He now had his eyes set on the cashier and he marched straight into the shop at the garage and grabbed the cashier by the throat and dragged him straight over the counter and threw him on the floor. The lads were doubled up with laughter.

Fish conscious of the fact that the man and cashier would suss their involvement tried to start the car but it wouldn't start as they had been there for hours playing the radio and the battery had died so the lads still stoned decided to get out and push. The car started to roll as Fish tried to bump start it but still no joy. With the lads still giggling and laughing the car rolled and then stopped on Charlie's foot. Charlie let out a loud scream and shouted "GET THE FUCKING CAR OFF ME FOOT YOU SILLY BASTARDS!"

In all the commotion with Charlie's foot they totally forgot about the angry man in the garage who had now got back in his car and driven past them at speed. The cashier who had picked himself off the floor and was nursing a bust nose shouted "You lot fucking caused this!" Fish by this time had managed to get the car going and Stephen and the lads drove off howling with laughter.

Not long after the little carwash incident they found themselves in the same car driving though Newcastle, when they saw a wagon with its back shutter halfway up and they were loading boxes of cigarettes into a newsagent. There were two men, one driver and one passenger making quite a few trips in and out of the shop. The lads waited to see if they were bringing any cash out with them. They then followed them to the next drop. They pulled onto Grainger Street in Newcastle's City centre and unloaded more cigarettes into a shop and left the shutters halfway up again as they went back and forth.

They were loading about a dozen or so into the shop at a time that they already had keys for and Stephen saw them open the shop up and then close it. He got out of the car and walked past the wagon and had a good look in. It was packed full of cigarettes. Fortunately for him the delivery man had removed the padlock and placed it in the back of the wagon until his return.

When he returned there was no padlock because Stephen had taken it knowing that he now couldn't lock the shutters. The delivery men had a puzzled look on their faces as they tried to work out where they had misplaced the lock. It was a waiting game for Stephen and the lads now. They were wondering where the next drop was now. They didn't have to wonder any longer as one of the drivers shouted over that they would have to get off to their next drop in Leeds. The lads didn't have enough petrol in the tank or the patience to go to Leeds so they needed a plan B.

So, they started driving down the Bigg Market but were stuck in slow moving traffic right behind the wagon. They knew they only had a certain length of time as the wagon had only stopped until the lights changed again. Stephen and Pie jumped out of the car and headed towards the wagon as casually as they could. As they approached the wagon, they pulled the shutters up ready for the 'jump up' which is where you jump up at a vehicle and take the valuables. They jumped straight in and started moving a lot of cigarette boxes to the back door. They got four or so in the car boot and went back again to get some more. They got a dozen boxes in total of which amounted to 70,000 cigarettes. The car was full.

Charlie then waited till the wagon drove off. They followed it to the lights and then turned left as they turned right. They drove in and out of the cars to get out from the city centre as quickly as possible and headed straight to the West end. They headed to a shop that belonged to a good friend who bought the cigarettes straight away. They opened the back gates and parked the car in his back yard, closing the gates behind them and then moved the cigarettes into his premises. Pie and Charlie then got rid of any evidence. Remember there were no DNA tests in those days. Stephen also had a friend at the time that had his own scrap yard and he could call him to collect any car used in a crime. Sometimes these cars had been burned out depending on the severity of the crime or link but either way for him it was valuable scrap. The 'jump up' was a good tickle for Stephen and the lads They cashed up for a grand a piece from the cigarettes. They put £100 back into the kitty to buy a new car which were ten a penny in those days.

They headed to Wheelers night club in Gateshead that night which was located just over the Tyne bridge where the Hilton hotel is now. They had new clothes on their backs, money in their pockets and women to chase. Life was good. It was a big daring adventure and the more daring you were the bigger the prize. It was how they made a living back then.

Stephen and his pals did not specialize in one particular crime. They were like pirates but with more scruples. They took anything and everything they wanted. They enjoyed it but most importantly were very good at it.

Chapter Ten: The Missing Cross

During the mid-eighties Stephen had hit his 20s and you could say he and his brothers were making the transition from boys to men.

Stephen was at his Mam's house in York street having a cup of tea with his good friend Tom Brayson one day when John turned up to see what they were up to. They left York Street and went to the pub that used to be at the top of the street called the 'Blue Man'. They were in there for about 15 minutes before Stephen went to the toilet. He could not get in as someone had their back to the door so he put a bit of pressure on it. He could hear voices and a few heated words and all of a sudden, the door opened and he heard a voice saying 'Stephen I'm sorry I didn't know it was you.' This fella had something in a bag which looked very suspect which in his agitated state he dropped on the floor. It was a white engraved ivory cross about a foot long.

Stephen asked him what it was and this man proceeded to tell him that it was a religious artefact that had been stolen from St Nicholas Cathedral in Newcastle. Stephen was disgusted that anybody could stoop so low. He had a few choice words with the low life and let's just say there was a decision made and he left the toilet with the cross under his arm.

Stephen showed John and told him what had been said and John suggested they visit their solicitor who at the time was Rowe and Scott. They then contacted the Priest at the church which was across the road from the solicitor's office. Then they went across to the church and met the Priest and they passed the bag over to him. He checked the contents and he could not thank them enough for returning the cross.

The local newspaper were there to capture the occasion and the Priest was only too happy to write a letter of commendation for the Sayers brothers whom 'the city of Newcastle owed a huge debt.'

The Sayers brothers liked the sound of that.

STATEMENT OF CANON PETER STRANGE

I, Canon Peter Strange of the Cathedral of St Nicholas, Newcastle upon Tyne, state as follows:-

In 1986 there was a theft from the cathedral, when the Bishop's Crozier was taken from the cathedral. The Crozier was presented to the cathedral over one hundred years ago and is of great value to not only the cathedral, but the City of Newcastle upon Tyne as part of its heritage.

The theft of the Crozier was reported to the Police, but before they were able to assist, the Crozier was returned undamaged by Stephen Sayers, who had retrieved it from a man who was trying to sell it.

The cathedral and indeed the City, as well as the population of Newcastle, owed and indeed still owe a debt of gratitude to Stephen Sayers for his help in returning the Crozier.

Signature .... *P. R. Strange*

P. R. STRANGE

Statement of Canon Peter Strange of Newcastle St Nicholas Cathedral

Chapter Eleven: Toe To Toe With The Sayers

In the Eighties The Sayers would often go to a fun pub named '42nd Street' in Newcastle. The pub would be packed from 4pm till 8pm most nights then the crowd would die off. They used to run a great happy hour on trebles.

On this particular night Stephen Sayers was celebrating a close friend's birthday Richy Hall. The alcohol was flowing and there were a few people worse for wear. There was about eight of them in total including Stephen, cousin 'Legs Lennie' and his other cousin Tony Sayers.

The lads left '42nd Street at 9pm as it was quiet and as they headed out to another bar the fresh air hit them and took them to another level. It took them about two and a half hours or so of staggering to arrive at 'Walker's Nightclub' that was only about a quarter of a mile away. The walk had helped them sober up a bit and inside Stephen was talking to his Aunty and Uncle who were with a group of friends. Out of the corner of his eye Stephen noticed some kind of trouble. He saw two big men that looked full of themselves pumped up full of steroids about 18 stone and 6ft 2, pointing their fingers and looking very aggressively towards his cousin Tony Sayers and another good friend Derek Tams. Stephen then saw the roid head storm out of the club so he thought nothing more of it. Tony was not a violent or dishonest person he was quite the opposite. Nevertheless, he was a Sayers and he was loyal and more like a brother then a cousin.

It turned out that the roid head (Steroid taker) had approached Tony and Derek and started with them for no reason. He kept saying 'Do you want to fight me; do you want to fight me?' Derek said no at first but the lad just wouldn't leave it. So, when Derek finally agreed to go outside with the man, he marched ahead of him tearing his shirt off ready for battle clearly having some sort of roid rage. Derek didn't bother going after him. Instead he headed to the bar to get another drink.

The would-be attacker must have stood waiting for about ten minutes before he realized that he was being stood up. The roid head came bounding back into the club again and this time approached Tony and demanded to know where Derek had gone and why hadn't he come outside. Tony told him he didn't know and turned away from him. So now the big roid head and his friend started on Tony and started asking him if he wanted a go. Tony calmly faced the mug and said look mate I really don't want to fight you…but…I know somebody that will. Tony then lead the two lumps to the other side of the club where Stephen was enjoying his night with not a care in the world. Tony pointed over to Stephen and said "That's' him there mate." All of a sudden this big mug has put his big finger in Stephen's face shouting at the top of his voice, " Do you want to fucking fight me?" Stephens' first reaction was to laugh at him. 'Is this a joke?' He asked him. The man poked Stephen really hard from the side with his finger in his cheek.

This was like a red rag to a bull. Stephen head butted him straight in the face and then reigned punches into his body winding him. The lad managed to recover and put Stephen in a head lock and tried to roll him like a wrestler. He managed to pull Stephens head towards him and had his full nose in his mouth. He did not realize he was creating a biting frenzy that was about to backfire on him. He started to bite hard on Stephens nose. Stephen managed to punch him in his windpipe and he released his nose but now the lad had bitten Stephen again this time on the arm hurting him. His friend also tried to get involved by restraining Stephen. Tony then jumped in and tried to wrestle the pair of them off his cousin. He hadn't had a fight since junior school but was as game as a badger. By now it was looking like a war zone. In the melee Stephen managed to latch on with his teeth to the closest thing he could find which unfortunately was Tony's stomach just below his rib and he started biting like a Pit Bull would and he wasn't letting go for anyone. He thought he was getting one over on the two lads but the screams he could hear were Tony's! When he realised his mistake, he let go!

One of the lads then kicked Tony in the chest causing him to grab the man's foot and he ended up pulling the man's shoe off. Tony threw the shoe behind the counter with temper and smashed the optics making the bar staff duck for cover. He then kept a hold of the man's leg and pulled his sock off. He was screaming towards the man's foot still obviously in a lot of pain from Stephen biting his stomach and started to bite the man's big toe as hard as he could. The screams were blood curdling! You'd think he was getting tortured. Stephen managed to break free from the other bloke and started to boot him over and over again whilst Tony had lock jaw on this bloke's big toe. The door staff arrived to break them up and a few of their mates were on the scene too. Tony and Stephen dusted themselves down and looked at each other and then laughed, looking back it was the funniest scrap they had ever had.

On another occasion in Walkers Stephen ran into the SPG officer who had beaten him as a 10-year-old and caused him to lose his football. As soon as he clocked Stephen he ran to the toilet and locked himself in a cubicle and started screaming he was sorry and that he wasn't a policeman any more. Stephen did not touch him. In Stephen's own words, "I just watched him scream like a woman in labour as I give him a piece of my mind. He had showed his true colours. He hid behind a uniform; without it he was simply a coward."

Chapter Twelve: Hard Times And Humour

The sun was beaming down on the car windscreen as Stephen and Michael 'Pie' Curtly drove down Diana street. They were on their way to the Greyhound Pub in Newcastle's West End. Stephen's window was open when he heard someone shouting his name but he could not see where it was coming from until he turned around. He saw a small blue Escort van behind them with two of his friends in who were telling them to pull over. So, as they stopped, they pulled alongside them and said "Nitto it's our graft," then drove on. Stephen and 'Pie' looked at each other and their initial reaction was confusion as to what they were talking about. It then clicked that the car they had been following must have been carrying cash or valuables and the lads thought they were trying to nick their graft.

They let the traffic pass then they pulled out and carried on driving along the street turned right and they were on Pitt street and heading to the Pub. As they drove down there, they saw their two friends again in the blue escort van double parked alongside a blue Morris Ital Car. A deluxe version of a Maurice Marina. They were nice cars but easy to break into. Anyone with a house key or a piece of metal could get into them within seconds. Stephen and 'Pie' pulled up a couple of cars behind them and watched as their friends jumped out of the passenger side. They took a second or two to put a blade into the lock and jiggle it. The car boot opened and he removed five big boxes of cigarettes which was the equivalent to 30,000 cigarettes, which would be about 150 sleeves today. All in all, a good little mornings thieving for the two lads. Stephen and 'Pie' reversed back up the street and left the area before they got a pull. They were gutted that they had missed out on this piece of work but wouldn't miss out again. The cars all had a sticker on the back with the company logo on so they knew what to look for.

By now the lads were both hungry and the petrol light was flashing and they needed petrol immediately so they found themselves driving around Percy Street in the City centre to a multi-story car park. They drove around the carpark until they found what they were looking for. A big Datsun. It was brand new and the occupants were just getting out so they pulled up at the side of them. Then they casually got out of the car and opened the Datsun's petrol cap with a blade. They then put a tube into their petrol tank and started siphoning the petrol from the Datsun into their car. With a half full tank, they were now looking for something to fill their bellies to stop them rumbling.

Stephen clocked someone carrying some shopping bags from Marks and Spencer food hall. They placed them on the back seat of their Range Rover and then locked the doors and headed off. Stephen watched them leave and then headed over to the car. He jiggled the lock open in seconds and looked through the bags and removed the food that needed to be oven cooked. He now had two bags full of goodies and a packet of napkins that he had found next to them with two bottles of sparkling Lambrusco. He casually got back into the car started it up and drove away towards Leazes Park which was a five minute drive from the City centre. The lads drove into the Park and parked the car up. It was a lovely summers day. They could not have chosen a better day for a picnic. They found themselves a lovely little table in the sun where they placed their spread out and got stuck in. They sat there for an hour or so until some students decided to join them at the table. Their bellies full it was time to make a few quid so they left the remainder of the food and wine with the students, and they were delighted with it.

As the day went on, they didn't seem to get any further forward so they called it a day and decided to meet up later for a few pints and a couple of joints. In those days they always used to carry a police radio scanner with them. They were using scanners in Newcastle years before anyone else in the country. In those days the Police were always very naive on the radio. They didn't realize who was listening in and would give away a lot of information. That night the lads ended up in a flat in the West end worse for wear after smoking and drinking for a few hours. They decided to listen to the Police radio scanner just to pass the time and kill their boredom. They were listening to different radio transmissions and this one came over from a Mr and Mrs Jackson from Gateshead who were reporting a burglary that was taking place across the road in a cash and carry from where they lived. From what Stephen could make out it was on top for the lads carrying the crime out as the Police were on route.

As Stephen and 'Pie' were such good criminal Samaritans they decided to give these lads a heads up so they could get away. Not only did the police give this couples name out but they also give out their address. So, Stephen called up directory enquiries on 192 and gave the operator their name and address and asked for the phone number which they gave him. Now for some fun.

On Tyneside there is a slang word used for leaving a scene and it's 'nashing'. When a criminal is active and wanted their partner in crime to leave immediately, he would give the shortened version which was 'Nash' which means run. So, Stephen phoned up Mrs Jackson who reported the burglary and had been back on the phone three times since giving a detailed account of what was occurring at the cash and carry.

She obviously thought it was the Police responding to her emergency call that she had only made moments earlier. The first thing she said when she answered the call was and 'about time too' in a well to do voice. She had obviously been drinking. Stephen asked her "Can you see these people?" She said "Yes we can see them, there are three of them and they are trying to force the door open with something that resembles a crow bar".
So, Stephen then asked her where she and her husband were situated in the house. She said they were both looking through the upstairs bedroom window and that the thieves were no more than 30 yards away. So, he explained to her

that Officer 'Nash' was on scene but was having difficulties with his radio. She had taken the bait and asked what she could do to help. She was loving it and was now sharing the telephone with her husband Mr Jackson and they were both now speaking down the phone. Stephen told them to open their bedroom window and switch on their bedroom light. He told them it was their job to scare the burglars in the direction of Officer 'Nash' so they agreed.

Stephen was struggling to keep his laugh in as he heard them open their window with the bedroom light on and shouting at the top of their voices 'NASH!' Stephen managed to pull himself together and then ask Mrs Jackson what was happening. 'Well they are just staring at us officer' she said. The lads by this time were creased and laughing uncontrollably. Stephen reminded them that Officer 'Nash' was in place and he was waiting for the burglars to be chased in his direction. The Jacksons were then asked to repeat what they were about to be told and to do it word for word. Mr and Mrs Jackson said they would do anything to assist and help. So, Stephen told them to hold the telephone in one hand and go to the window. They agreed and confirmed they were at the window. 'We haven't moved and neither have the burglars' said Mrs Jackson. All of a sudden Stephen heard them screaming at the top of their voices 'We have phoned the Police and they are on their way. NASH! NASH! NASH!" This did the trick and the lads were off. Villains 1 Police 0. The lads carried on smoking that night and couldn't stop giggling.

They still had the scanner on and had been aware of a certain individual that had been repeatedly contacting the Police and reporting anything and anybody. He would report people who he thought were drink driving or innocent people just walking home minding their own business. Some people dream of winning the lottery, some dream about being a star, but this man dreamed of being a crown prosecution witness. He was ripe for the picking and Stephen had heard his name come over the radio reporting things for quite a few weeks now. He seemed to have a bit of an attitude as well and you could tell that even the Police were sick of his constant phone calls.

This night Mr Bell's name came up at least three times in the space of half an hour, reporting different incidents that he believed were going to happen. It was time to teach this bloke a lesson and for once Stephen and the lads were going to do the Police a favour. One of the other lads dialled 192 and went through same process that they had gone through with the Jacksons.

The call was made to Mr Bell's home and within seconds it was answered by a very abrupt and aggressive Mr Bell who obviously thought that he was speaking to the Police who were returning his calls. He demanded to know why they had not been responding to his tip offs and why no arrests had been made. The response from one of the lads was simple. "Because we are fucking sick of you!" This certainly fuelled the fire, Mr Bell screamed down the phone "How dare you speak to me like that, I have assisted you for over twenty eight years now and I have not had so much as a thank you it's disgusting!"

Stephen's mate had him on a hook. "Have you not heard of insurance companies, sir? We have CID to investigate these crimes. This is what keeps us in a job, so we have to turn a blind eye now and then."

Mr Bell was foaming. "I am reporting you what's your number!"

The calm reply to Mr Bell was "Well if you do bonny lad we have your address and there is a few of the lads going out on the drink for the derby on Sunday and we will make it our business to issue a search warrant for your home and you will gain first-hand experience of the finest police brutality" One of the other lads shouted "I'll personally get you three year in the jail for the drugs I'll plant in your house you nosey old bastard"

Mr Bell couldn't believe what he was hearing and replied with a completely different tone of voice and asked "Is this a joke?"

Stephen's mate continued "I'm going to tell you this once and once only, there is a cracking young tanned blonde big chested woman Police Officer on duty tonight and not only do I fancy my chances but I think our lass has cottoned on to it. Can I say to my wife when I get home that I have been round yours investigating one of your countless accusations"?

Mr Bell replied with anger shouting "I cannot believe this I am going to call the police!" "But we are the police you silly cunt now get ya head down and go to sleep and mind ya own businesses and let people try and get a living"

"I want your name and badge number now!" Mr Bell screamed.

It just so happened that the lad on the phone had been pulled over a few days earlier and still had the producer leaflet on him with a coppers details on so he read them down the line. Mr Bell continued "I am going to see my local MP about you!" The criminal Samaritans wished Mr. Bell the best of luck and hung up. They never heard Mr. Bell on the scanner again. So, it looked like their tactics had put paid to the local busy body and that probably saved a lot of people from getting nicked.

Chapter Thirteen: G and M Vending

G and M vending was the name of a cigarette vending company owned by Stephen his older brother John Henry and their friend Davey Lancaster. G and M stood for the previous two owners' wives' first initials. At the time, the lads thought it would be a good idea to cash in a little on the back of their growing reputation. So, they decided to invest in the cigarette business.

On paper it all seemed to be going well but the previous owners, two of whom were still working for the lads, forgot to mention to them that the majority of the vending machines they bought were stolen and the company was already under investigation and receiving a lot of attention from the police.

Everybody back then in the licensing trade knew the name Sayers and they took full advantage of the situation and they 'told' them they were placing their cigarette machines in their licensed premises. There were no complaints. The only problem the Sayers brothers encountered was supply and demand. They were expanding at such a rate that they needed more machines and quickly. They asked the former owners to pull in a few favours and get some more machines. Once again, unbeknown to Stephen and John they supplied them with machines freshly stolen from local pubs.

They now found themselves with 80 to 100 licensed premises and had another 50 orders, so were looking for more machines and at that time they were expensive, around £1400 each. So, Stephen spoke to another lad that worked for them called Pat and asked him to see what he could get. He said he could get them some cheap second-hand machines. Six weeks later Stephen found 25 to 30 machines downstairs in his dad's hostel.
He was over the moon. Pat had done well and no doubt had saved the lads a few quid into the bargain. The money continued to roll in for a few months until one day the police turned up and arrested the lads and took 100 machines away. Stephen, John, Davey and Pat were up at court the next day. Pat was so scared you could see his face shaking. It was all just too much for him and that didn't help them at all. It also didn't help that the prosecution as part of their case alleged that the company initials G and M actually stood for Guns and Money. Some may say very apt but a complete fabrication. The four of them were found guilty. Stephen, John and Davey received a sentence of 15 months each and Pat got 12 months.

A couple of days later Stephen was lying in his bed in his cell when the screw knocked on his cell door. Stephen asked him what he wanted. He told him to get ready sharpish as he was up in Court again. The judge had summoned the three of them back to Newcastle crown court but they had no idea why. It turned out to be good news. The Judge reduced Stephen and Davey's sentences to 12 months each as they had proved that they had legitimately bought some of the machines and they weren't all stolen. So that was the end of G and M. It was time to look for other money-making opportunities.

Chapter Fourteen: A Good Card Marker

There was a certain group of professional blaggers from the West end of Newcastle who were very active throughout their criminal careers who specialised in major robberies. They were well trained, disciplined and very experienced. They had a good combination of brains, brawn and extreme bravery. They knew how to work as one....as a unit.

One day the word came through amongst the boys that they had a good 'card marker'. A 'card marker' is an individual on the 'inside' who knows about the timings of large cash movements. The graft is only as good as your card marker's knowledge and if he or she has first-hand information from working there it does not get any better proving this person is co-operating.

Back in the 1980s nearly everyone got paid in cash. We didn't have the card system that we have today. If someone found a business where a few hundred people were working villains would know there was a large amount of money being moved there to be distributed. This particular 'card marker' gave the lads a heads up about the money that was being transferred to pay the Nurses and cleaning staff at the 8 hospitals in the area. The money would be picked up from a security cash depot in Washington and taken to 'Pritchard's security' depot in Gateshead. The lads were on it and plans were set in place.

They watched the vehicles movements over a pro-longed period of time and the only problem they would have to overcome as far as they could see was when the vehicle left the cash depot it would drive approximately 500 meters until it got to a roundabout. Here there was a choice of two or three exits but the security van never took the same route. What it did do was drive 500 meters to that roundabout each time so that is where the lads decided to strike.

At 8'clock on a Wednesday morning in late March 1987 the lads headed to Washington and were ready and waiting. The lads were sitting in the vehicle with the windows steamed trying not to draw attention to themselves. They sat there for five or ten minutes when the radio started crackling. One of the lads picked the radio up and said "Repeat, Repeat" and a message came back "It's on its way". Everybody knew what to do. These boys had been down this road many times before. The balaclavas were rolled down their heads and the pump-action shotguns were being cocked with the safeties removed. These boys meant business and nobody was about to stop them. As the security van approached the roundabout, they noticed a car very close to them. Within a split second there was now a car at the front and back of the security van boxing the security van in and forcing it to a standstill.

Two armed, masked gunmen ran towards the van and pointed the guns at the driver and passenger in the van and told them to get out of the van. There were three security at the front of the van and one at the back of the van. The man in the back of the van was refusing to open the door. The three front seat occupants were now laying down face first on the ground with their hands on their heads. One of the lads dragged one of the security guards from off the grass verge and asked the security man at the back of the van to watch as he placed the gun against the other security guards head and he told him if he did not open the door he was going to blow his head off. The security guard at the back of the van had a change of heart and decided to open the van door where he was dragged out by the scruff of the neck and placed to the ground with a gun to his head.

There were half a dozen vehicles behind the security van with all the occupants watching events unfold. One of the lads ran over to the cars and pointed the gun at them and demanded they threw their keys out of their windows. All the occupants did as he said with no hesitation. At the same time another lad had got into the back of the security van. He emptied it in moments taking five boxes. In no time at all they were in their vehicles and they were off. There was no stopping them. They switched cars twice, both times setting the previous car ablaze to prevent the Police planting evidence. They then headed to the 'slaughter' to share out the wages.

The boxes felt a bit light as they headed into the house and there was a feeling that the half a million haul that they were expecting was not what they had managed to get away with. When the boxes were opened the contents didn't even look like 50k. The radio was on at the time in the background and a newsflash was on that 'a firm of armed robbers had stopped and successfully robbed a security van on a daring day light raid.' It carried on to say that they had successfully escaped with £300,000. The money had been compressed by a machine and it had steel bands around it. When one of the lads cut the bands off the money instantly expanded.

Not a bad mornings work for a four-man team each clearing £75,000 minus the expenses such as the 'card marker', cars, safe house, boiler suits etc. Once the money was shared out the gang went there separate ways.

That night the robbery hit the local news on a regional news show called 'Northern Life'. Northumbria Police released a statement which was short and simple. "We are now dealing with a new breed of criminal."

Chapter Fifteen: Ain't Nothing Better Than An Honest Days Thieving

On 12th August 1987, Stephen Sayers 22nd Birthday, at approximately 10:30 am in the morning a group of carefully selected armed robbers met up. The lads had been specifically brought together for a robbery due to the different skillsets they possessed. They knew it was going to be big, but what they didn't know at the time was how big.
This was going to be Britain's biggest Post Office robbery.

A Royal mail train was going to be delivering a large amount of cash to Newcastle train station and then it would be moved to a main sorting office in Newcastle Orchard Street. It would send the money from Newcastle City centre to the outer lying districts in the North East and Sunderland was going to be one of them. They would be given a lump of money once a week on a Wednesday to supply the people of Sunderland and some small communities that surrounded it.

There was one big problem. The security van was followed by armed police from Orchard Street to Sunderland. The plan was for the robbery to take place at the Post Office depot where the vehicle would be arriving under heavy security and it would be unloading, in the closed compound, large amounts of money, sackfuls of it. Because of the Police escort there had been a couple of abandoned attempts to pull off this job but the lads were nothing if not determined.

The spotters were out and everybody was in position once again. They were getting notifications that the police car who's job it was to protect this vehicle was still behind the van until it came to the junction next to the bridge leading into Sunderland city centre. This was the stage where everything was in the balance. For whatever reason on this occasion the Police didn't follow the van through the city centre. Nobody will ever know why but the Police themselves. The heavily armed robbers were hiding in the back of a vehicle with other men from the firm plotted up in their positions waiting for notifications that it was on. Everyone was sat in silence when the message came over the radio, 'The dog has made its own way home, I repeat the owner has lost his dog.'

Everyone knew their job. Nobody spoke a word. The only noise that could be heard was the noise from the pump action shotguns being loaded with heavy shot. Heartbeats were thudding twenty to the dozen, balaclavas were being pulled down and the robbers were getting ready to strike. Now for the part that made this work so special, the split-second timing of it. Without this timing it would have never of been successfully completed. The van was now in the depot and the big double gates were shut behind it and four or five security guards came out into the compound to give it some extra security. There were two vehicles parking a little bit further up from the depot on the street. The boys were sitting in their vehicles ready; they knew that in any second it was going to be all systems go. Seconds were turning into minutes and the minutes turned into tens of minutes. Everyone was on action stations until the word came through. "Go! Go! Go!" This in turn sent these men's hearts racing, their pupils inflated and the adrenaline was pumping through their veins.

Suddenly a big Range Rover came from behind the transit van at high speed and proceeded to ram though the heavy reinforced security gates propelling two security guards who were standing at the gates across the yard. The Range Rover was in the depot now, alongside the cash van. The lads opened the doors and were out and into the yard. There they stumbled across a wheelbarrow with sacks of money in. Two of the lads dragged the barrow towards the van and started throwing money inside it.

As they were at work four or five security guards were placed face down on the ground with pump action shot gun placed on the back of their heads and the gunman was shouting, " If you want to be a hero you die a fucking hero, now touch the fucking ground with your noses." They did as they were told. At this point there was a group of post office workers who were walking past as the robbery was taking place. They made an attempt to try and get involved and prevent the robbery from happening but the robbers were not having it. The one at the front was stopped in his tracks with a gunman pointing the pump action shot gun at his head saying "Lie down on the ground or I'll blow ya fucking head off."

As all of this had been going on the other lads had been stacking up the cash and they were finished ahead of schedule. They then sped off in the back of the van with great big sacks of money and every radio station on the scanner blasting into their ears. "Major armed robbery committed all vehicles to attend." The lads had a head start though and had changed vehicles, burned the other ones out and were on their way to the safe house to share out the loot.

How many were on the graft we will never know and exactly how much was taken will never be known either but the boys made history that day and one thing is for certain, Northumbria Police were in no mood to celebrate. But Stephen Sayers, as I mentioned earlier, it was his 22nd birthday and he had made arrangements to go out that night.

The police wasted no time deciding who they were going to blame for this robbery and the Sayers brothers were right at the top of their list. Two days later they had arrested John Henry Sayers and had raided the home of Ken Sanvid who lived in Chapel Park in the West End of Newcastle and Stephen's cousin Tony 'Legs' Lenny who lived in Heaton. Stephen was next. They arrived in numbers at 13 York Street where Yvonne was doing her latest word puzzle testing her mental agility as she did regularly as a member of Mensa. Stephen however was nowhere to be seen.

Chapter Sixteen: On The Run

Stephen was in a taxi on the way to Walkers nightclub in Newcastle. The taxi driver couldn't stop talking about the Sunderland robbery. There was a sense of a pat on the back from the general public for the underdog. Of course, he had no idea who his passenger was. The reputation of the Sayers brothers was spreading like wild fire now but nobody really knew their faces outside the West End and they always kept a low profile because they were brought up not to seek attention. When you are a hoister the last thing you want is to be recognized. The taxi driver continued to talk about the Sayers brothers and told Stephen that they now ran Newcastle and had an army of armed men at their disposal. Stephen afforded himself a smile as he paid him and thanked him and gave him his best tip of the night.

As he arrived at Walkers there was a queue as long as the building. He walked straight to the front door and saw the doorman who gave him a nod. Stephen and his girlfriend at the time passed all security hand in hand. The club was full with over 2000 people all dancing and having a good time. He was centre of attention and not just because it was his 22nd birthday.
The Champagne was flowing and there was a party atmosphere. People could not have been more generous and respectful. Stephen didn't have to put his hand in his pocket. He partied the night away with his girlfriend and other couples and close friends. A good night was had by all.

A couple of days later Stephen's phone rang and a good friend told him that his Mam's house was being raided. Armed Police were ransacking her house and the street was closed off with a dozen vehicles all with blue lights flashing. The police were there to arrest him. At the same time, they had managed to arrest John.

Stephen had received legal advice to leave Newcastle as he was going to be fitted up for the robbery. Over the course of the next two days John and Ken Sanvid were charged with the armed robbery at Sunnyside sorting office which was confirmed as Britain's biggest post office robbery.

At a hastily arranged ID parade the calibre of witnesses left a lot to be desired. The first witness pointed at John in the line-up and said that it wasn't him but it looked very much like him. Another witness picked John out saying he had attended the robbery just moments after it happened and seen John with a boiler suit on, a pump action shotgun, and a balaclava on his head rolled up so you could see his face and he was smoking a big old pipe that looked like it belonged to Sherlock Holmes.

There was not a shred of evidence linking Stephen or John to the robbery but his brother got remanded in custody and would find himself behind bars for the next 13 months. Stephen on the other hand was not prepared to be fitted up and spend 20 years in jail for a crime that he didn't commit thanks to fabricated evidence. He was parked up at a safe house down South with trusted friends.

Meanwhile back home the publicity that the robbery received was crazy. A reward of £75,000, 10% of the money that was stolen, was put up by the Post Office. That was a nice earner for anyone especially a straight goer.

Stephen's cousin Tony 'Legs' Lennie was also a wanted man. Word came through that the police had raided Tony' s mothers house looking for him but he had gone. On hearing this news Stephen knew he had to find him. Remember that in those days there were no mobile phones. It took around four days and 20 separate phone boxes and call after call filled with codes before Stephen tracked him down. They finally agreed to meet up on Weymouth beach on England's sunny south coast in the middle of August.

Stephen was there first and saw his cousin walk past looking for him but he didn't acknowledge him at first. Stephen was on edge constantly looking for the police. He then started to follow him without him knowing. He did this for a short distance checking that nobody was following him. When it became clear he was not being followed Stephen approached him as he arrived at a nearby café. They looked at each other and burst out laughing and hugged each other. They were both in the same predicament but could still raise a smile.
Tony stood back and looked at Stephen and asked him 'Where should we go cuz?'
"I don't know but I think we should book a hotel", Stephen replied.
They found one close to the beach. It was beautiful with big glass windows and sea views. As they were sat having a meal in the hotel that evening a 'Crimewatch' preview came on the television in the dining room. The BBC announcer could be heard saying 'Coming up tonight after the news on 'Crimewatch' you can help catch Britain's most wanted men.'
Legs and Stephen looked at each other. It sent a shiver down both of their spines. They paid for their meals and returned to their room to put 'Crimewatch' on. They packed their bags and were prepared to leave just in case their faces were on the show.

Luckily, they weren't featured and felt safe for another month at least. They spent a bit of that time at that hotel and on the coast during the holiday season. It was easy to blend in as it was so busy. As the holiday season came to an end though they had to think of a new hiding place. The only winter resorts in Britain at the time that they were aware of was Aviemore in Scotland or Blackpool in England. They weighed up the situation and the two choices. Snowy Scotland or rainy Blackpool? Blackpool got the nod. They enjoyed the sea air and the fish and chips too much! 'Legs' had wanted to go to Scotland but there was no way in the world Stephen was going anywhere that cold and he'd heard that there were plenty fun pubs in Blackpool.
So they headed back up North.

It took them a full day to get from the South coast to Blackpool. 'Legs' spent the whole journey trying to convince Stephen to keep going but he'd made his mind up. When they arrived, they found a hotel and booked in. They went straight to the room where Stephen put on the TV just in time for the news at 5:45pm. The newsreader announced that the Conservative Party were holding their conference in Blackpool. At the time the IRA were bombing the mainland and threats had been made towards Margaret Thatcher who was the Prime Minister at the time. Security was a top priority the report said and they showed dozens of Police walking along the sands and promenades and even a mini battleship in the sea! Scotland suddenly felt really appealing to Stephen.

No sooner had they booked in then they were leaving. Stephen contacted a traveling family who lived close to Blackpool and they headed there for the night. They made the lads welcome, fed them and gave them a bed for the night. When they woke up the next morning they talked about their plans with the family and they offered them food and shelter for as long as they needed. The lads took them up on their kind offer. The camp was their home for the next three months.

Despite living on the camp, the lads still managed to grab a few nights out in Blackpool. One-night Stephen was standing in a nightclub which was packed full of Scottish people. Stephen was talking to a beautiful dark lass whose family originated from Newcastle. He went over to the bar to get this girl and 'Legs' a drink. He'd been served and was heading back with the three drinks. All of a sudden, he heard a loud roar as if he was at a football match. There were people shouting for Celtic and others for Rangers on opposite sides of the dance floor. A big gap appeared and the crowd went to either side. The chants got louder and louder until the two groups of about 50 or so on each side started fighting with one another. It wasn't long before they were battering the living daylights out of each other with chairs and bottles flying across the room. All of a sudden the two massive groups were headed towards where Stephen was standing with 'Legs' and the young girl. This wasn't a good place for them to be. Normally the lads would be in amongst a bit frisk like this but they were wanted men and couldn't afford to get nicked.

People had been hit with glasses and bottles and had been seriously hurt. There was blood everywhere. The police would arrive in no time. Stephen tried to leave with the girl through the fire exit to escape the madness. The Doorman stopped them in their tracks and said that nobody was getting out until the Police arrived. Stephen told him his 'girlfriend' was pregnant and he gave him a £20 note. The doorman smiled and opened the door and they legged it over to a waiting taxi just in the nick of time. A police van pulled up outside the club with the blues on and 6 coppers headed into the club.

The taxi driver asked Stephen if he was Scottish. He told him he was a 'Geordie' and to put his mind at rest that the madness had nothing to do with him. The taxi driver went onto to explain that it was an annual event. He said the Scots were good spenders but that once they'd all had a good drink they'd fall out over football and the Police would wade in. The taxi driver dropped them off at 'Rumours' next to 'Yates Wine Lodge' and Stephen could see 'Legs' at the window waiting for them. He had scarpered as soon as he saw the Scots kick off which was a wise move. The girl had to head off so they said their goodbyes and 'Legs' and Stephen decided to have one for the road before heading back to the camp. Stephen got the round in and waited for 'Legs' who had nipped to the toilet. He waited and waited but 'Legs' didn't come back. Stephen went to the front door and asked the doorman if he had been thrown out. They couldn't even remember 'Legs' going in so the mystery deepened.

The club closed and Stephen headed back to his hotel hoping 'Legs' was there but he wasn't. The following day came and went but still no sign of him and Stephen was beginning to fear the worst. In this situation there wasn't much he could really do. He packed their bags and was starting to get restless and a little paranoid. He was like a caged lion pacing the room. Mind ticking over twenty to the dozen. He decided to stay one more day. He was lying having a cat nap when he heard a fumbling at the door. He jumped up immediately and ran over to the door and opened it. False alarm. There was a stranger standing there with a key in his hand. He was drunk and was looking for another room. Stephen was feeling down and concerned about 'Legs,' but he had made up his mind that he was going to leave the next morning. He had an uneasy sleep that night tossing and turning thinking through the various scenarios. Had he been arrested? Had he lost his key and forgotten where they were staying? Stephen was worried sick, but he knew he had the spare key as he had asked for it and it was on top on the television the night they had gone out. In that case if the Police did have him they didn't have the key with the hotel name on so he knew there was no chance of them turning up and walking in uninvited.

He got a few hours kip and woke up in the morning and went down to have his breakfast. He came back up and had a shower and prepared to leave the hotel when all of a sudden there was a knock at the door. He thought it was the cleaner that had just passed in the hotel passage. When he opened the door to his surprise it was 'Legs'. He was so happy and relieved to see him and to his surprise he was standing with their good friend John Brooks 'Brooksy'. Stephen asked him "Where the fuck have you been!" 'Legs' said, "Cuz you won't believe what happened to me, I went outside to smoke a spliff and I heard someone shout my name and when I turn around to my surprise there was Brooksy in a car. I went over to him and he told me to get in, so I did." Brooksy had apparently found the love of his life and 'Legs' had decided to head off with him without telling Stephen. He was starting to feel angry with him for leaving him for days but then 'Brooksy' chipped in explaining that it was his fault. They had been on a two-day bender and 'Brooksy' had been in bed most of the time with a girl who he said was as brown as a berry with hair down to her ankles and a waist like a wasp with legs up to her armpits called Montinique. He went on to say that she had a friend who gave a cracking massage. Stephen's anger disappeared as they headed downstairs into a waiting taxi to meet Montinique and her talented friend.

Chapter Seventeen: On The Run In The Sun

With boredom in rainy Blackpool setting in, the lads decided to head home to Newcastle and a good friend Frankie Slater came and picked them up and took them to a safe house. He drove them into Newcastle in the back of a van. They couldn't see a thing, but more importantly nobody could see them. They were happy to be back in Newcastle. Their aim was to recharge their batteries and catch up with friends and family and get their affairs in order before heading off to their next destination. Another mate was going to sort them some passports out. Back in the eighties you could go with fake paper work with any name on in any post office and get a 12-month passport over the counter in ten minutes or so.

Frankie brought back some lamb and cooked them a nice dinner on their first night at the safe house. They spent two or three days in Newcastle before deciding to take the trip abroad. Tenerife was the chosen destination and 24 hours later 'Legs', 'Slats' and Stephen were looking out of a plane window waving goodbye to Blighty. Another chapter was about to begin.

The plane came to a halt on the runway in Tenerife. They had booked their tickets separately and had agreed to hook up once outside the terminal. They took their time getting off the plane and headed towards baggage collection and then customs. There seemed to be an issue at customs with officials running backwards and forwards and one or two of them looking in Stephen's direction, or was he just being paranoid? Then across the airport tannoy came an announcement and he could clearly make out the name 'Sayers'. This wasn't good. He waited in line trying not to arouse any suspicion or look concerned but this really didn't look good. Again, the same announcement came across the tannoy and there it was again as clear as day 'Sayers.' Then to Stephen's left a group of officials came walking directly towards him. This was it. The game was up.

At the back of the group was a female official with a young child. To his right he became aware of a woman in tears running towards the group. The boy ran towards the woman and into her arms. It turned out that the 'Sayers' family had lost their little boy in the airport and that's what all the fuss had been about. Stephen breathed a huge sigh of relief. By this time, he could see the lads behind him in the line and they exchanged a few winks and smiles. They all got through customs unscathed and as they walked outside of the terminal the sun was beaming down on their faces.

They jumped in a taxi and headed straight to the infamous 'Veronicas' complex. It was time to have some fun. They headed to the first bar and ordered three large beers. They didn't last long and then they ordered another three. They started talking to the bar staff asking if there were any apartments for rent and they were quite helpful and gave the lads a few phone numbers. As they were talking a group of lairy pissed up cockneys started shouting over towards them and were taking the piss asking if Stephen and the lads had the bottle to play them at pool. The leader with the big mouth was about 15 stone and about six foot two and was obviously juiced up. He was looking for trouble and started calling the lads 'Geordie Maggots' a term used in the past by armed robber John McVicar.

He must have mistaken the lads for holiday makers, well he was about to realise the error of his ways and discover how a Westender deals with a big mouthed cockney. Stephen walked over to him with the lads watching his back. He looked at Stephen still giving it the big one and asked him if he had any money to gamble with. Stephen told him that he only had his holiday money. The cockney said good as they were playing pool for £20 a game. He was trying to intimidate Stephen and impress his mates. He told Stephen to put his £20 on the table. Stephen agreed and pulled it out of his pocket. He had watched him earlier spinning a coin to decide who would break and sure enough as he put his money on the table next to Stephen's he said 'I'll spin you for the break Geordie.' He took the coin off the table and flicked it up. As he followed the coin up and then down with his head Stephen caught him with a peach of a right uppercut and knocked him out. As he hit the floor knocking over tables and glasses Tony 'Legs' and Frankie 'Slats' came steaming in with pool cues and started battering his mates.

The bar staff ran for cover and the manager was about to call the Police when another cockney lad came over and told him not to. This man's mates scattered leaving him lying in a pool of blood and broken glass. This other bloke seemed okay and must have had something to do with the complex as he offered to get Stephen and the lads some drinks and got the staff to clean up the mess. The guy was impressed how they had handled the bully. He had been causing him a few issues and had been waiting for somebody to teach him a lesson. He asked how he could help Stephen and the lads. Stephen told him they needed a roof over their heads so he said he would fix them up with an apartment.

By this time the bully was starting to come round. He didn't know what had hit him. As he staggered out of the bar dazed, it was clear that his jaw was broken. He would not make the same mistake again. With a roof over their heads and a few quid in their pockets they made the most of their new home.

They were partying hard and life was good in the sunshine. Before they knew it four months had passed and the funds were beginning to run out. They all had their own ideas on how to raise some cash but they went with Frankie's plan after he had stumbled across a safe full of cash at the car hire place next to their apartment.

The place also exchanged money and when they had been in to hire a car, he had clocked about 12k in notes in the safe that stood wide open most of the day. The cockney lads who they had sorted out on their arrival were still on the scene and had started drinking with Stephen and the lads most days so Frankie put the bit of work to them. It turned out that they were a little firm back home in South London and were well up for it. The safe was attached to an outside wall so Frankie's plan was to get the lads to scrape away the cement between the bricks on that wall and then remove the bricks and then the safe. The London lads had other ideas though and had plundered a few tools including a steel bar and a pick axe from a local building site. They got to the wall that night and started laying into with brute strength and the noise was attracting attention.

It didn't take long for a local man to come over and start shouting at them. Then another, and another. The lads panicked and dropped their tools and started running from the scene. Frankie and another mate of theirs Dave were sitting at a local bar waiting for the lads to get back with the wages. Instead he got the lads shouting 'It's come on top Frankie' and a group of irate Spanish locals chasing them.

Frankie and Dave were now in big trouble. One of the Spaniards nutted poor Dave flush in the face so hard it put him on his arse but he was an ex-boxer and he got straight back up and got stuck into them. There was now six of them and a dog which bit poor Dave a couple of times and Frankie who was unfit, overweight and who had been partying for four months. They managed to get away from the mob and ran through a few back streets and headed down an embankment to the apartment and to safety. When Stephen saw the clip of the pair of them and they told him what had happened he couldn't stop laughing.

Dave had a broken nose and had lost a few teeth to go with his cuts and bruises and dog bites and Frankie wasn't looking much better. The tears were streaming down Stephen's face as the young cockneys arrived and Frankie started shouting and bawling at them for bringing the trouble to them. They didn't see Dave again after that. He got himself some new friends. You can't really blame him, can you?

The lads stayed for just short of seven months in Tenerife but when it's time to move on its time to move on. Stephen, Frankie and Tony started to pack. It was time to make their way back to England.

Chapter Eighteen: Back To Blighty

They arrived in Luton, it was windy and raining. They were already missing the sun on their backs. They headed to London and booked into a hotel. It didn't take them long to sink into a depression about their situation and within a few days Tony and Frankie were going stir crazy and fighting each other over nothing. On one occasion the noise was that bad that the hotel manager came to the room door and started threatening the lads with the police. Frankie opened the door. The manager took one look at them and said that he would let them calm down and be back in ten minutes and that they had better clean up the mess that they had made. They weren't daft. They knew this meant that he was going to call the police so they packed up their things and got ready to leave the hotel.

Tony and Frankie were still punching the living daylights out of each other in the lift. Stephen just stood there and let them get on with it. The lift stopped and the door opened to reveal Tony biting Frankie's shin. He was screaming and both of them had blood all over their faces. The people who were standing waiting to get in the lift took a step back with shock. They couldn't believe what they were seeing and how violent the fight was. The lift door closed and it then reached reception. Stephen managed to get them apart and out of the lift. Frankie jumped in the first taxi with Stephen and Tony jumped in the one behind and both cars sped off in opposite directions. So, after months together they had now lost each other in the middle of London.

There was no doubt they needed a break from each other but not like this. After of a couple of days in London Stephen got talking to a man from Sunderland who was heading up North the next day to make a delivery in Gateshead. They both agreed to head home and next day the man dropped them off at a friend's place in Darlington. After a night there an uncle of Stephen's George 'Blow' Shotton came to pick them up and take them back to Newcastle. He got the nickname 'Blow' through the number of safes he blew in the sixties. He was never trained in the use of dynamite so it was very much trial and error with him. He liked to think he was in charge and used to boast about his time in the army despite the fact he spent more time in the dock for desertion than he did defending the country.

Health and safety didn't really come into it. 'Blow' and his firm were at the top of their game and had slowly worked their way up the criminal ladder. Electronic security was in its infancy, and while the many of these premises were still very secure, the lads would always find a way in. They also found it easier to peel off the back of these safes and get their loot out than trying to carry the safe away.

On one occasion they found a nice piece of work from a pal of theirs. They gained entry through a back door and were delighted to find not one but two safes. One was huge and the lad's eyes lit up. The bigger the safe the bigger the haul they were thinking. 'Blow' set to work packing the two safes with dynamite that they had taken from an old quarry. The idea was to blow the two safes together. With the fuses set the lads headed out of the building. They were in no rush. They had done this many times. However, the small safes fuse was quicker than the lads imagined and there was a huge explosion which blew the safe through the window.

There were half crowns, ten bobs and two bobs scattered all over the street. If the first explosion didn't wake the neighbours then the second one did. The explosion was so powerful that it blew the supporting wall down and the floor above that and all the change that had been in the safe was damaged due to the explosion. That's how George got the name 'Blow'.

Blow told the lads he was going to look after them and he told Stephen that he had a boat on the Isle of Bute on the West coast and that Stephen and Frankie could stay there but he also said it needed a bit of a lick of paint. He also gave them a three-year-old transit which was on the hit list for the finance.

They got to work in no time and they 'rung' the transit van and then got hold of a generator, television and a video after one of Stephens's cousins had screwed the local video shop! Stephen bought them all off him and then they made their way to Scotland with the words of 'Blow' echoing in their minds, 'Make sure the ropes are tight', meaning the ropes which tethered the boat to the shore.

It took them two weeks to sort the boat out. In the meantime, Stephen, Frankie and George stayed in a bed and breakfast and it was laugh a minute. George, according to Stephen was a really good liar and his stories were always very interesting. He did not need to move up to Scotland for those two weeks but he did it to make sure the lads got settled in and the right people were there in case they needed help.

With the boat finally finished the lads got settled in on the boat which was when boredom started to kick in. It didn't take long before they were at each other's throats and Frankie decided he needed a change of scenery. So, Stephen took him on the ferry and then took him to the station. It was sad for Stephen to see him leave, he had devoted eight months of his life to him and for that he, in his own words, is 'always grateful'.

It started to get a bit lonely for Stephen on the boat and there was nothing to do apart from drink. He used to drink in the pub on the harbour and was always one of the last to leave and stagger over to the boat, not always in a straight line. This particular night he'd had had a good drink and he noticed that he was having to jump on the boat as it was about four foot away from shore and the words of 'Blow' were echoing in his ears again. 'Make sure the ropes are tight!' The rope was as thick as his leg he thought, how on earth was he expected to do that? As much as he tried, he couldn't move them at all so he went to bed and fell into a drunken sleep.

Next thing he knew he was on the cabin floor after being thrown out of his bed as the boat was leaning to one side. With the rope slipping and the tide going out the boat had moved further away from the harbour and a ferry was just coming in.

Stephen had the hangover from hell as he got onto the deck. People getting off the ferry were pointing and staring. He didn't need this kind of attention. There was still a £75k reward for his capture. He managed to get the boat steadied and back to its original position. Panic over. Later that day he got word through that the lads had been given a trial date so there was light at the end of the tunnel and it would not be long till he could return home.

After getting the news Stephen managed to get a message to his cousin Philip Riley who dropped everything and drove up to get him and take him back North to another safe camp. Philip was a sight for sore eyes after so much time alone. He told Stephen how the camp had been raided by over two hundred Police looking for him and Tony. Stephen stayed with him for a couple of days and then he moved to another camp for a couple of days. It was just good to be around people again instead of being on the boat. He moved from camp to camp for a few months but with the trial date on the horizon he felt that the time was right to head back home to Newcastle. A safe house was sorted and he headed up the A1 to a hero's welcome. He was pleased to be back home.

John was also wanted for questioning over a Post office burglary and the attempted murder of two Police officers. It was suggested that he and two other associates were disturbed whilst carrying out the burglary and during their escape a crowbar was thrown through the windscreen of a Police van which had arrived on the scene causing the vehicle to crash into another car.

There is a law in Scotland stating that if you do not get produced from police custody to court in 101 days your charges are dropped, so while John was on remand for the Sunderland robbery which happened to be Britain's' biggest Post office robbery he was due up at court in Scotland. They applied to have him transferred up but due to the severity of the robbery (£750,000) the judge declined to move him saying that the Sunderland robbery was more severe. Three quarters of a million pound might not seem a lot now but in line with inflation that would amount to £1.9 Million today.

Chapter Nineteen: In The Clear

The back end of August 1988 Stephen Sayers was 23 years of age, 12 stone and very fit to go with it. He had spent the last four months in a safe house on Tyneside waiting for his brother's trial to finish. He was bored rigid and was living in a downstairs flat with another one of his cousins who came to his aid in his time of need.

He didn't venture out of the house leading up to the trial. To kill the boredom, he would do body circuits and peddle a bike until he was exhausted. On a couple of occasions, he passed out.

One particular day he was sitting in the flat trying to catch his breath after a hard training session whilst listening to the radio and a newsflash came over the radio. 'John Henry Sayers and Ken Sanvid have just been acquitted for Britain's biggest Post Office robbery'. (It became Britain's biggest ever Post Office robbery as the great train robbery was on a train). Then the radio went into detail about the circumstances of the robbery saying that it had been done with 'SAS' style planning and split-second timing. Stephen jumped that high that he punched the ceiling. He then went outside for some fresh air and felt a massive relief and a sense of liberty. It was as if the world had been lifted from his shoulders. He now knew that Northumbria police had no chance of a conviction after failing to convict his brother and co-accused.

Stephen's cousin who was helping him was shopping at the time but had also heard the newsflash on the radio and immediately bought two bottles of champagne and came running round to the flat with another cousin who was there and who was just about to change shifts watching him. They bumped into Stephen in the back lane where he was still jumping for joy. They popped the corks and started spraying him from head to toe with the champagne.

The following day Stephen and his cousin Tony 'Legs' Lennie handed themselves into the local Police station. Stephen was arrested and given a brief interview that took about half an hour. All the police got was no replies. The interview was terminated and he was held at the station for a court appearance the next morning for a driving offence and failure to produce documents. He got bail with no further action on the Sunderland robbery.

Having beaten the robbery case John was arrested again with another couple of associates and taken to Scotland for questioning but he again he chose to say nothing and the 101-day ruling was in his favour. He was released on bail and would have to appear at Sheriffs court a week later. The case came to nothing and John was a free man once again.

When John arrived home from Scotland his friends and family threw him a huge party in the 'Balmoral Pub'. All his friends from Elswick and the West End were there and a few well-known faces too. Word travelled fast across Tyneside and the rest of the country. Messages of congratulations were flooding in from Glasgow to Parkhurst to the Sayers family home in York Street. The villains of Tyneside were finally getting some national recognition and about time too.

Chapter Twenty: Sayers 1 Psycho 0

It was a sunny Sunday morning early September 1988. Stephen was at his Mam's house to see her and get himself a cup of tea and a sarnie. He was going out for a drink that day and thought he'd put a lining on his stomach. While he was there a few of the lads called in to see him. John Mac, Tom Brayson and his cousin Frankie Kelly. They all had food and then left York Street with her words ringing in his ears "Promise to stay out of trouble my boys".

Stephen shouted back "Don't worry ma!", and the lads shouted "Don't worry he's with us!" and they strolled up to the 'Balmoral pub' on Westgate road which was only a five-minute walk from his Mams.

They got to the pub at half twelve where they met up with another fifty lads from the West End. Amongst the crowd were Tony Chambers, Charlie and Davey Huggens, Snake Mains, Jimmy Hardy, Fish Tams, to name a few. They had a good days drinking, and left the 'Balmoral at 8:30pm and headed to 'Raffles bar' in Pink Lane.

Pink Lane was infamous for prostitution in the 50s and 60s but the area had been cleaned up. The group was about 30 handed now with most of the group from Elswick and they were all a bit worse for wear. They headed to the lounge bar and were all having a good night when a friend of Stephen's called Malcolm Balmer asked him to speak to somebody on the telephone. As he walked through the bar to get to the phone, he could see a stocky little man talking and looking in his direction out of the corner of his eye. He did not take much notice of him. He took the call and then when it finished hung up and started talking to Malcolm again. Stephen and Malcolm were engrossed in conversation when he heard a voice say "Hello Malcolm what are you doing with him?" It was the stocky man who had been eyeing him up earlier. The voice came from a man called Jimmy Summerville also known as 'Psycho'. This man was extremely violent and dangerous. He was 37 years of age, 5,11 in height, 17 and a half stone and loved to fight.

Three years previous he had tried to bully Michael Sayers and his co-accused while they were in Durham prison. He had such a fierce reputation throughout Tyneside that everyone refused to fight him but Stephen's criminal CV was growing quicker than the average bad lad. Not only did he love going hoisting (thieving) but he also loved a fight. He feared nobody.

'Psycho' made his move towards Stephen, but he was too slow and Stephen hit him with a right hander. It was full of bad intentions and broke his nose. There was blood all over his face. He staggered back but did not go down. This wasn't going to be a one punch fight. He came back at Stephen and caught him with a couple of good clean blows but Stephen caught him again just below the ribs winding him. This was turning into a real battle. Pain can weaken some people but it seemed to make this Sayers brother stronger as Jimmy was finding out. He was roughly 5 stone heavier than

Stephen and although he was weakening that was his one advantage. He tried to grab Stephen in a bear hug but he managed to pull away and started shouting at him. "Come On then, Come On!" The 50 or so people in the bar weren't getting involved but the barmaids started screaming 'Do him Stephen.' He steamed in again with a four-punch combination striking with power and accuracy. His left eye was beginning to close now and they both had bust lips as 'Psycho' tried to attack Stephen again.

The momentum carried them both towards the door and one of the barmaids shouted "Take it outside lads". Hearing this Stephen dropped his guard and said 'Come on then Psycho outside.' He took advantage of this error and grabbed him and got him in a headlock. Jimmy's trademark was biting his victims' noses or ears and now he had Stephen's nose in his mouth and was biting hard. Stephen managed to get his full finger in his eye and tried to pull it out. He heard a scream of pain then 'Psycho' released his nose. This was his big error. He was leaning over Stephen so he jumped up and caught him flush with a headbutt which rocked him. He then ran at him, grabbed him and butted him again and again. He was on top now. Jimmy staggered and fell against the bar so Stephen jumped on him and was pulling his head up and butting him again and again. Stephen's nose was throbbing but the pain was driving him on. 'Psycho' was fading so Stephen decided to give this bully a taste of his own medicine by biting his nose. He was struggling trying to pull away but Stephen got a lock on and he was showing no mercy. Fortunately for 'Psycho' Stephen had lost a tooth and he couldn't quite get the grip required to pull the nose clean off. He did enough though and it was hanging off on one side as he released his grip. His opponent still wasn't finished though. His sheer strength and determination kept him on his feet. Stephen head butted him again and then followed that up with a good body combination. The fight was now his for the taking. It is hard to believe that this took place in front of a bar full of witnesses.

They looked like two pit bulls by now, shirts were ripped off and they were both covered in blood. Stephen now caught 'Psycho' with another couple of punches and he finally dropped him to his knees. "TRY AND FUCKING BULLY ME PSYCHO, COME ON PSYCHO, BULLY ME!!" Stephen shouted at the top of his voice. Suddenly he felt a lot of arms around him and could hear people saying "Stephen stop you're going to kill him." The crowd who were screaming for him to do him in were now screaming for him to stop. His friends were picking him up and trying to drag him off but he was breaking free and going back to do 'Psycho' again.

They finally got him outside giving 'Psycho' a much-needed breather and time to lick his wounds. By now he had come to his senses and was looking at Stephen through the big glass windows. It was like pouring petrol on a fire. Stephen broke free from his friends and ran into the bar and shouted "COME ON PSYCHO COME ON!" But 'Psycho' had no more to give. He looked at him and said "No more Stephen. You have done me, no more." He stood back and said "Tell them then. I'm not sure they heard you." He looked up and said, "He has done me fair and square."

Stephen could hear the pain in his voice and see the tears in his eyes. His nose looked really bad and he needed a trip to hospital. He then turned to Stephen and apologized and he offered him his hand to shake. Stephen accepted his apology and shook his hand. There was a feeling of mutual respect. He was handed a towel by one of the barmaids and wrapped it around his face for the bleeding and headed off to hospital whilst Stephen and the lads went back to the Balmoral pub to celebrate his victory.

Chapter Twenty One: The Shooting of 'Big Billy' Robinson

Stephen Sayers was having a night out in Newcastle city centre, in Bentleys nightclub 1989. The place was bouncing and there was a good atmosphere. Billy Robinson from Gateshead was also there with his entourage. Billy was about 6ft 3 and twenty stone of muscle. A former heavyweight fighter who was very agile and nobody's fool. In those days Billy was not shy to lift his hands to anyone he came across. He was a man who had a fierce fighting reputation throughout the North East and was looked upon by many as the best fighting man around. 'Big Billy' was Viv Graham's mentor.

Billy saw Stephen in the club with about half a dozen Westenders and one person from Gateshead. Billy immediately made a beeline to the person from Gateshead shouting disrespecting things to him about Gateshead people being with Westenders. Billy then attacked the man from Gateshead. The scuffle was broken up quite quickly. The man from Gateshead was not happy and had a blade about a foot long and wanted to stick it in Billy but Stephen took the knife off him and hid it. He may not have been from the Westend but he was in Stephen's company and he felt obliged to look after his friend. They carried on with their night and ended up at a party in Gateshead in a two-bedroom downstairs flat with friends 'Fish' Tams, Davey Hindmarsh and a few others. The house belonged to a lass called Carol.

About an hour or so later Billy arrived. He didn't like the fact that the Westenders were at a party in his area of Gateshead. Billy was in no mood to reason with anyone and had a reputation for knocking people out. He approached Stephen and asked him what he was doing there. Stephen wasn't intimidated and told him that he was looking for somebody. This got Billy's back up and he asked him who. Stephen told him he was looking for a man called Jimmy Fear. Billy explained that he was getting paid for looking after Jimmy and if anyone had a problem with Jimmy then they'd have to go through him first. Stephen wasn't happy and had a firm grip on a razor-sharp foot long blade hidden down the back of his coat. It was the same blade he'd taken from the man 'Big Billy' had attacked earlier in the evening.

Stephen looked him in the eye and said 'My advice to you, is don't stand too close to Jimmy because when we do Jimmy we will do you next!' He immediately waved his bear like hand towards Stephen and then he started removing his ring from his finger while telling him to follow him into the kitchen. Stephen followed him into the kitchen but it was full of people off their nuts on 'E' so Billy told him to 'Get outside' so he obliged.

As Stephen walked out behind him, he heard Billy say 'I know someone is there'. Stephen was confused and didn't know what he meant until he saw a man with a balaclava on and a sawn-off shot gun in his hand. It seemed to all happen in slow motion then. Billy grabbed a hold of Stephen by the shoulders and pushed him towards the gunman who shouted 'Stephen Move, Move!' Billy was using Stephen as a human shield.

Stephen struggled for about 10 or 15 seconds before he managed to push Billy away from him and towards the backdoor that they had come out of. They both managed to scramble into the house. The gunman discharged his first shot and missed the big man but it went off very close to Stephen's left side. Stephen had his hands raised up high which probably stopped him getting hit. The blast and the flash of the light was dazzling in the pitch-black backyard.

Billy went back out of the flat into the yard and shouted to the gun man who was still standing there in the same position. 'You will never walk in this town again son'. The gunman wasn't going to miss a second time. He shot Billy in the leg just above the knee cap and then fled the scene. Stephen was in a state of shock and was thanking his lucky stars that he had not been hit.

Billy now had a very big hole in his leg and was losing a lot of blood. The colour was draining from his face but he managed to hobble over to the door. Two of his friends ran outside and started charging towards Stephen thinking he had shot him. Stephen knocked one of them out and his friend Davey Hindmarsh floored the other. The rest of the party goers were still dancing in the kitchen oblivious to what had just happened a few yards from them.

They couldn't get a phone to call an ambulance or a taxi so Stephen offered to take Billy in his car. Even though he was in excruciating pain Billy was concerned because he thought he was about to be taken away and finished off but Stephen was only offering to drive him to the hospital. As Stephen was in a bad state of shock, they got Billy into Fish Tams car and he took him to the hospital instead. Stephen remained at the party and was joined by a few more car loads of Westenders who had got word that he had trouble and had jumped in taxis to back him up. When they arrived, they were told about the nights events and partied into the early hours.

Chapter Twenty Two: Meet Viv Graham

In the late 1980s Newcastle's nightlife was opening up like never before. Gone were the old men sitting with their cloth caps on and bottles of stout and whippets. The dolly birds had arrived and the bars were bouncing. The clubs were full to the rafters and tough guys were making a reputation for themselves. Money was flowing through the tills and in those days, you never had the areas such as Jesmond, the Quayside or the Gate. The Bigg market was the heart of the party and anybody who was anybody would be seen there. It was not unusual to see 50 or 60 people queuing up outside of the pubs and clubs. Newcastle had more licensed premises than any other city centre in the country. With crowds came trouble. In certain pubs on certain nights of the week it was like the wild west with the two big groups of people in one square mile battering the living day lights out of each other. For a lot of years there was a massive divide between the West End of the City and any doormen. Westenders didn't like any person in the position of authority especially when they weren't from the West End. When violence was used both sides suffered casualties.

There was one man that stood out amongst them all, not just by his physical size but also his ability to knock people out which he did on a regular basis. He had been a good amateur boxer, very strong, 13 and a half stone was his fighting weight until he came across a man called Andy Webb. What Andy didn't know about body building is not worth knowing. If anyone can take credit for giving Viv Graham his strength and size it has to be Andy. Andy 'roided' Viv up with 3 and a half stone of muscle in all of the right places, which changed him from being extremely dangerous into a lethal weapon. He was starting to get a reputation for battering anyone who stood up to him. The Westenders though were certainly not afraid of him.

With the City thriving, work flooded in for the likes of Viv and his associates. His solution was very effective. It consisted of punching whoever stood up against him unconscious. Quite simple really. His reputation spread very quickly a bit like his hands. It was not difficult to see that this man was a little bit different.

'Viv' had risen up the ranks and the bar managers in Newcastle had taken notice. They needed somebody to stop the 'Westenders' wreaking havoc. By taking on 'Viv's services they were fighting fire with fire. Violence with violence. Viv looked down on 'Westenders.' He had a real dislike of the West End because he could not control the west end or the people who lived there. There were a lot of Westenders that made much more money than 'Viv'. They had pockets full of money and were good spenders, they were not 9 to 5 workers, 90% of them were criminals involved in serious crimes such as armed robberies and murders.

Newcastle has had plenty of tough fighting men over the years but Viv seemed to tick all the boxes and his name was coming back to Stephen Sayers all the time with stories of him beating this one up and knocking that one out. He seemed to have a firm grip over a lot of the city. It was time to see what this 'Viv' was all about.

'Viv' had risen to power whilst Stephen had been on the run and John had been facing robbery charges, but now Stephen was back home and keen to have normal service resume. 'Viv' would normally drive round to his various premises to see the doormen in his 'Ford Sierra' making sure they were OK before heading to 'Zoots' Nightclub.

Stephen decided to head down to 'Zoots' to see 'Viv' and make his presence felt. His friends had organised a homecoming at the 'Balmoral' that evening, but he left the 150 strong party and headed down to 'Zoots' with his good friend Fish Tams. When they got to the door Viv saw Stephen and headed over to him and gave him a big cuddle and welcomed him home. They had met before at 'Wheelers' Nightclub in Gateshead where he started working the doors under the watchful eye of Paddy Leonard and Billy Robinson.

Stephen mentioned that he had just left a party at the 'Balmoral' and that his guests would all be heading down to join him. 'Viv' had no issues and let the door lads know the score. He was as good as his word as each guest was admitted to the club free of charge and 'Viv' got each one a drink.

Many of Stephen's friends couldn't understand why Stephen was being so friendly with this man who had taken liberties with a lot of their friends, but Stephen didn't care, he had his own agenda and was keen on diffusing the tension. That night 'Viv' could not have been a better host. His sixth sense had served him well. There were a lot of drugged up and tooled up psychopathic people who enjoyed violence in the club that night who were looking to settle a score. It would have just taken one person to light the blue touch paper and that place would have exploded. Those free drinks had given him some breathing space.

Feeling quite uncomfortable with all eyes on him 'Viv' spent a lot of time on Stephen's shoulder that night talking to him about certain things. He was testing the water and obviously sizing him up as his 'competition'. He knew Stephen and his brothers were the figureheads in the West end, they flew the flag and were tried and tested at the highest level.

As the night reached an end one person really had 'Viv' concerned. The person in question was staring directly at 'Viv' from the moment he had entered the club. 'Viv' asked Stephen what the guy's issue was and why was he staring at him all of the time. Stephen took a drink from his pint glass and turned slowly to 'Viv' and said 'Because he wants to do you.' For the first time there was a look of fear in 'Viv's face. No man had ever put it on him as strongly as that before. Stephen had given the new kid in town plenty to think about. The night came to an end and there were no big problems until a big Scotsman and his friend were very disrespectful to Stephen's friend's wife and sister. 'Viv' was across in seconds and knocked the two big Scotsmen out. There was a sense of a truce between 'Viv' and the 'Westenders.' It was not going to last.

A few nights later on the 22nd August Peter Logan Donnelly a cousin of the Sayers family, walked into a restaurant in the Bigg Market called 'Santinos' with two of his associates. The place was full and they were well served. He had white fluffy socks on his hands no mask and was holding a shotgun and began shouting for 'Viv'. He then pointed the gun at 'Viv' and told him to head to the back room.

Ordinary punters were shaking and screaming. Donnelly seemed to be in control. Then in a flash Viv grabbed the gun and threw it against the wall. A fight broke out. Donnelly's friend attacked Ian Bell but was knocked unconscious by someone smashing a chair over his head. Bell and Donnelly got stuck into each other in the back alley of the restaurant. The fight ended as quickly as it started when Bell fell to the ground with blood pumping out of stab wounds. He had been stabbed through the heart and in the shoulder. Viv arrived on the scene and struck Donnelly on the jaw breaking it. He then tried to save his friend Bell by giving him first aid. He did a great job. He managed to stem the flow of blood until the ambulance arrived and helped save his life. One of Donnelly's mates ran away whilst the other was receiving a terrible beating from former boxer Paul Lister. Lister was at the peak of fitness and had just recently fought for the British Heavyweight title. As blue lights lit up 'Santinos' 'Viv' and Lister left the scene. If there was ever any sort of truce between the 'Westenders' and the city doormen it could have been well and truly shattered with this incident.

Little was said after that between Donnelly and his cousins. The Sayers did not need the heat of being associated with him. Once Bell was sitting up in his hospital bed, he wasted no time in naming Donnelly as his attacker. Bell and Viv gave statements. Donnelly was subsequently charged with attempted murder, wounding with intent, possessing a firearm with intent of endangering life and possession without a firearm license. He was remanded. It was alleged that Bell took a bung not to go through with his evidence at court. In the witness box his mind went blank as did Viv's and Donnelly was found not guilty on all charges and he was released back onto the streets.

'Zoots' was a big venue and absolutely bouncing at the weekends with over 1200 people on most nights so there was a lot of trouble. On one occasion the Westenders led by Stephen Sayers and 20 or so doormen (not all of them working), teamed up against a big stag party. At least a dozen or so Westenders had been attacked and that couldn't go unpunished. Despite being outnumbered 3 to 1 they were still game. They gathered in the lounge part of the club and confronted about a dozen or so of the stag party. Bottles and stools started to fly. It was like a scene from a western. One bottle narrowly missed Stephen as everybody in the vicinity got sprayed with glass and alcohol. The big lad who had thrown the bottle was their top boy and he picked up another bottle to try and do the same again. This time Stephen picked up a stool and whacked it over the kid's head knocking him unconscious. The sight of the big man falling to the floor put the other lads on the back foot and Stephen and the lads made easy work of his pals. They hadn't realized that trouble had also kicked off elsewhere in the club. In the passage way leading to the exit Viv was stuck into a few lads and had already knocked a few out. The fight continued onto Waterloo Street outside of the club it was now a mass brawl involving about 200 people.

The locals had collected the pool balls from the pool table downstairs in Zoots and they were putting the pool balls in their socks and battering the living daylights out of the out of towners. Cars boots were getting opened and weapons were being removed. Viv was shocked when he saw how fast the Westenders operated and acted as one and within moments they were all ready, tooled up, and ready for war.

Stephen got next to his good mate Hally. The Westenders stood side by side grouping together whilst the visitors started coming towards them. They threw bottles and glasses and anything they could get their hands on and then started running towards Stephen and co. It was like a scene in Zulu. Stephen took charge and shouted, "Stand! Stay together and let them run at us." They were gathering speed and were getting closer and closer. Stephen waited patiently and knew what to do. He shouted again, "Get ready, get ready!" They continued to stand their ground. As they got closer Stephen could see at the front the man, he had knocked spark out earlier in the lounge with the stool. Stephen still had half the smashed stool in his hand. They were now a few feet away. Stephen shouted for the final time, "CHARGE!" He had eyes for one man only. For the second time in the space of an hour he smashed him over the head and knocked him spark out with the remaining part of the stool. The visitors who it turned out were a rugby team were beginning to wish they hadn't been in such a rush to join the Westenders outside as they were given a right pasting. Viv had by now seen what was going on outside and had waded in too. He took out at least six on his own. The Elswick war cry went up 'Take no prisoners' which brought a smile to Stephen's face. This was the battle cry they used in their early teens.

The secret to being in a mass brawl is to not give in, and keep fighting and fighting. Do the biggest and best first. Divide them and hit them until they run away. Your unity is your strength. There were now dozens of men lying on the floor some screaming in agony some either unconscious or semi-conscious. These men had come for a fight and they certainly got one. The fighting must have lasted 15 minutes or more whereas an average fight lasts a couple of minutes if that. The Westenders went back into the club and finished what they had started with the Rugby players in the lounge. At least 14 ambulances attended the scene along with the local police.

Miraculously there were no serious casualties and no arrests and everyone seemed to dust themselves down, including Stephen's nemesis carrying a bad head and a few bumps, cuts and bruises, and they carried on with their nights out.

Stephen recalled after the event, "To this day I have never seen so many bodies unconscious in a street. I remember looking down the street and seeing the big lad I had levelled twice back on his feet giving it what for with a pack of about 8 Westenders surrounding him and attacking him. It reminded me of something from a David Attenborough documentary where a pack of lions are attacking an Elephant." On the plus side Viv had proved his worth to Stephen once again. There was no doubt that having him as friend was going to be useful moving forward.

Chapter Twenty Three: Hobo's

Stephen Sayers was drinking in 'Zoots' nightclub with his friends Fish Tams and Davey Lancaster and they met up with Viv and his good friend Rob Armstrong. Later that night someone Stephen knew passed him a message saying that some doorman had said that all the Sayers and their associates were barred from a nightclub at the bottom of Bath Lane. The nightclub was called 'Hobos'. Stephen was not going to stand for that but didn't want to spoil his night out so decided to put the 'slight' to the back of his mind as he ordered another round. As the night passed, he started thinking about what the doorman had said. It was not a club the lads went to but that wasn't the point. So he sent a friend down to the club to test the water. The doormen would not let him in explaining that the police had barred the Sayers family and associates and they were not allowed in. So, it was true. This was a direct challenge to Stephen and his brothers.

By now Stephen was at 'Walkers' nightclub. Viv had received a call from his doormen there telling him that there was trouble inside the club so they had jumped into Davy Lancaster's Shogun jeep and headed over. The three of them went in and Viv was told who was working themselves and he just walked over and knocked the two big steroid heads spark out. It was just another night at the office for Viv. They then had a quick drink in there and left in the Shogun and drove out onto the back lane of 'Walkers' and onto Bath Lane. They parked outside of 'Hobos', and were joined by a few more friends including 'Fish' Tams. The next part can be seen on a video on YouTube from a BBC TV documentary they made about Viv.

The lads approached the door and just walked in. When they walked in, they walked straight into the reception area. Shocked staff tried to explain that they were barred. Then out of nowhere Viv sees a doorman called Stuart Watson and starts to lay into him with a flurry of punches before getting him in a pressure hold. The fight continued onto the dance floor scattering punters including some undercover police officers. As the lads left the club the CCTV captured them all. The woman on reception can be seen mopping up Watson's blood and Stephen explaining that the issue was, 'private'.

The police had other ideas. This was far from a private matter. After all they had told the venue not to let the Sayers in. This was a challenge to their authority. Warrants were made for their arrests and they were rounded up hours later. During interview it was made quite clear to Viv and the lads that their association with Stephen and the Sayers family was the reason everyone was being arrested. They were all charged and taken to Newcastle magistrates court the following day. Stephen stood in the dock alongside Alan 'Fish' Tams, Davey Lancaster, John 'Nodge' Thompson, Rob Armstrong and Viv Graham.

'Nodge' was unlucky to be in the dock at all. He had absolutely nothing to do with what happened that night. He had seen Davey Lancaster's jeep pull up outside the nightclub and he had stopped his car and parked behind them and followed them in and the fight broke out. They were all remanded to stand trial and were sent to Durham Jail.

Chapter Twenty Four: Banged Up

Stephen and the lads settled straight into the 'jail' routine. Every morning they would open their cell doors and would be greeted by a chorus of "Please release me let me go I don't want to be here anymore" by Rob Armstrong at the top of his voice which would echo throughout the prison. Then give it ten seconds and you would hear an old screw screaming "ARMSTRONG SHUT UP". To say it put a smile on the lad's faces was an understatement. Little victories were good for morale.

While remanded to custody, the prisoners had to give permission for the magistrate to remand them over 7 days without attending court. If they refused, they had to be taken to court every 7 days for up to 4 months. It served no purpose at all if they had wasted bail applications. When they were taken from Durham jail the escort was completely over the top. People must have thought it was the train robbers!

With Stephen locked up, the police now arrested and charged his brother John with the robbery of two security vans, one containing £300,000. They then charged John and Stephen with GBH torture and kidnapping. This charge came from allegations made by a registered heroin addict. This person said that he was tied and gagged back to back with another man and was then beaten to a pulp with various instruments. He then claimed he was untied and released but that on his way home he was kidnapped again. He claimed that he was then tied to railway lines like you see in the westerns but that he survived as the train was re-routed. What are the chances of getting kidnapped twice in one day? This was the calibre of the witnesses the police were using against the Sayers brothers. It was something they were going to have to get used to.

On a return trip to court the lads were in the back of a police van and Stephen was double cuffed to another prisoner whilst 'Fish' and Davey Lancaster were also in the van and cuffed but not to each other. They were sitting to the side of Stephen. There were also four SPG (special patrol group) officers watching their every move. When Stephen had first got into the van a policeman had poked him really hard in the side of his body under his rib cage and laughed. Stephen looked at him and said "Wait until I get these handcuffs off and try and do that again." The van started up and began its journey with the sirens blaring.

They were category B prisoners but were being treated like they were category A prisoners for a fight in a nightclub. They were followed by the police helicopter and an armed escort with blue lights flashing. As they approached Birtley the policeman who had poked Stephen earlier looked at Stephen and Fish and said, "No speaking in the van!" 'Fish' looked straight at him told him where to go whilst Stephen put a cigarette in his mouth and lit it. He was just inhaling the first draw of his cigarette when he felt a thump on the side of his face which knocked him, and the lad he was cuffed to, off the seat. One of the SPG had blindsided him and was now trying to choke him out from behind whilst another had decided to get in on the action too so he now had two of them attacking him.

Davey Lancaster still cuffed tried his best to help Stephen as the two coppers started to lay into him with their fists, then 'Fish' jumped up and put his cuffed hands over the top of one of the coppers necks and started to give him a bear hug. Stephen was really distressed at this point and could feel his face going bright red as the police choked him. Then he heard 'Fish' shout "Let's see how you like being fucking choked you fucking dog!" The policeman started screaming for assistance.

"Stop the van escape in progress!" By now they were all wrestling and fighting in the back of the transit van and the roles had been reversed as the policeman was now getting choked and over powered by 'Fish'. The radio crackled into action with shouts from the Police saying 'DO NOT STOP...I repeat Do not stop!' The closest police armed escort that was following the van had its front bumper touching the back doors of the van to prevent the van doors from being opened and anyone from escaping but the lads were not trying to escape they had been defending themselves from police brutality.

The policeman still had his arm around Stephen's wind pipe and was punching him again as hard as he could in the ribs. He was receiving another beating but 'Fish' managed to use his weight to pull him off and they fell back over towards the backdoors, giving Stephen time to get his breath back. When he looked up 'Fish' had hit the metal part of the van door whilst the policeman crashed straight into the van's safety glass window. He put a big dint in it as he landed and it took the wind out of him. The fight had lasted around fifteen minutes and it finished as quickly as it had started. As they were approaching HMP Durham Prison the policeman who had started all the trouble was now trying to be the peacemaker and said "Just forget about it and calm down lads okay." He had obviously realised the error of his ways.

Stephen sat calmly for ten or fifteen seconds staring at him, 'Fish' then said, "When you take these cuffs off me I don't care what you do for a living I am going to do a lot worse to you than you have just done to me."

These words were enough to start it all off again but this time the other police officers in the van opted to restrain the prisoners using reasonable force as they drove through the old prison gates. As they parked up the now calm officer was going a whiter shade of pale and was starting to shake. He was sitting directly opposite Stephen who was staring him straight in the eyes and said, "You have just taken a liberty with me you cowardly cunt." There was no reply. Instead the doors opened and he rediscovered his sadistic streak and dragged Stephen and the lad he was cuffed to out of the van and tried to knee him in the ribs. 'Fish' could see what was going on and still cuffed he broke free of his escort and ran up to him and kicked him straight in the balls knocking the fight out of him. This gave Stephen a chance to pull himself together again. The riot bell started to sound in the prison and soon there were 20 screws outside the van surrounding them. The SO (Senior Officer) at Durham was a man called Montgomery and he soon assessed the situation. He knew what had gone on in the back of the van and knew that it had 'got out of hand', so he detained everybody including the police officers and screws to get their side of the story.

At HMP Durham there are metal stairs leading up to reception and they are hard solid ones with lots of sharp and blunt edges. The SO Montgomery ordered that the lads should be un-cuffed immediately. The police all looked at him disapprovingly. As Stephen was getting un-cuffed the sadistic copper had made his way to the top of the stairs. Another prisoner who hadn't travelled with them took it upon himself to take a run and jump at him and he caught him sweet as a nut and knocked him flying down the stairs. The riot alarm which had just been switched off was set off again and more screws rushed down to reception. The Governor arrived to see the copper at the bottom of the stairs being brought round with smelling salts. The Governor asked what was going on and naturally the police lied and said Stephen and the lads had attacked them in the van and then they had tried to restrain them. The Governor said, "I want everyone who has an injury to be checked over by the doctor immediately." When Stephen was checked over the doctor found over fifty bruises that he had received all over his body. He was still in a lot of pain when the doctor walked out of the room and then returned with the Governor. Stephen was standing in just his boxer shorts. The Governor took one look at his body and shared the same opinion as the doctor and he said, "You should press charges and have the police officers arrested for what they have done to you." Stephen looked at him and told him and the doctor that he didn't want to press charges against anyone but that he did wish to keep a medical record for a later date just in case they tried to charge him for the assault of a police officer. Davey and 'Fish' were unmarked.

In the reception in Durham there are four holding rooms all with clear plastic windows so you can see through. Stephen, 'Fish' and Davey were sitting there for a short while and started to smoke a spliff that one of the lads in reception handed them. Ten minutes or so had passed when the sadistic police man walked in from the doctor's room looking like he had just had a lifesaving operation. He was placed in the room next to the lads and he was sitting with his head in his hands. Stephen shouted to him "Give me two seconds and I'll get that screw to put me in there with you!" The policeman looked away. Once the Governor was satisfied with his investigation the police were allowed to go home and Stephen and the lads were given a shower and something to eat and were then stocked up with their new prison clothes. They then made their way to the cells. The screw opened the door to Stephen and Davey's pad and they were greeted with the sight of 'Viv' lying on his bed covered in chocolate wrappers and crumbs. Stephen, Davey and the screw burst out laughing and Stephen shouted "Captured you eating all the goodies eh! Could you not just have two bars like everybody else?" 'Viv' tried to respond but couldn't because he'd crammed a full bar of chocolate into his mouth. The screw locked them all up and they embraced each other and then got settled for a quiet night in and started recalling the day's events. 'Viv' was gutted that he had missed it.

Three weeks had passed when early one morning the cell door was opened and the lads saw an old screw from years back who knew Davey. The screw came in the cell and clicked the lock and said "Hello young Lancaster back, again are you?" He then told Davey that he was going to be arrested for fighting with the police alongside 'Fish,' and that they were going to court that day. Stephen looked at Davey who was sitting up in his bed. He had pulled out a packet of twenty menthol cigarettes from under his pillow and in that packet was a ready rolled spliff and two hundred pounds in cash. Davey lit up the spliff in front of the screw who just stood looking at Davey who was now blowing the smoke directly into his face. The screw told him to cut it out, whilst 'Viv' was cuddled up under the blankets giggling like a little school kid. The size of 'Viv' made this even funnier. Davey gave the screw thirty pounds and asked him to go and get him 200 menthol cigarettes. The screw took the money and walked out of the door. Ten minutes later the screw came back and said "Get your stuff Lancaster your late for court". The screws had also opened 'Fish's' cell. They both had their flasks filled, had a cup of tea, and then headed off with shouts of encouragement from Stephen and 'Viv'. They stayed behind the door that afternoon and smoked the day away. When the lads returned, they were as high as kites. They had been charged with assault on three police officers. Stephen looked at Viv and he looked at Stephen and then started to giggle. Fish and Davey both straight faced looked bemused at the reaction. Fish then said, "You think that's bad I'm charged with assaulting two inspectors as well." That was it they both burst out laughing. The cannabis had certainly taken its toll on the lads they left behind.

Stephen had been remanded for five months by now with a number of charges that saw him go to court week after week. He was playing the system. He was given technical bail on one charge but refused bail on the other charges so he was going nowhere. On the various court visits the lads would get packs of pre-packed food sent in from 'Marks and Spencers'. They had meats, peppers, asparagus, sauces and much more. They decided to hold onto these and try and find out who was number one in the kitchen because the food they were getting wasn't up to scratch and they fancied something special. As the kitchen lads came out from work Stephen asked one of the inmates who the number one orderly was. He pointed to a big man called Jenkins who stood at 6ft 3 and was quite thin. He approached Jenkins and spoke to him and asked if they could do some 'business' with their goodies in the kitchen to which he had access. This proposal seemed to upset Jenkins and he started to raise his voice. He managed just two words before he was grabbed by the scruff of the neck and dragged into a cell. The two inmates who were sitting there having their tea were shocked but they knew who Stephen and 'Viv' were and they just sat their minding their own business. They did not want to get involved.

'Viv' had a hold of Jenkins by the scruff of the neck and he was squeezing the living daylights out of him. Stephen pointed at Viv and then pointed at the kitchen and said "You either fuck Viv in a fight or you fuck the kitchen out of stock." Jenkins's replied "I'd prefer, if it's ok with you two lads to go with the second option." It was a wise move. Jenkins asked Stephen what they wanted. Stephen told him they wanted six fillet steaks. "Where do you think I'm going to pull six fillet steaks from we are in Durham prison" he said. Stephen smiled and replied "We need to see more enthusiasm Jenkins and you need to improvise."

Getting cocky now Jenkins said, "You will be asking me for the joint of meat I'm just about to cook for D-wing's dinner next." Stephen and Viv looked at each other and both turned to him and said "That will do nicely." Jenkins realised he'd dropped a right clanger and tried to back track. "Oh no you can't do this to me what I am going to feed them? There's 147 prisoners wanting beef on their dinner." "Viv said "Fuck them! Give them corn beef." The doors opened to the kitchen and the lads saw their opportunity and walked straight in. There was the big lump of beef that was getting cooked for D-wing. They grabbed it and wrapped it up in a clean towel and 'Viv' said "Here I'll carry it and I'll take it back and if anyone asks what I've got I'll tell them it's my dinner." The screws were wary of them all but especially Viv. The lads needed some salt and pepper for seasoning so Stephen grabbed some. They then made their way back to the cell thanking Jenkins on the way giving him a spliff for his troubles. When Stephen and Viv returned to the cell Davey burst out laughing when he saw the big lump of meat. He instantly knew what to do. He was an old prison lag and new all the tricks of the trade. Before bang up they got a hold of two metal trays for cooking and then Davey showed the lads the basics of how to cook in a cell.

They waited until the screws had done their count and went home so there was only a skeleton staff on the night shift and then they got cracking. The oven was made by placing a metal tray on a hard table. They then got four tins of equal size and placed the other tray on top of them and then ripped a length of bed sheet which Davey wrapped up in a ball around his finger. He slowly pulled his hand out leaving a small gap and he squirted olive oil over the top of it. He then placed it in between the two trays that were supported by the four tins and he lit it. The top essentially became a frying pan. They then used a makeshift knife which was a razor blade melted into a toothbrush handle to slice the meat. With the pan heating up 'Viv' placed three large slices of meat in. He had the door blocked with newspapers to stop the smell of the cooking going down the landing. He was quite nervous about the whole thing but his stomach kept him motivated. You see on the outside Viv was a 100% straight man. He was no criminal in anyway shape or form, he was an honest lad who could have a fight, so Davey and Stephen took over the cooking whilst 'Viv' kept lookout.

The stack was sizzling by now so they opened a tin of beans and they opened a tin of beans and they still had the pre-packed goodies that Stephen's Dad had managed to take in for him on their trips to court. The first steak was ready and was cut into three pieces. They had them with coleslaw, potatoes, salad and some bread and butter with a nice hot cup of tea as someone had stolen the kettle from the education block so they had bought it from them to make a brew! They had it wired up to the light as it was the only source of electricity in the cell. 'Fish' started shouting from next door, "You have the jail stinking off your cooking you'd better be careful." Stephen replied "How would you like your steak?" and he burst out laughing. He then said "It will be an hour or so mate I've still got some more to cook." Stephen, Davey and 'Viv' tucked into their food with big smiles on their faces. Little victories are sweet in jail and this was certainly a little victory for them. It went down that well that the cooking in the cell became a regular occurrence with no interference from the screws. Everyone on the wing could smell it but the screws just turned a blind eye to it all. The screws were more concerned about other matters and they certainly did not want to confront Stephen, 'Viv' and co. As the time went by the bond between 'Viv' and Stephen became stronger. They played cards together, cooked together, went to the gym together. They were a good team and got to see different sides of each other.

Back in those days a visitor could just turn up and didn't need to be approved and the screws would just come and tell prisoners that they had a visitor. One day a screw opened the lads cell door and told them all that they were all on visits. They made their way down to the visiting rooms passing all the faces on the way and catching up with the local gossip. As Stephen approached his table, he saw his ex-sister in law and his oldest daughter Rebecca Liza. His ex-sister in law told him that her sister, his ex was moving away to another country and it was going to be many years before he was going to get to see his daughter Rebecca again. This news was every Dad's nightmare and it caught him off guard. He was devastated. Rebecca was only two at the time, so as his ex-sister in law went to the canteen, she handed over his daughter. Stephen looked down at the innocent child's face and he began to cry. A tear dropped on her face. He forgot where he was for a moment before reality hit and he regained his composure. He could not show any weakness in jail.

'Viv' knew Stephen was upset as he was on the table next to him and had overheard the conversation. He walked over to him and gave him a big bear hug. He told him not to worry because he would see his daughter again and that things would be ok in the long run. Viv had a big heart and he was very family orientated. The visit finished and they all said their goodbyes.

Time ticked by. Stephen and Davey knew they were up for judge in chambers but had no idea when. Their cell door was always open which was great if they wanted to go out and see other friends or socialize but the downside was that they would have every ponce in the prison at the door because 'Viv' was as green as grass and would give them everything and anything if they had a hard luck story.

One afternoon Stephen and Davey had just been sitting smoking and playing cards with 'Viv' and when their game finished, they decided to go for a wander. When they came back Stephen kicked the door closed and it locked to stop any callers. Stephen jumped onto his bed and rolled a spliff and then started to smoke it. He had got a hold of some good jail weed which gets you sleepy and chilled whilst you listen to your music. An hour later he was disturbed by somebody shouting his name again and again. He tried to stand up but was disorientated and completely stoned. The voice was faint but they were definitely shouting for Stephen. He decided to shout back, "Who is it? What do you want?" There was no reply so he decided he must be hearing things and he lay back down on his bed. Then the voice started again but this time it was closer and this time he recognized the voice.

This time he got up off his bunk bed and placed the chair next to the window so he could look out of it and see outside of the cell window and he heard the voice again. It was his girlfriend Donna who was shouting. He put his hand out of the window to indicate he was there and he shouted "What's the matter?" She shouted back and told him that he and Davey had been given judge in chambers and would be bailed. Stephen was buzzing. He thanked her and told her he'd see her in a couple of hours. Davey arrived back in the cell and was delighted at what Stephen had to tell him. 'Viv' and 'Fish' came into the cell and the lads told them that they would be leaving them the next day, they were happy for them and wished them well. An hour or so passed and the screws came to get them and they said their goodbyes. It had taken the system long enough. They had been remanded for over six months for a fight in a nightclub and the injured party wasn't pressing charges.

They released Stephen and Davey on bail and they were put on a curfew. They were on bail for three months and then back at court for trial. The trial was stop start until a deal was put to them to plead guilty on the lesser charge of ABH instead of GBH. They all discussed the offer and decided that it was the best thing to do. 'Viv' pleaded guilty and admitted to being the sole person for the beating up of Stuart Watson and got an 18-month sentence. He also received 18 months for another charge of beating up a doorman at 'Madisons' nightclub. Stephen, 'Fish' David and Rob pleaded guilty to ABH on the grounds that, through their presence, they lead encouragement and they all received a sentence of two and a half years for witnessing the fight. The Sayers would have to get use to this type of treatment.

Chapter Twenty Five: The Duffer

Lee Duffy was a young man from Middlesbrough who was 17 stone, naturally built, a good amateur boxer and an excellent street fighter. Stephen had a lot of time for him and a lot of respect. He classed him as a close friend. He had heard about Duffy's fearsome reputation for violence. Unlike Viv, Duffy fought on the Sayers side of the fence. They first met as youngsters in the Low Newton Remand Centre in 1982 in the block. At first, they could only talk through the crack in their windows and their friendship developed over the first few days. Stephen would often hear Lee punching walls with towels wrapped around his hands. He also saw him lay into screws two at a time on more than one occasion.

They hooked up again when Stephen was on home leave from Acklington where he served his sentence for the 'Hobos' nightclub case. Stephen had a party in 'Masters bar' which is 'Tup Tup' these days. There was about 200 of Stephen's friends and family in attendance and it was a really good atmosphere. A lot of his travelling cousins turned up with their friends from Bedlington and Ashington.

Stephen was in the toilet when one of his brothers Michael walked in with Lee Duffy and they were re-introduced. Duffy went into the toilet cubicle and produced a big bag of cocaine. He and a few others sniffed a line and then asked Stephen if he wanted one. Stephen declined but a few others joined in with him. As this was going on 3 doormen from another venue walked in to use the toilet. When one of the door lads realized what Duffy and his mates were doing, he said, "You can't do that in here mate." Stephen asked him if he worked there. The doorman replied "No". So, Stephen said 'Well what the fuck does this have to do with you!' The doormen did not recognise his face. 'Can you fight?' Stephen asked him. There was a Mexican stand off for a few seconds which ended with Duffy springing forward like a coiled spring and throwing a combination of punches. Duffy wiped out the three doormen. Stephen was taken aback and was really impressed with Lee's fighting ability and gameness. Duffy smiled and started shouting to anyone that wanted to listen "Go and get 'Viv' Graham and I'll do the same to him". There was no doubt in Stephen's mind that Duffy would be more than a match for 'Viv'.

A few minutes later the 'Masters' doormen carried out the other doormen from the toilet. They were all conscious and nursing their injuries. One of the doormen pointed at Stephen and Michael and was explaining that it was them who they had the run in with. When they were told who they had the trouble with they decided to put it down to experience. Duffy being Duffy he had to be held back as he was wanting to knock the other doormen out as well. He was shouting 'Go and get ya fighting men I'll do the best of them,' but the last thing these people wanted was more trouble. The whole place could have gone up.

The manager at 'Masters' now had 200 guests wanting to fight with the doormen. Stephen reminded people he was on home leave and had been arrested in the first place for fighting in nightclubs. He defused the situation with the doormen that had been beaten up and they headed over to apologise and shake hands before buying them a bottle of champagne and leaving. The night ended without further incident

Stephen still had a few days home leave left so he decided to take up Lee's invite of a night out in 'Boro. They ended up in a 'Blues' that night which is basically a house in a terraced street that has been turned in to a bar/ drug den and a whore house. These places sprung up in the eighties in various cities across England such as Bristol, Birmingham and Manchester and they all had a very similar feel about them. Danger.

Lee introduced Stephen to another fighting man that night Brian Cockerill. In Lee's own words Brian was the hardest man he'd ever come across in his life. Brian was a special fighter and, on his day, nobody would have even come close to beating him. When Lee, Brian, Stephen and Co. arrived they bumped into a certain firm of men that Duffy did not get along with. He wasn't one for conversation so he attacked them and knocked quite a few of them out. A week later at the same 'Blues' somebody shouted for Duffy to come outside. The man had a Geordie accent. Duffy was shot in the leg. The injury wasn't life threatening but this was clearly a warning from somebody. Duffy foolishly signed himself out of hospital within a few days and travelled to Newcastle to see Stephen who insisted he stayed with them for a few days.

They put him up in one of their houses and got a young lady to look after him which was counterproductive. Duffy was there for rest and relaxation. She was there to lift his spirits but she drained the life out of him and he looked in a worse condition after three days with her then he did after being shot, so Stephen replaced her with her friend who was, unfortunately for Lee, not as forthcoming. One of the lads' mothers was cooking for him. Plenty of old-fashioned homemade food that brought colour back into his cheeks. His mind was certainly on the mend, but physically the shooting had taken its toll.

Despite Stephen telling his guest he could stay as long as he wanted, Lee was beginning to get homesick. He wanted to head back to Middlesbrough. Trying to keep him in Newcastle was very difficult. He had a heart like a lion. He was a proud man and he wanted revenge. The biggest problem he faced was knowing who had shot him as he'd had that much trouble. He asked Stephen to put the feelers out and to speak to certain people which he did. Before he returned home, he thanked Stephen for his friendship. Stephen gave him a gift...a bullet proof vest.

There was a lot going for the Sayers in Newcastle at that time. They had their fingers in a lot of pies. Business was booming and the clubs were full of happy clubbers all loving each other on 'E's. Duffy had arrived back in the 'Boro and Stephen received a phone call from his good friend Lee Harrison who told him that him and his Dad Tommy Harrison were going to take Duffy under their wing and look after him until his injuries healed. Lee and Tommy were close friends of Duffy and he always spoke well of them. He looked at old Tommy as a father figure and you could see they had a close bond.

The next time Stephen saw him a couple of weeks later he looked a lot better and he had a bag with a couple of guns in. A hand gun and a shot gun. Stephen asked him if the guns were really necessary. He told Stephen that he believed his life was in danger and that those people were going to come back and kill him. He then asked Stephen for his opinion on the situation. Stephen told him "I would rather be judged by 12 then carried by 6 anytime," 12 being 12 jurors and the 6 being 6 pallbearers carrying the coffin. Duffy smiled at that and gave Stephen a wink and was gone.

Over time Lee Duffy made it very clear that he wanted to fight Viv Graham. Lee was a natural heavyweight. 6ft 3, 17 stones and no steroids as opposed to Viv who was 5ft 11, a natural middleweight going on to be a light heavyweight when he wasn't on the gear. Duffy would always say in the boxing game that a good big one will always beat a good little one from a lower weight division. Viv had beaten all comers but had not come across anyone like Duffy before. Stephen decided that the time was right to put Lee's theory to the test.

Chapter Twenty Six: The Greatest Fight That Never Happened

Lee Duffy first met Michael Sayers when they had both received four-year prison sentences the same day for unrelated crimes and they met up in jail and became firm friends. Duffy got out six months later and their friendship continued. Lee feared no man, loved a scrap and when he was out in Newcastle he represented the West End. He was on a collision course with Viv and they all knew it and Lee was not shy in telling anyone who was listening that he wanted a straightener with Viv. This news travelled back to Viv and he was in no doubt that Duffy was different and dangerous to others that he had faced and he was wary of him.

At this time there was a certain high-ranking Policeman who had taken it upon himself to try and bar The Sayers and Duffy from the city. It was discrimination, of that, there is no doubt. The Sayers would always do their rounds of the bars and the clubs and finish the night off at 'Walkers'. They had also started drinking in a place called 'Buzz bar' which was located near Central Station. There was quite a few of them out on this particular night and word came round that the bizzies's and Viv Graham were saying that they were not allowed in a place called 'Maceys'. The lads were waiting for something like this happening. It was like putting petrol on the fire anybody telling them that they weren't allowed in anywhere.

There was no CCTV about in those days and they were as game as can be and knew a lot of doormen who fancied themselves as fighters that would be drinking in Maceys that night so they let the night just tick along until they were all ready. Stephen Sayers looked at his watch and gave his brother and Duffy the nod and told them its time. They knew instinctively what he meant and began the short journey to the 'Bigg Market,' twenty handed.

These lads stood back and were waiting to be called upon if needed. Stephen, Michael and Lee made their way down to 'Maceys.' They headed up the back lane and walked up to the doormen and Stephen said, "Who the fuck says the Sayers Brothers are barred from here?" There was a lot of them maybe twenty or so drinking and another five or so working the front door. There was a man from the West End who had it with a lot of doormen and was not well liked amongst the West End lads his name was Barry. Duffy struck him first. He went down like a sack of potatoes and so did three or four others. It was off and there was no holding Duffy back. This had now become the Duffy show and he was knocking them out for fun. You have to bear in mind that some of these lads were twenty stone plus. In the middle of all this mayhem one of the doormen who was standing next to the window shouted 'Come on Duffy I will fight yer.' Duffy reacted to this doorman's challenge by springing forward and sparking him out too. He then turned, springs back and knocks the other two doormen out who were standing next to him.

Duffy put eight doormen on their backsides that night and knocked as many out. Stephen said, "They were like loads of baby dinosaurs lying on the street." As they walked away from the bar Duffy was shouting that he was with the Sayers brothers and that he wanted to fight Viv Graham to anybody who could hear him. So, having battered Viv's door team and telling everyone in earshot that he wanted Viv next it became a waiting game. You could imagine the reports that Viv got back that night from his pals.

Viv knew he had a major problem on his hands. In Brian Cockerill's book 'The Resurrection Of Brian Cockerill' by Jamie Boyle he claims that the group then headed to another bar where Stuey Watson, Geoff Brown, and Steve 'The Hammer', were working. They were allowed in despite Duffy wearing shorts. He started dancing on tables, shadow boxing on the dancefloor and doing one legged squats. He met no resistance.

The next morning Stephen was awoken by the phone. He answered. It was his Dad and he wanted to see Stephen at his house urgently. Stephen headed over, head thumping and as he walked into his front room He was greeted by the sight of his Dad and Viv. Stephen's hangover cleared quickly. John Brian Sayers explained that Viv had come to see him asking if he could straighten things out with Duffy and him. He could not understand what he had done to upset him and wanted to make the peace. Stephen's Dad has always been a fair man and had agreed to speak to all parties. He then rang Duffy and after explaining the situation he passed the phone to Viv. He then pulled Stephen to one side and told him that this should be an end to this particular issue. Viv looked relieved as he handed the receiver back to John. Nothing more was said. They all exchanged handshakes and Viv was gone. The fight that many would have paid to see would now never take place.

Another well-known doorman wasn't as lucky. Howard Mills was a former professional boxer who had fought for the British middleweight title against Roy Gumbs in 1981 in Piccadilly losing by TKO. He had settled on Tyneside and was head doorman at 'Hanrahans' bar on the quayside which was where 'Sambuccas' is now just off the Swing Bridge. Mills had been shot with a shotgun on July 24th 1989 whilst leaving work. He had clearly upset the wrong people on Tyneside. Part of his right leg was amputated. To his credit he returned to the doors a few months later but came face to face with Lee Duffy who banged him in the mouth with the palm of his hand and pointed to his leg told him that he had got that for being a grass and now he had a 'slap off the Duffer,'

The Police meanwhile continued their campaign against the Sayers family. They started speaking to individual doormen, telling them that if they let the Sayers family in that they could lose their jobs in town. That didn't work so the next tactic was to tell the bar owners that they could lose their license if they allowed the family onto their premises. This didn't work either as some of the Sayers would turn up at the licensee's home asking them why they weren't letting them in. This always seemed to have the desired effect. So, the Police went back to the drawing board and came up with the idea of licensing doormen. They also created a scheme called pub watch. They decided that the only way they could deal with the Sayers was to change the laws of land.

Over the next few months Stephen kept asking Duffy to move to Newcastle but he would not have it. He would say that he'd love to but he couldn't because it would look like he was running away from the troubles he was having in 'Boro at that time. He wanted to face things head on. It was the only way he knew. He ended up getting shot again on two occasions. He got shot outside of a 'blues' in 'Boro by a lone gunman but wasn't seriously injured and on another occasion, he was confronted by three people two of which had guns. When Duffy set eyes on these people he knew they had bad intentions. He struck first and attacked them and knocked two of the three out and then wrestled with the third one. Duffy managed to get his hands on the gun and force the direction of the gun from his head down over but unfortunately the gunman discharged the gun hitting Duffy in the foot. The gunman should count himself lucky that the bullet hit Duffy that night or he would have no doubt suffered a beating.

Sadly, Duffy's luck was about to end. He got himself involved in a fight with people from the 'Boro outside another 'Blues club' and was stabbed in the back and sadly died in the street. He was a soldier and a warrior and had the heart of a lion. It did not take long for the news to filter through to the Sayers brothers on Tyneside and they were devastated. Stephen and Michael were in the 'Bay Horse Inn' in Newcastle recovering from another night out. One man started singing 'One Lee Duffy', and soon the hundred or so punters were joining in. The atmosphere was emotionally charged. Later that week Stephen, his Dad, Manny Burgo and cousins Michael and Terry Patters went through to pay their respects and speak to Lee's family. His brother was there and his Mam and they were inconsolable.

On the day of the funeral it felt like the whole of the West End wanted to pay its respects. Stephen booked a fifty-six-seater coach and a sixteen-seater mini bus. There was a pickup truck full of flowers and another twenty or so cars that made the journey about 120 people in total. The 'Duffers' funeral was by far the biggest the 'Boro had ever seen. It's the first and only funeral where crash barriers had to be put up for the crowds gathering. The church was full and there was any amount of people outside the church and lined up from the church to the cemetery which was a couple of miles away. 1500 People were lining the streets to pay their respects. Stephen and Lee's best friend Neil Booth were amongst the pallbearers. The service went off without any issues and everyone toasted his memory. This was such a tragic waste of life. Lee Duffy was only 26-years-old.

Chapter Twenty Seven: Pritchards: BlagDone

As the winter closed in and the dark nights arrived word was going around that there was a big bit of work in the offing. If it was true then this was going to take the lads who did the job to the next level. This was the big one, a potential retirement fund. The job was plotted up in a safe bar in Gateshead. The possible haul was in the region of £5M, enough to put a smile on any villain's face. The money was to be picked up from a depot in Washington and transferred under heavy security to Pritchards security depot in Gateshead. The timings of the vehicle were known so the lads got to work.

Two lads were assigned to monitor every movement the cash van made over a month-long period. Any deviations from route or change in times were noted and recorded. Another meet took place and they shared their information with the rest of the gang. It wasn't good news. The van was always followed by two undercover police vehicles with three occupants in one vehicle and four in the other, there was also police on a motor bike also undercover. There was an uncomfortable silence amongst the lads. They realised that there was no chance of stopping this van without a massive shoot out with the police. The only other option was to do the depot. The two lads were set a new task which was a find a way in. Another meet was set for a months' time.

The lads turned up at a safe house for the meet. The two lads who had been staking out the depot were already there and the smiles on their faces said it all. "This graft is ours, lads, we can get in". The lads had noticed that when the security staff would leave the building there was no security staff to lock the door after them and they could see the second door was wedged open and had been every time the front door had been opened. This was music to the gang's ears. It was not a high security door and if it was the staff were not following the correct procedures and this meant the door could be smashed open. The graft was on and they were going to go for it. They had a five-man team which made it a million pound a head. The graft was put together and the cars were put in place. The first cars which were to be used for the robbery were a Sierra Cosworth and a big wide top of the range Audi. These vehicles were specifically chosen because of their speed, power and the size of their boots to stick the haul in. Both cars were white to resemble police vehicles which would help in the getaway.

On the day of the robbery the five-man team of blaggers were plotted up in a car park about half a mile away or so from the depot. Two spotter vehicles were used on the day and as they returned, they gave the lads the green light. The two vehicles made their way to the security depot while the two spotter vehicles stayed in the vicinity in case of any unforeseen circumstances that might occur. The lads drove to the depot and pulled up just outside.

The balaclavas were rolled down and the shotguns were cocked. The staff had no idea what was going to hit them. The lads reversed into the car park. The boots and back doors of the vehicles had been opened.

All five men got out of the cars. One man stood on guard with a pump action shotgun cocked ready and waiting for anyone that dared to challenge them. The four-man team approached the door. This was second nature to these lads. One of the lads took aim at the door with a sledge hammer and let fly. It gave way but was still secure so the door was hit for a second time which forced it open. The lads ran into the building. There were three rooms with staff in each room.

The lads took a room each and told the staff to get face down on the floor. There were no heroes and all fifteen members of staff were face down in seconds. There was a gunman stood in the passage way with a pump action shotgun in his hand cocked with his finger on the trigger waiting to put any hero in their place without a second thought. These people would control with the fear factor and in a split second they would react to any hostility whatsoever with a no-nonsense approach. There were five big safes in the depot and four of them were already open and full to the brim with boxes of money approximately 6ft high and 3 foot wide. The lads wasted no time and started emptying the safes. They would grab as much as they could and then run to the cars outside and throw the large bags into the car boots and then back again for more. The two car boots were full when the call came over "TIME, TIME". Everyone knew what that meant. It had just come over the scanner, 'Armed robbery in progress all armed vehicles to attend Prichard security depot Gateshead.' The lads had all decided to stay on the work until the police were notified. It was time to leave. The lads jumped into the cars and spun off at high speed over the Gateshead flyover with blue lights flashing on the inside of their vehicles.

This part of the plan worked to perfection. As it was dark people who saw two white cars with blue flashing lights presumed, they were the police and moved out of the bad lads' way. As they drove along the flyover, they passed armed police who were rushing towards the depot. Priceless. As they came to the Tyne Bridge the traffic lights were all green which suited the lads perfectly as they were hitting 100 mile an hour plus coming towards the Swan House roundabout. At another set of lights they found themselves blocked by two cars so they had to bump one out of the way to get through. They then turned off and headed into an estate in Byker which was appropriately named Blagdone Close.

The Police scanner was going haywire as the lads were unloading the bags into a transit van. They knew they had gotten away with a few quid but they didn't know how much, but the sacks stretched from the seats at the front of the van to the doors at the back. With the van packed they then set off for a safe house in Heaton. When they arrived, they discreetly pulled into a back lane and pulled the vehicle to the side of the adjoining garage where they proceeded to empty the van as quickly and as quietly as possible. The garage was a lovely bit smother (secluded) so nobody could see them. Once the van was empty it was taken away and destroyed. The lads headed into the sitting room to start counting the money out but the bulb had gone and there was no light so one of the lads pulled out a torch and was shining it around. This was where things went pear shaped. The lad who had given them the keys for the house hadn't told his daughter who lived over the road that people would be using his house. She just happened to be in her own sitting room that night looking outside when she saw a light in her Dad's sitting room. She picked up her phone and called the Police presuming her Dads house was being burgled.

The police arrived quite quickly and headed to the front door. The two lads inside trusted with counting the money, Alan Minniken and Surtees Fisher heard them outside and tried to escape but were arrested in the backyard. The Police walked into the house and were amazed to find millions of pounds in bags lying on the floor. This was a great result for Northumbria Police. They had got the money back and nabbed two of the robbers to boot. For the lads it was like winning the lottery and then realizing you'd lost your ticket. Minniken and Surtees were charged with the £300k armed robbery. This was laughable. The card marker was quite clear that the haul would be in the millions not thousands and the fact that the haul filled the back of a transit tells you its own story. They got the money back but allegedly tried to claim that they had only had £300k stolen to stop their insurance premiums rocketing. It seems that it's not just blaggers that are dishonest! All this left a bitter taste in the lad's mouths. Talk about bad luck.

A few weeks went by and it was no surprise that John Henry Sayers was getting some special attention from the regional crime squad. At Prime Minister's Question time that was held in the House of Commons a local MP stood up and said he wished to re-name Tyneside 'bandit country'. As per population there was more robbery committed on Tyneside than anywhere else in the country. This just put more pressure on the Police and they needed to find a scapegoat. They chose John Henry Sayers.

At the time of the robbery Stephen Sayers was on remand for the incident in Hobo's night club with Viv Graham, Fish Tams etc whilst John was on Police bail for some minor traffic offence. He was due to attend the police station to answer bail but when he got there the regional crime squad had other ideas. They arrested him and kept him for a couple of days and then charged him with the robbery of the Pritchard security van. George McFadyen and Geoffrey Whelans were also arrested and charged alongside Surtees and Minniken who would also stand trial. John was interviewed and then taken back to his cell where one of the policemen tried to start up a conversation with him. He told him there had been three million three hundred thousand pounds stolen in the robbery and that they had come close to catching them after the robbery but had lost them on the Tyne Bridge. He continued that they had been instructed to shoot the robbers if they caught up with them. That order came, allegedly, from above. These comments got no response from John and he went back to his cell. He was then hit with a voluntary bill of inditement which meant that he would miss all minor court appearances and would be fast tracked to crown court which was unheard of at the time. It left his legal team scratching their heads too. It left him 7 weeks to prepare his defence. A High Court judge was assigned to the case, Justice Leonard. The evidence against John was very weak but the Police had another trick up their sleeve. A handpicked witness who they had managed to get onside to say exactly what they wanted.

Philip Bourke was a former security guard who had worked for Pritchards. Bourke was on remand in HMP Armley Prison in Leeds and while he was there, he repeatedly told anyone that would listen that he was in for the crime of armed robbery. The Police said he was the man who was guilty of supplying the inside information about the robbery i.e. the card marker. Whilst he was in prison on the exercise yard he seemed to mix in his own little crowd and he would tell his fellow inmates who became his friends that the Police showed him a photograph of a man he had never seen before and this man's name was John Henry Sayers. They had told him that if he did not pick John Henry Sayers out on of an identification parade and give evidence against him that he would receive a custodial sentence of fifteen years but if he did do as he was told then he would receive a sentence of two years.

This must have been on his mind 24/7 because he would mention the same story and each time stated the same thing, that he had never met John Henry Sayers before. That was music to John's solicitor's ears. Three of Bourkes friends all made the same statement to their own solicitors verifying the same thing that Philip Bourke had confirmed many times to them that he had never met John. When the trial began in 1989 Stephen had been released so he headed to court to give John support.

John went on trial for the depot and van at Washington at the same time. What is known as a half time submission was lodged and John was acquitted of the Washington robbery which meant that the jury should have been discharged and a new trial started. That didn't happen.

It was full of undercover policemen all shaking their heads at any words that came out of John's defence barrister's mouth. This was clearly an attempt to influence the jury. John called his witnesses and his witness statements were also read out. The Judge dismissed Johns' witnesses and assured the jury that no deal whatsoever had been made by the Police or Phillip Bourke. The defence were then handed a tape of DI Barry Lambert and DC David Hales talking to Bourke and showing him holiday snaps of John, Stephen and others on holiday in Tenerife which was quite improper. The police put two statements in together about continuity except they were different. The officer was called to give evidence and at the crucial moment Justice Leonard said he was ill and left the bench. The next morning everything was smoothed over.

Half way through the trial there was an application by Johns' defence team which was led by Mr Richard Louden to have the case thrown out due to lack of evidence but again the Judge ignored the defences plea. The trial came to a close with both sides stating their case in the final speeches and then the jury went out. The Sayers family watching on felt confident and the jury returned and the foreman of the jury was asked if they had made a decision on all of the defendants. They had. John and George were found guilty of all charges and sentenced to 15 years apiece. They were seen as the ringleaders. Alan and Geoff fared slightly better getting 13 years whilst Fisher got 3 years for his part. There was a lot of murmuring but not much reaction in the public gallery but the police were grinning like Cheshire cats.

The brothers stared at each other across the court and nodded and winked but showed no other emotion. The MP's had got their scape goat and the Police had got their man. As Stephen walked out of the courtroom, he was greeted in the hallway by about 15 or so policemen all celebrating as if their team had just won the FA cup final. Those celebrations went on well into the night. Stephen headed back to Newcastle and to his Mother's house. He parked at the top of York Street and as he walked to the front door she was pulling up in the car. She got out and started walking towards him. Nobody knows you better than your mother and she took one look at Stephen and she knew straight away. She collapsed to the ground and started screaming relentlessly. Stephen had never seen his Mother like this before. She was inconsolable. She had lost her first child still born and this to her was like losing another son.

Stephen managed to get her indoors where her friends and family arrived to show their support. It was a heart wrenching experience. It made Stephen realise that the career they had chosen did not just affect the lads personally but it hurt their loved ones at home when things did not go to plan. The phone was ringing constantly over the next day or so with messages from all over the country sending their best wishes and support. Stephen was gutted and his head was battered. The Sayers had lost this battle but they hadn't lost the war.

Raid was timed to the second

By LINDA RICHARDS

THE raid on the Pritchard security firm's Gateshead offices sparked a major police inquiry involving police forces around the country.

It is the biggest wages robbery in the North-East to date and inquiries spanning 10 months took policemen to Yorkshire, Scotland and Liverpool.

Police officers clocked up thousands of miles gathering evidence and information for the inquiry, collating hundreds of pieces of information which were all fed into a Home Office computer to build up a composite picture of what happened on the night of February 15 last year.

All leads and every piece of information, even the flimsiest snippets, were followed through to piece together step by step the gang's movements.

What emerged from months of tireless investigations was a picture of a terrifyingly well-executed military-style operation timed to the last second.

From the moment the gang burst into the Durham Road offices, wearing horror masks and balaclavas, and wielding guns, sledgehammers and pickaxe handles, until they fled carrying £150,000 in banknotes, the operation went like clockwork, just as it had been drawn up in detail on paper in the planning — until fate took a hand.

Normal

It was a normal Wednesday night when security office staff, mainly women, were compiling wage packets for the following day, when the six-man armed gang smashed their way in with sledgehammers.

Staff were herded into a back room and forced to lie on the floor as the gang ransacked the premises.

Meanwhile, a security guard who drove up in the middle of the raid, had a sawn-off shotgun smashed through the van window before being dragged from his vehicle and forced on the floor with a gun at his head.

When he heard an order from one of the robbers to a gunman to blow his legs off, he managed to roll to safety under his van and escape harm.

Next the gang sped off in two stolen cars towards the east end of Newcastle, where, in Blagdon Close, they switched vehicles, threatening passers-by at gunpoint.

They abandoned the two getaway vehicles, transferring to a hire van, which was driven to a "safe house" in Trewhitt Road, Heaton, where the up-till-then perfectly executed plan fell apart.

Mistake

It was there that a minor mistake led to major repercussions and gave police the breakthrough they needed to put them on the trail of the robbers.

At Trewhitt Road, an empty flat had been carefully chosen to stash the money until the heat died down and the haul could be shared out.

But it was there that fate took a hand and the flat owner's daughter saw lights in the flat, thought it was being burglared and alerted police.

Uniformed officers from Clifford Street, Byker, raced to the flat, where they found all the money except £5,000 and three guns — two sawn-off shotguns and a machinegun-style shotgun — abandoned by the robbers in their hasty bid for freedom.

Bank tellers and cashiers, used to handling vast amounts of money, were called in to assist police and count the thousands of recovered banknotes.

Two men were arrested nearby after a police chase and then followed a long protracted inquiry and exhaustive investigation which has cost thousands of pounds itself, in officers' overtime, travelling expenses and the protection of witnesses.

Security was a major feature of the subsequent court appearances and trial, with Gateshead CID officers teaming up with the Northumbria Special Patrol Group and colleagues in the Durham Police Force to put an armed dragnet around the courts.

One of the senior officers involved in the inquiry, Det Chief Insp Reg Johnson, deputy head of Gateshead CID, said: "This is one of the most serious robberies in the North-East, not just because of the high value of the money taken but because of the sophisticated planning by the gang and the breadth of the investigation and security measures at the subsequent trial."

The planning of the robbery read like a cops and robbers thriller, with every gang member having his own role to play in the jigsaw.

There was Mr Big, who masterminded the entire raid; The Planner, who meticulously planned every detail of the strike; The Firearms Man, who organised the hardware; The Wheelmen, who arranged the transport and drove the getaway vehicles; and the "foot soldiers," who wielded the guns and terrorised the staff.

There was also the gang member who arranged the "safe house" and the "inside man," the former guard who passed on vital information to make the robbery possible.

The police file on the robbery is not yet closed. Det Chief Insp Johnson said: "Police inquiries have not been concluded.

"Inquiries are still on-going to trace other members of the gang who made good their escape that night."

GANG leader John Henry Sayers, 26, of Coquet Terrace, Newcastle, an unemployed fruiterer, whose family own a hostel in the west end of Newcastle, probably used his short spell in the Parachute Regiment to help organise the raid with military precision.

George McFadyen, 42, of East Acres, Dinnington, who helped mastermind the robbery, was planning to set up in business in Malta, but his plans were thwarted by his arrest. His scrapyard on Newcastle Quayside has burned down since his arrest.

Alan Minniken, 30, of Grosvenor Court, and Geoffrey Whelans, 30, of Greenway, both Chapel Park, Newcastle, are both family men who have lived in the Newburn and Lemington areas all their lives.

Also in the dock was Surtees Fisher, 52, of Trewitt Road, Heaton, Newcastle, who provided the safe house.

How the Evening Chronicle reported the robbery

Chapter Twenty Eight: The Free John Sayers March

After the initial disappointment of John receiving a fifteen-year sentence, minds were firmly focused on his appeal. Prior to the appeal in 1990 there was a lot of talk amongst the lads about creating some publicity for this. They had a couple of journalists interested in their next move which was a good start. They all came to the decision to join together and have a march through Newcastle City Centre. There is a lot of preparation needed for that kind of thing, you can't just march through the streets. So, the family went to the solicitors and he told them that they would have to register the march with the Police to keep everything legal. With this news they expected problems but they ticked all the boxes and were granted permission. Next, they had to prepare the banners. This was difficult. None of them were budding Tony Harts or had spent hours watching 'how to make the perfect banner' on 'Blue Peter'. They scrapped a few but eventually got them right. Another hurdle had been overcome.

On the day of the march about six or seven hundred people turned up at the starting point which was on Elswick road. The crowd stretched from the 'Blue Man Pub' to 'The Dodds Arms.' It was a 1pm start but Stephen Sayers had made sure that everyone had arrived by midday. There was a strong positive and uplifting atmosphere amongst the crowd. Stephen had moved the starting point of the march without telling the Police due to the vast numbers of people that had turned up. It was more for safety than anything else but one copper took the hump and started shouting at him to get the crowd back to the arranged spot. The crowd as I have already mentioned were in a good mood but started booing the copper and shouting back at him which he didn't find amusing.

Freddy Mills better known locally as 'Fred the Head' then came running past Stephen with one of the 8-foot-long poles that the banners were being held up with. Freddy darted past the crowds with this pole in the air and immediately started chasing this out spoken policeman around his police car a couple of times. Even though the policeman had not been harmed whatsoever he was screaming at the top of his voice. It was unbelievably embarrassing for this man who had just tried to intimidate the crowd. As 1pm approached the crowds were growing longer and longer. Another overzealous policeman decided to drive along the road and pass the crowd at high speed and then put on his brakes and come to a skidding halt. He immediately jumped out of his car and slammed the door while shouting very aggressively that he was personally going to stop this march. He was pulled to one side by an Inspector who told him to stop making a fool of himself.

Stephen spoke to the crowd using a loud hailer and he told them that they were ready to start and told them which route they were going to take. He led the march with John's oldest daughter. They walked along Elswick Road and then down the Westgate hill. The crowd was growing all the time as they made their way through Newcastle city centre. By the time they got to Northumberland Street there were over 2,000 people and the City was at a standstill. The police asked them to speed the march up. Stephen told them it will be finished when it is finished. This didn't go down to well with them and one policeman threatened him. Stephen stormed towards him and could see the fear in his face. He reminded him, man to man, that he was incapable of doing anything with him. The march continued along Percy Street. As many people were leaving to go about their business, others were joining to show their support. There was a lot of noise and a lot of animosity shown towards the Police who were trying to provoke a reaction. The Sayers did the best they could and the march was as successful as it could have been. The march finished back where they had started on Elswick Road where Stephen thanked everyone for attending on the loud hailer. They got a great write up in the papers the following day and there was a follow up article in the Chronicle when a banner was draped on the Tyne Bridge and photographed as the Great North Run took place. John was quoted speaking from Whitemoor Prison saying, "No matter how long it takes I will prove my innocence." Now it was time to focus on the appeal itself.

John Henry had decided to hire the services of Michael Mansfield QC who was looked upon at the time as one of the top QC's in the country. He was to look at the PACE Act (Police And Criminal Evidence Act). This was brought in specifically to prevent miscarriages of justice and they felt this case fell into that category. The day for the appeal arrived. Stephen and co. had set off for London the day before and had stayed in a hotel for the night. There was about 30 of them and their hopes were high.

The appeal started and Mr Mansfield presented the case like any expert would. He clearly proved that the PACE act had been broken on numerous occasions by the Police but unfortunately this fell on deaf ears with the appeal court judges and they took no notice of Mr Mansfield as it appeared, they had their own agenda. It is amazing to think that the law of the land would install a procedure to prevent miscarriages of justice taking place but when these procedures are totally disregarded by the Police it makes you wonder why this PACE act was put into place to start with.

As I have said the judges had their own agenda, the decision had already been made. John lost his appeal and it was a very sad day for all concerned. Stephen, Michael and the rest of the family were devastated. John was taken back to prison and they headed home.

FREE ME FROM NIGHTMARE, SAYS CONVICT

JOHN SAYERS IS INNOCENT ... say posters across the Tyne Bridge during the Great North Run.

DEMO ON BRIDGE FOR ROBBER JOHN

By NIGEL GREEN

CONVICTED armed robber John Sayers this afternoon told of his nightmare world in a high-security prison. I pledged: "I will be free!"

And, after a banner-waving demonstration during yesterday's Great North Run, he promised to prove his innocence – by taking Northumbria Police to court.

The 29-year-old was branded as the North East's most notorious criminal suspected

by detectives of having carried out the biggest-ever raid in Sunderland.

The former para-trooper was arrested for the £750,000 robbery at West Sunniside Post Office four years ago, but later cleared by a jury at Durham Crown Court.

The armed gang, who rammed open the post office gates with a Range Rover, had operated with "military precision".

But, despite his acquittal, Sayers was later convicted of a £300,000 robbery on a security van in Gateshead – and jailed for 15 years.

He has lost an appeal against conviction and leave to appeal against sentence.

But now he plans legal action against Northumbria Police, claiming they breached the Police and Criminal Evidence Act in showing a witness photographs of Sayers.

Speaking from White Moor maximum security prison, near Cambridge, he said: "I will prove my innocence – no matter how long it takes.

VERY BITTER

"It's hell being shifted from prison to prison, hundreds of miles away from my wife and three little girls. I feel very bitter and very angry."

John, a fruit and veg merchant, from the West End of Newcastle, is backed by his wife

JOHN SAYERS ... when he was in the Parachute Regiment.

Yvonne, and their three daughters, as well as his brothers, Michael and Stephen.

Two years ago, after his conviction for the Gateshead robbery, nearly 1,000 people, took part in a march around Newcastle, chanting: "Free John Sayers."

Yesterday, at the start of the Great North Run, banners were dropped from the Tyne Bridge by supporters. Three men were arrested for alleged public disorder, but released without charge.

Sayers told the Echo his fight to see his name been forgotten.

"I have been in seven prisons since I was convicted."

How the Evening Chronicle reported the march

Chapter Twenty Nine: The Shooting Of Robert Smith

In the early 90's Stephen moved back to the West end of Newcastle after being absent for many years. He lived in a two-bedroom downstairs flat in Stanton Street with his common law wife Donna and his two children at the time, young Stephen aka Moe and Stevie Lee.

The flat itself was like most flats, too small. He decided to buy a house on Grange Road in Fenham which had three bedrooms and two sitting rooms. It was semi-detached and a very spacious house with big gardens at the back and a car park at the front. It did not take them long to get settled in and find their feet. There was a pub not far from them in Cowgate called the Ord which was owned by a friend of his called Cecil Levy. Cecil was a kind natured lad and as strong as a bull. He was so strong as a young lad he could get a six-inch nail and bend it in half. Michael Sayers was using this bar at that time as his local and there was a few of the lads going in there like, Tommy Dillon, Richy Hall, Billy Dixon and various others. The bar itself was not flash or fancy. That kind of bar just wouldn't have suited the locals if you know what I mean. Kick offs were a common occurrence and I'm not just talking about blokes. Most Monday lunchtimes you would see a woman screaming at her bloke outside the boozer because he had just blown the families money on a dodgy tip or pissed it up the wall over the weekend. Some lasses wouldn't waste their time screaming but would just attack their man with different things like ashtrays, glass bottles and any other item they could get their hands on to use as a weapon. Madness.

A friend of the Sayers family Nigel Abadom had just recently been released from prison and he didn't have a place to stay so Stephen asked Cecil if he could have the flat above the bar for a while until Nigel got himself back on his feet and found himself some accommodation. Cecil had no issues with that and he gave Nigel a set of keys. On the day he moved in Stephen, Michael and a few of the lads met up in the bar and went through to the lounge area to wait for Nigel to get ready and come down to join them. They had a couple of drinks whilst the old ladies in the bar enjoyed their game of bingo. Someone was messing about with the water supply whilst Nigel was trying to get a shower. The water was going hot and then cold. Not happy he came downstairs with his towel wrapped around his waist to complain. As he was talking to Cecil about the situation somebody whisked his towel away from his waist leaving him standing starker's in the middle of the bar. The old woman who were playing their quiet game of bingo were now witnessing a 6ft naked black man with nothing on but the soap suds on his head. Some of the old dears found it mortifying but most of them were whistling and clapping their hands shouting "We didn't know you we putting strippers on Cecil". The lads were howling.

Nigel managed to get ready and they headed into town about 12 handed. They all had a good drink and ended up back in Cecil's bar for a lock in. Everybody was in the lounge part of the bar when there was a knock at the door. As Stephen looked out of the side window to see who it was, he saw a man who he knew well. Robert Smith was a friend of Michael but Stephen kept him at arm's length. Smith was the type of man who had a reputation for being lairy and he fancied himself as bit of a fighter. He could be outspoken and insulting at times to people he thought he could do it to.

The previous week Stephen had overheard a conversation with him and Michael and heard him say quite clearly "I will fight your brother Stephen." Stephen had put his drink down, walked over to him and said "Get outside bigmouth!". A silence came over the bar for a few seconds and a few people got between them and Stephen made it perfectly clear that any time he wanted a fight that all he had to do was to go and see him instead of pulling his brother to one side.

A voice shouted "Stephen you're wanted on the bars telephone". He walked away from the window and went to take the call. He then saw a certain man who I don't wish to name so I will call him Mr X. (This man later became a police informer). On a couple of previous occasions this man had asked Stephen if he could be his minder. Stephen had heard a few stories about this man's use of extreme violence and this man was certainly handy if any incident arose. In those days Stephen's philosophy on life was to fight fire with fire. He went behind the bar to take the call and when it had finished, he was making his way back though the bar when he was approached by Mr X who told him that Robert Smith was now in the bar and he was working himself with people. Stephen was just in the mood to give him a good old-fashioned licking. So, he made his way through to the lounge part of the bar. Mr X was walking in front of him and as soon as Robert set eyes on Stephen the first thing he did was insult him. He had just given Stephen the perfect excuse to set about him but he never got the chance. Mr X stood in front of him lifted his arm and in the same breath says to Robert "We have had enough of you, arsehole". To Stephen's surprise he was holding a handgun.

Stephen was stood directly behind the shoulder of Mr X. He could see his hand clenching the gun which was cocked back and directly pointed at Robert Smiths' head at point blank range. Mr X proceeded to slowly but surely pull the trigger. Now fortunately for Robert Smith he had a bizarre habit of jumping from side to side spontaneously and he did it when the gun went off and as a result, the bullet hit Robert Smith in the side of the head just above the temple and through the other side in-between his skull and scalp then exiting out the back of his head. This all happened within seconds. Stephen had only wanted to bash Robert up he didn't want to kill him. He made a be-line for the gun and grabbed it out of Mr X's hands and told him to make himself scarce whilst looking around to see if any of Smith's friends were going to get involved.

Those who had come in the bar with him that night wisely stayed in their seats. Stephen managed to defuse the situation and have a look at Roberts injuries which miraculously weren't life threatening. Naturally Robert was complaining about the pain in his head. The blood was gushing out so

Stephen went to get Robert a towel to try and stem the flow. He passed the gun on to be disposed of then looked at Smith's injuries and told him it was not life threatening but he needed a doctor and quickly. In the meantime, he wrapped the white towel around his head and sat up. He asked for a pint of lager before he went to the hospital. He had his pint and took a bag of cocaine from his pocket and proceeded to pour it on his injury insisting it would numb the pain. One of the lads in the bar volunteered to give Robert a lift to Newcastle's RVI hospital which was no more than a mile away.

With Smith gone and the mess mopped up the lock in continued and Stephen sat and supped a few more pints till the sun came up with Billy Dixon and Tommy Dillon. You might find that a little strange after what he had just witnessed but this kind of thing was water off a ducks back to Stephen. If there was anything good to come out of this night it was that he never got another bad word out of Robert Smith again.

Chapter Thirty: The Wild West End

Between 1991 and 92, Stephen was living with his partner in Stanhope Street, Newcastle. One day he was waiting for Michael to arrive to pick him up. He was half an hour late. Stephen kept pacing backwards and forwards at his front door. He hates being late. Finally, there was a knock at the front door. 'About time' he said as he answered the door. When he opened the door, it was not his brother it was his friend Yanhal. He told him that Michael had broken down up the street and his car had overheated and asked him for a kettle full of water. Stephen went into the kitchen to get the kettle. His partner had just bought this kettle only a week previous and she wouldn't be too pleased with him taking it out but what she didn't know wouldn't hurt her. When he reached the broken down car he could see the bonnet was open and steam was pouring from the engine. He emptied the kettle of water into the radiator. Hopefully that would sort out the problem. They gave it a few minutes and turned the car over a couple of times before it kicked in. They were off. They started driving along Newmills Road which is in the West End when suddenly the engine made a really loud noise. Whatever Michael had done to the car earlier it wasn't happy and it came to a grinding halt outside the 'Darnell Pub'. This heap of scrap was going nowhere. They had no other option but to dump it there.

They decided to pop into the pub. Stephen was too late for his meeting now anyway. It would keep for another day. 'The Darnell' wasn't a popular bar in Newcastle at that time. The pub was owned by Vaux breweries which were based in Sunderland whereas most bars in Newcastle were owned by Scottish And Newcastle. The football fans would always swerve the pub because of that link to Sunderland. They were greeted by a man called Charlie and he told Stephen and Michael that the pub was up for grabs if they were interested. They were wanting 18 grand all in for the fixtures and fittings and 10 grand deposit but Stephen told them he wouldn't give them that for the building it just wasn't worth it. Charlie could see the glint in Stephen's eye though so he offered them a chance to take it over and pay as they went. That was much more appealing. Stephen and Michael had a quick chat and agreed to give it a go. They shook hands with Charlie to seal the deal. Maybe that car breaking down outside was fate.

The bar itself was taking between £500 - £700 per week which wasn't covering the expenses such as staff wages and bills. Despite this, there was no doubt the place had potential. The lads couldn't understand why the place wasn't making money. They took over with immediate effect. The staff seemed happy that they had taken over and were all happy to stay on. That night they had a bit crack with them and the few locals getting in to see what they felt were the real issues. Many said that the kids around the doors were waiting to see who went in and were then screwing their houses. The lads would sharp put a stop to that. Over the next few hours, and pints, they plotted how they were going to turn the boozer into a gold mine. Stephen headed home just before closing time and left Michael to lock up. He hadn't got far along the street when his partner appeared in front of him asking him where he had been and where the hell was her new kettle. Michael hearing the noise had popped his head out of the door and shouted that the kettle was wedged under the back wheel of the motor because the handbrake didn't work. That did not go down well.

Word spread like wild fire that the lads had taken over the bar and over the first month they managed to get the takings up with the assistance of good match day trade and some major overnight lock ins. They never really closed the bar and were averaging £8 grand per week. In one particular lock in there was approximately 100 people or so and they had been partying for one of the lad's birthdays, Tommy Dillon who was one of the Dillon brothers from the West End of Newcastle. There was a good atmosphere in the bar that night and the last person left at 9 o'clock in the morning. The area manager from Vaux breweries arrived an hour later to see Stephen to tell him that because of the large amount of alcohol that they had been buying from them that they had decided to make them a better deal. They told Stephen to scrap the idea of paying for fixtures and fittings on the bar and that they had another two bars and wanted to know if they would be interested in running them too. He put his cards on the table and told Stephen straight " Head office can't believe how much alcohol you have been buying," he continued to tell him that they had ordered a £5000 dray beer order for delivery on the Monday and got another £6000 order only days later on the Thursday of the same week and that those kinds of figures were second to none. This certainly had created a big impression and got the Sayers brothers noticed for doing something right for a change.

There were stables in the back of the bar which had not been used for years but they were still suitable for horses. Stephen had been given a horse as a gift from one of his traveling cousins. He was drunk that night and he had it in the back of a horse box which was becoming an inconvenience to him so Stephen accepted the horse and put it in the stable. It started to became a novelty act in the lock ins and you could guarantee someone drunk in the bar would offer one of the girls to see the horse and off to the stable they went.

Anyway, getting back to the area manager. If they took on the other two pubs as well as the Darnell, they would not have to pay any bills, so no rent, no gas and no electric just their alcohol bill. He told Stephen he was going to spend £70 grand on the Darnel but the refurbishment had to be done by the people from the brewery so there was no earner on that part for the lads. Stephen took this all in and then told him that he'd take the three bars on but he wouldn't need £70k spent on a refurb as the place was perfect the way it was. He told him that he wanted a reduction on the price of beer they were buying from them though for all three pubs. The area manager went away made a phone call and came back and struck the deal with him. Stephen was very happy indeed.

As they signed the deal the area manager looked at Stephen in a quizzical way and asked him, "What is your secret?" Stephen sat back and savoured the moment. He looked at him and said "To be honest there is only one way to describe it," and he asked "What?" He was hanging on his every word. "Please tell me the suspense is killing me what is your secret?" He was just about to open his mouth and the word 'Respect' was coming off his tongue when the door to the bar lounge opened and in wandered the horse with a girl sat upon the back of it wearing nothing but a pair of high heels and cowboy hat. The horse clearly startled ran into the bar slipped on the wet floor and knocked all the tables over like dominos flinging the girl off the horse and onto the floor. The area manager tried to help this beautiful naked girl up off the floor. She thanked him and asked who he was. Stephen told her it was the horse owner. The area manager was just shaking his head in disbelief with a big silly smile on his face.

So in the space of a few months the Sayers Brothers now had three pubs and were buying in cheap drink and turning over a good profit. The Darnel was still their main bar though and the parties were relentless. The atmosphere was always the same in that place. Plenty of laughs but a few rucks as well. The lads tended to let people sort out their disputes and clean up afterwards. It was that type of place.

On one particular evening Stephen arranged to meet a lady in the Darnel who was working for a local Newspaper at the time. He found this woman very down to earth, well-educated and a genuinely nice person. When she said she was going to do something then she would do it. She stuck by her word and had done a write up about the march that they had held for John Henry. That night a fight broke out between two men in the pub who had been out on the drink together. The two of them proceeded to punch the living day lights out of each other. The young lady in question started to look concerned and said "Aren't you going to break the fight up and stop them? Stephen said "I am most certainly not." She said, "Break it up Stephen they are really hurting each other". So, he said "Don't be alarmed this is not unusual. They fight better in this bar". She looked shocked and said "Why is that?" He replied "because in this bar winner stays in." The lady did see the funny side.

Night became day in that bar and day become night. All the lads would come and use the place. The Sayers would put a lot of free food on at the bar for the old age pensioners and those less fortunate. People could go to the bar get some hot food, in a warm place with some good company in a safe environment and watch television if they wanted. If anyone went in the bar drunk working themselves and looking for a fight which happened from time to time in the West End of Newcastle then they'd end up unconscious after a right hander from Stephen or Michael. They were fearless and nobody could take one of them on never mind two of them.

They were also hitting the beer hard and partying every night and

doing what red blooded males do. One-night Stephen was lying in bed at his house on Stanton Street that was only five minutes from the bar when his phone rang in the house and his partner answered. She started screaming.
Stephen jumped out of bed and took the phone off her and placed it to his ear. He could just hear somebody saying "He's dead cuz he's dead." Stephen replied, "Who the fuck is this and who is dead?" It was someone calling him from the bar and they were hysterical. All he could hear was screaming in the background, it sounded like complete chaos. Once the caller regained their composure this person told Stephen that his younger brother Michael was dead along with a couple of others in the bar.

Stephen got ready straight away and put a bullet proof vest on that he had in the cupboard. He put a coat on and got in his car and headed for the pub. As he arrived at the bar there was a lot of police activity and people nosing. The air was full of sirens and flashing blue lights. About half a dozen policemen were shouting "Stop him! Stop him!" as Stephen got out of his car and headed towards the doors. He was stopped dead in his tracks by armed police with guns pointing towards his head shouting "Show us your hands." They asked who he was. He told them he was Stephen Sayers and he explained that he had received a phone call about his younger brother. They told him that he had been taken to hospital but that they were not sure if he was still alive or not. Stephen turned around without hesitation and jumped in his car and drove to the hospital at high speed. His mind was racing and he was thinking to himself that they would not take Michael to hospital if he was dead so there was still a flicker of hope in his mind that his younger brother was still alive.

Stephen screeched to a halt at the hospital and jumped straight out of the car and left the lights on, the keys in and the engine still running but it didn't cross his mind. All he wanted to know was if Michael was alive and if he was going to be ok and of course who was responsible. As he was running into the hospital looking for him, he was stopped by two armed policemen who pointed their guns towards his head. This was the second time in just under five minutes he'd had guns pointed at his head and his life threatened by armed police despite his brother being the victim. They started to search him and found that he was wearing the vest. One now had a machine gun placed right on the temple of his head shouting for him to slowly raise his hands and asking him if he was armed. He was screaming at Stephen to drop on the floor. Stephen lowered to his knees with his head forced against a wall with the gun now at the back of his head and they slowly took the vest off him. They asked who he was and what he was doing there so he explained that he had just received a phone call that his younger brother had been shot and he was there to find him and see how he was as he had been told that his brother was dead.

Stephen was getting nowhere fast with the officers and despite having a gun pointed at his head was beginning to lose his patience with the two of them. The situation was defused by a Sergeant who was walking past and felt that their behaviour was uncalled for. He spoke to them and they removed the gun from Stephen's head and allowed him to stand up. The sarge then gave him permission to go on his way. Stephen left carrying the vest under his arm. His heart was racing. Not because of the police but because of the uncertainty over his brother. He went down one corridor and then another until he reached A and E and heard a familiar voice. It was his brothers voice. He made a be-line to the cubicle and barged his way in. To his amazement he was sat up and actually looked perfectly normal considering he had been shot seven times. He didn't seem bothered in the slightest he was laughing and was even cracking jokes with the nurses. Stephen looked him in the eyes and asked him if he was really ok and with a smile on his face he said, 'Apart from my bullet wounds I'm perfect' and laughed out loud. He then said 'Poor harry though', Stephen said, 'Poor Harry who?' He said 'Poor Harry Orange their Dads cousin had been mistaken for Stephen and he had been shot five times and they had him on the operation table fighting for his life. Fortunately for Harry he was a big strong 18 stone man and survived. He was lucky but not as lucky as Stephen for not being there. Once Stephen had established that Michael was ok, he asked him the million-dollar question. "Did you see who it was?" His reply was short but simple. "Yes".

Before Stephen left the hospital, he saw a good friend Richy Hall and pulled him to one side and asked him if he'd seen what happened and he said he had. He told Stephen that when people were arriving or leaving the lock in at the pub for some reason Michael was letting them in and out which he didn't normally do as the brothers had someone employed to do that. The bar had been quite full with about thirty people or so. There had been a group of girls sat right next to the window just moments prior to the gunman's arrival and fortunately the girls had moved and decided to sit down elsewhere. There had been a tap at the window and Michael had lifted the curtain up and there was a gun man stood on the opposite side of the window. The gunman recognised him and discharged his firearm at point blank range hitting Michael in the shoulder and knocking him back over. Michael being Michael though and not wanting to shy away from a bit of trouble decided to charge again at the gunman so he shot him twice again which forced him back onto the ground. Amazingly Michael got back up and tried to charge again and got shot for a fourth time. The would-be assassin pointed at his second target who he believed to be Stephen but in fact was their Dad's cousin Harry Orange who received five bullets into the core of his body. When the gunman fled Michael had sat down on the floor. When the ambulance arrived, he refused to get in it as he did not want to go to hospital. When he had eventually arrived at the hospital, he didn't want to go in but his Dad persuaded him and then had to restrain him to stop him leaving. The doctor gave him drugs to sedate him and calm him down.

When Stephen left the hospital, he headed home where some of his friends were waiting for him and checking the house to see if Donna and his children were safe. He moved them all to a safe house. His head was battered. These would be assassins were still on the loose and the question was would they come looking for Stephen?

His cousin owned a caravan which was parked across the road from his house and it was parked outside of his front door. It was a perfect smother as it blocked the view for any potential ambush. Stephen jammed the halogen light to stay on and opened his front door. It was about 3 o'clock in the morning. This was a deliberate attempt to draw attention to show his front door was open with passage lights on as well. Stephen had a car at the top of the street with a few lads in and a car full at the bottom of the street too. These lads could box in any cars that pulled up outside Stephen's house. There were also people in the caravan and in the house. Everyone was tooled up. There was going to be no mercy shown. Hours and hours went by and cars went back and forth. But not with the occupants that they were looking for. Revenge would have to keep.

Michael was operated on that night with his Dad and his solicitor McKeag by his side. He wanted to leave immediately but was persuaded to stay one more night by his family. The shooting had mentally affected him. He felt insecure, paranoid and could not sit still. He couldn't stay in the same place for any amount of time. He started to experiment with cocaine, Valium and speed and was having relationships with three different women. His life and others around him were never going to be the same again.

Chapter Thirty One: No More Viv

If Lee Duffy's death had sent shockwaves through the 'Boro in 1991 the death of Viv Graham was to have a similar effect on Tyneside. Viv had not led a quiet life by any stretch of the imagination and it was fair to say that he had a few enemies gunning for him before his untimely death. In fact there had been another attempt made on his life a few years earlier. In *Fog On The Tyne by Bernard O'Mahoney* there is a story about an attempt on Viv's life in 1988. In February 1988 Viv was involved in an attack on Carl Wattler. Viv was working on the door at Baxters in Newcastle and he asked Carl amongst others to drink up. He didn't drink up quick enough for Viv's liking so Viv punched him in the face. He was then put out of the bar. When Viv left to go home Wattler was waiting for him at the exit and a fight broke out between them. Wattler was apparently getting the better of the fight until one of Viv's doormen came out of the shadows and clumped him with a metal bar knocking him unconscious. He was left for dead in the street. He was rushed to hospital and a CT scan showed a large blood clot at bottom of his skull. He went under the knife and had a lengthy spell in intensive care on a ventilator to help him breathe. After the attack the book claimed that 'Skinny' Gary Thompson tried to shoot Viv as revenge for the beating. The other suggestion was that he tried to kill him because he had enough of his bullying behaviour.

Viv and his close friend Rob Armstrong were walking from the Quayside to Manhattan's Nightclub and were unaware of a Black Nissan car following them. In seconds the car passed them and the driver slammed on the brakes whilst a gunman opened fire with a pump action shotgun. Armstrong shouted at Viv, 'Move' but the big man was rooted to the spot so Armstrong, with his back to the gunman, took drastic action and jumped on top of Viv causing them both to fall to the pavement. He was shot in the back and sustained other injuries for his trouble. An innocent bystander was also injured sustaining facial injuries. 'Skinny' was arrested and questioned, but released without charge. In court Viv pleaded guilty to the assault on Wattler and showed remorse for his actions. The Judge took this into consideration and sentenced him to 18 months suspended for 18 months. He also had to pay Wattler £500 in compensation. Wattler now walked with a limp, suffered constant migraines and had blurred vision in one eye. Hardly justice.

Viv was then involved in the Hobo's attack with Stephen Sayers and co against Stuart Watson which he served time for and there was the fight with the Sayers cousin Donnelly which I have covered earlier in this book. There were also run ins with both Michael Sayers and one of the Conroys in separate incidents. There were a lot of people who had a motive to kill Viv.

On the day of the shooting 31st December 1993, Viv planned to visit family to wish them Happy New year. He also intended to visit his doors to see his door staff to make sure everything was ok. He was then planning a night out with his partner Anna Connolly in Wallsend to see the New Year in. That day

Anna received a few silent calls at home. Doorman and close friend Terry Scott also visited the home to ask where Viv was as he needed to see him. Viv then received a call at the New Anchor pub which shook him up. It was allegedly a death threat. He then headed to the Queen's Head pub and stayed there until 6:05pm when he headed to the corner shop to buy dog food and cigarettes. He wished the owner Happy New Year and gave his change to a young girl who was behind him in the queue. He then headed out towards his car. As he approached the car he saw that his car had a broken window. As he was inspecting the damage there was the sound of a car approaching at speed and then somebody shouted out at him "Happy New Year Viv". The young girl who he had given the change heard three loud bangs as she left the shop and saw Viv falling to his knees. He had been shot. The car drove off and Terry Scott who had reached the pub via Anna's house rushed over to Viv who was lying in the road trying to crawl away. The shopkeeper tried to assist his customer until the ambulance arrived. Viv travelled to the hospital with a policeman trying to get him to name the people who had done this to him but to no avail. Viv died in North Tyneside Hospital in North Shields with Anna by his side. He had fought for his life in typical Viv style and had said "Don't worry I'll be ok," before he passed away.

The aftermath saw big changes in Newcastle on both sides of the law. A meeting was called a couple of weeks later by the doormen in town at 'Maceys' where they discussed the way forward whilst the police and council set plans in place to legally register doormen in the city to get rid of the criminal element in the pubs and clubs once and for all. Despite early leads in the case the police found a wall of silence descend over Tyneside with regards to the murder. Rumours of Italian hitmen flying in from Spain, and Viv having various contracts on his head clouded the investigation.

Since the murder two people have made vastly different statements regarding the shooting. Lee Watson's statement which is referred to later in this book in 'Operation Insight" claims that the Sayers were behind the plot but hired friends to put the plan into operation. The first person to make a false statement about the murder of Viv Graham was Davey Glover who claimed that he had driven the car after the murder and that Michael Sayers had pulled the trigger. He has since retracted this statement claiming he was under duress from a third party. The case remains unsolved but open to this day.

Chapter Thirty Two: The Shooting of John Brian Sayers

In January 1995 John Brian Sayers was approached by a man by the name of Robert Stokoe. This man seemed to have quite a bit of knowledge on his son John Henrys trial for the Pritchards' robbery. He claimed he had personally seen evidence on a computer which indicated that during John's identity parade that the prosecution witness Phillip Bourke who I mentioned earlier, had been shown photographs of John prior to the identification parade.

Stokoe told John Brian that he had not only seen this on a computer but he could get this evidence downloaded. The words coming out of this man's mouth were very convincing. He claimed he was downloading the information from the national computer. When the paperwork was obtained it was handed over for legal advice to see if it would be useful in the forthcoming appeal for John Henry. This went on for a couple of months back and forth with more paperwork forthcoming followed by more convincing stories from Stokoe.

This man had convinced John Brian Sayers that he was going to download a statement made by a member of Northumbria Police stating that he had personally witnessed Philip Bourke being shown pictures of John Henry prior to the identification parade. If this information was correct it would have a major baring and possibly sway the judgement on the forthcoming appeal.

To cover himself John Brian asked the family solicitor Richard Haswell to visit him at home at 8pm and he informed him of the situation. Haswell told him that it was highly unlikely that these documents would come from the national computer. Richard Haswell insisted on speaking to Stokoe so they called him. Stokoe assured him that he had the information showing that the ID parade was a fit up. Haswell asked him to come forward and produce the evidence. With his work done he left John Brian's home. He was surprised to see a police helicopter hovering above the house but unperturbed got into his car and drove off. As he headed towards Jesmond on the motorway he was aware of car travelling at high speed behind him almost touching his bumper. It was a marked police car and he knew exactly what he was doing and who he was doing it to. Haswell unshaken carried on driving to his destination as the pursuer eventually pulled back and then disappeared into the night.

On January 16th Stephen was visiting his Dad with a copy of the 'Times' newspaper. They had just run an article written by Ian Burrell and Adrian Levy out of the blue implying that the Sayers family were indeed a crime syndicate. This is the article in full:

In the shadow of three bridges spanning the River Tyne, five well-dressed men strode through the lobby of a luxury hotel. They had come from Glasgow, Liverpool and London for an extraordinary business meeting at which they would bid for a share in a £360m market.

To hotel guests there were few clues to their common purpose. Only the men's hard and pitted faces seemed at odds with their executive suits as they relaxed in the marbled lounge of the riverside annexe.

The business associates were not alone. Their every movement was monitored by a surveillance team who noted with alarm the identities of those present: the five represented some of Britain's most powerful criminal groups, clans who normally confined their activities to jealously guarded local territories.

The host was one of Newcastle's ruling family networks which was holding an auction to supply drugs for distribution through the vast portfolio of nightclubs and pubs under their control. The gathering represented the high table of British crime and each man present had earned his place there by settling other contracts closer to home. Britain's criminal clans were burying their rivalries and finally learning to co-operate: this was a network of criminals turning traditional gangland "manors" into a national marketplace for drugs.

Executions in home territories had been carried out some weeks earlier as each clan demonstrated its regional supremacy. On a winter night in the East End of Glasgow, Paul Hamilton, a lieutenant for the feared Thompson family, was executed as he drove his Daimler. Hamilton's associates say he was one of the last survivors of the Thompson regime and had little respect for the new order now closing its grip on the city.

A few weeks after Hamilton was shot, another score was settled in Newcastle. Viv Graham, a former boxer, was gunned down as he walked to his Ford Sierra Cosworth. Graham had established a protection empire over 50 pubs and was raking in £ 250,000 a year. Detectives say he was once an enforcer for a leading crime family but had gone solo and took a share of their profits.

In the drinking clubs of Newcastle's West End and on Glasgow's Blackhill estate the two local hardmen were mourned as folk heroes. To detectives, the killings were a show of strength that indicated more than just who was in control in the two cities.

Police intelligence reports reveal that the Newcastle hotel meeting was one of a series of gatherings during the past year in Glasgow, Liverpool and London as Britain's criminal groups forge links to exploit the growing market for drugs. In a fourth-floor office in London's New Scotland Yard, intelligence development officers have plotted a new national crime map in which gangs are linked by arterial routes for cocaine, heroin and cannabis. "I cannot think of any recent job that we have done that we have not eventually linked to drugs. They are committing extortion, murder, armed robbery, but you keep coming back into drugs," said Commander John Grieve, head of Scotland Yard's intelligence unit, SO11, last week.

At the hub of the new drugs alliance are the crime families in London with their easy access to three airports, the key transit points for heroin and cocaine, and the Channel ports, where most Ecstasy and amphetamines are landed.

Having developed large stockpiles of drugs, they sought new markets in other cities run by other families, drawing on contacts made during jail sentences. "These people used to be at arm's length because they didn't trust each other," said Peter Walker, head of customs intelligence. "But they have found it's to their advantage to have a reliable line of distribution to people who are well-documented villains."

Liverpool has become a key staging post for drugs being moved into Newcastle and Scotland and a market in its own right. Local gangs are setting up importations themselves, often through Manchester airport or Liverpool docks. Before Christmas, customs officers arrested two Liverpool criminals in London with 110 kilograms of Ecstasy intended for northern clubs during the holiday period. It was their fifth such supply run.

The drug marketplaces have regional characteristics. In Newcastle the demand is for amphetamines and Ecstasy which local gangs dispense in pubs and clubs controlled by their army of doormen and "approved" dealers.

In Glasgow heroin and barbiturates are more popular, supplied through a network of mobile shops and ice-cream vans. Flats in tenement blocks have been converted into drug dens by pushers who receive their supplies by road and rail from the south.

The influx of drugs has also changed London's criminal geography by bridging the Thames. "It used to be that south and north London criminals would never have dealings," said Detective Superintendent Micky Banks, who has spent his career fighting the gangs. "Nowadays they all seem to know each other and are all doing business."

CHAMPAGNE corks popped at the Savoy hotel in London as 300 guests in tuxedos and cocktail dresses toasted the marriage of Johnny Brindle and Debbie Arif. The bride was related to the Arif brothers, notorious Turkish Cypriots who control much of south London crime, and the guest list at the £32,000 reception reflected their connections.

The hotel was a halfway point; south of the river was territory ruled by the five Arif brothers who, between them, have been sentenced to more than 70 years in prison. The brains behind the family's criminal empire is Dogan Arif, the second brother. Ozer, the eldest, was described by former associates as the "admin man", keeping the books and running the family's business affairs. Dennis, Bekir and Mehmet were the hardmen who won a reputation as armed robbers. From small beginnings on the Old Kent Road, their name is now respected by gangs as far away as Newcastle and Scotland.

"They are into everything," said a former associate. "They handed out some good beatings to put a bit of fear into people and after that they could just strut around."

Even though Dennis and Mehmet are serving 22 and 18 years respectively for an attempted 1million pound armed robbery, they are "running" D wing at Parkhurst and conducting business using prison issue phonecards.

The family's influence is greater than ever. The Arifs have recently invested in legitimate companies, including BD Enterprises, a car dealership, Team Oak, an import-export company, and NDM Ltd, an international freight and haulage firm. They have no qualms about flaunting their wealth and even invested £500,000 in Fisher Athletic, a non-league football team.

One police intelligence report from detectives monitoring the Arif wedding in 1990, which was later quoted at an Old Bailey court hearing, recorded that among those present were some of the capital's most "powerful families the Colemans, Frasers, Whites, Adamses and Hiscocks".
The old territories had new borders: north, south and east London were all represented, each drinking to the others' health and prosperity.

The Arifs now have good contacts across the Thames where a feared north London family network has established a business empire controlling pubs and clubs in Islington and Soho. That family has also recently acquired property in Marbella where it is being investigated by drugs intelligence officers; in Britain, possible links to the Brink's-Mat robbery are still being examined.
"They made much of their money from 'soldiering', sending loads of vans on burglaries around the M25," a London detective said last week. "They are virtually untouchable because you cannot get anybody to give evidence against them."

Detectives are also studying the family's connections with the contract killings of Terence Gooderham, a book-keeper, and Maxine Arnold, his girlfriend, who were found shot in a Mercedes car in Epping Forest. It is thought that Gooderham had been employed to detail the gang's accounts.

The men who finance the supply of drugs to the London families, customs sources say, are also beyond the law. Ronald Everett and John Mason are on the run in the Costa del Sol and have been wanted by police since the 7 million pounds Security Express robbery in London in 1983.

In east London, one crime group has sought to create its own drugs stockpile by setting up laboratories in the Essex countryside. Customs teams are monitoring William Blundell, from Essex, who was sentenced to eight years after masterminding a plan to produce 3.5million of amphetamine in 1984.

The booming drugs industry has lured some criminals out of "re-tirement". Eddie Richardson is serving 25 years for trying to import 43million pounds worth of cocaine and cannabis. After his release from prison in 1976 he claimed that he had gone straight and had abandoned the extortion and violence which characterised the empire he ran with his brother Charlie in the 1960s.

PART of the Richardson cocaine consignment was to have been sold in Merseyside. Intelligence sources have revealed that it was bound for Brian "Snowy" Jennings, who was one of the richest men in Liverpool but drove a second-hand car and lived in a council house. "He was worth a million but dressed like an unmade bed," said a close friend.

Jennings's partner was Tommy Comerford, a convicted armed robber who set up a drug smuggling empire stretching from Liverpool to Colombia, America, Pakistan and Amsterdam in the 1980s. Comerford, who at one stage was claiming social security while he cruised on the QE2, was recently released from prison after being jailed for 14 years for importing heroin. Customs say he is under investigation again.

Jennings, though, is no longer a danger. He died in Strangeways prison 18 months ago while awaiting trial over his role in the importation of cocaine worth £ 500 million into Britain.

The financier behind the pair, whose identity is known to The Sunday Times, is nicknamed The Fox and has never been charged with drug smuggling. He uses Athens as a meeting point for his heroin contacts from Pakistan, has £57 million in a bank account on the Isle of Man and recently placed £235,000 in cash into an Irish bank.

His client list also includes the Showers family, who were responsible for supplying heroin and cannabis to Merseyside for a decade. In the aftermath of the Toxteth riots in 1981 Michael Showers perfected his cover as a community worker and even appeared on BBC's Question Time to give his commentary about Liverpool's ills.

He drove around his blighted community in a gold Rolls-Royce but was caught in 1991 and jailed for 20 years. Delroy, his brother, is also a convicted drug smuggler and is believed to be putting together new shipments in Amsterdam where he is on the run from prison. The flood of drugs into Liverpool has since provoked a power struggle over supplies to the city's pubs and clubs. The war between rival armies of bouncers last week led to police mounting one of their biggest anti-drug operations. More than 200 officers from four counties raided 32 homes in an investigation into extortion, arson, kidnapping and the drug supply lines from Merseyside to the northeast.

One of the most influential gang leaders in Newcastle is Paddy Conroy, who faces charges of kidnapping and blackmail and is awaiting extradition from the Costa del Sol after going on the run from jail. One internal police memo warns that Conroy is the leader of "a very violent faction" in Newcastle, a group that has now established an international base at Benalmadena in Spain.

Conroy's rivals for control of the northeast are the Sayers, a gang led by John Henry Sayers from his cell in Frankland jail where he is serving 15 years for armed robbery. His younger brother, Stephen, is now out of jail having served a two-and-a-half-year sentence for beating a nightclub doorman who crossed him.

THE CATALYST for the new drugs alliance among city gangs was the Brink's-Mat robbery in 1983, when £ 26 million in gold bullion was stolen. The proceeds were used to buy into the international drugs trade, generating billions of pounds over the next decade and creating Britain's first criminal jet set. They formed bases in Spain and Holland and forged links with the Colombian cartels *and Turkish heroin syndicates.*

Today leading Scottish drug smugglers have set up on Spanish soil. One, who cannot be named for legal reasons, is wanted by police for masterminding a massive shipment of cocaine into Scotland from his base on the Costa del Sol. Customs sources revealed that his cocaine deal was financed by London criminals.

Scotland became awash with heroin and barbiturates during the reign of Arthur Thompson Snr, Glasgow's former godfather, who died of natural causes in 1993. Thompson's gamble with drugs cost him dear: his daughter Margaret died after a drugs binge while Arthur Jr was shot dead while on home release from an 11-year jail sentence for drug dealing.

The Thompson name is still revered by locals and the heir to the legacy is Billy, 27, the remaining son, due to be released from Barlinnie prison next month.

There are rivals for the turf. At the bar of the Caravelle Inn, a bunker-like drinking hole recently the target of a hand-grenade attack, associates of Paul Ferris raised a glass to crown him the new king of Glasgow's East End.

Ferris, who is well connected in England and Spain, is reluctant to accept the mantle. Police have him under 24-hour surveillance but Ferris, who has served only one prison term for firearms offences in the mid-1980s, claims he is being victimised. In 1992 he was charged with knee-capping, drug dealing and co-accused of the murder of Arthur Jr, but after the longest criminal trial in Scottish legal history, he walked free.

"I'm no gangster," he pleaded after a Manchester court fined him £ 250 for possession of crack cocaine last August. He claimed he smoked the drug to treat his sensitive skin.

In barely a decade drugs have gushed into Britain. Since 1983 the value of drugs seized by Customs and Excise has risen from less than £50 million to more than £500 million a year. Intelligence sources believe the value of the market to Britain's leading crime syndicates last year was at least six times that figure.

Glasgow detectives admit that they are being outflanked by the new network of alliances. "It used to be a big deal if Glasgow criminals were operating in Edinburgh, but now we are seeing groups up here from Liverpool, Tyneside and London," said Gordon Ferrie, a Strathclyde superintendent who co-ordinates the force's fight against organised crime.

So far, attempts to unite law-enforcement agencies in a single mission to break the new network have failed. "We have now got police, customs and the intelligence services tripping over each other," said a senior customs source, "so the criminals are winning hands down."

As they were discussing this article Stokoe phoned John Brian up. It was 11am. Stokoe asked if he could meet John in Birmingham later that day. Stephen who was listening into the call looked at his Dad and instantly shook his head. Then Stokoe asked if Leeds was easier for him. Stephen shook his head again. Stokoe was not to be put off so he said he would turn up the following afternoon with the vital information which the Sayers would need to help get John Henry out of his situation. After the call Stephen sat with his Dad and discussed Stokoe and the statement. Stephen asked his Dad if he trusted this man. He didn't answer. Instead he asked Stephen what he thought Stokoe could gain from this. Again, no answer was forthcoming. They came to the conclusion that if this man produced the paperwork that they would be extremely happy and he would deserve a few quid for his help.

Stephen left his Dad's house and made his way to Hartford camp to see his cousins Frankie, Phillip and Joe. When he arrived at the camp Joe was just pulling away. He had a horse van on the back of his van and he asked Stephen to go with him which he did. They went to Joe's stables where they got the horse from out of the box and they harnessed it up to the cart and spent the next couple of hours on the cart. After a relaxing couple of hours, they made their way back to the camp where Aunty Silvia made them their tea before Stephen headed home.

Whilst driving back to Newcastle Stephen picked up his cousins Edward Lennie and Tony Sayers and they went down to his Dad's hostel which was located in Newcastle city centre on Westmorland Road. The building which is derelict now was quite a large building and it had a large cellar to it which they had converted into a gym. The lads had been down the gym for an hour or so doing pad work and a bit of circuit training when Stephen heard someone shouting his name down the stairs. With their tone of voice, he knew instantly that there was something wrong. He heard someone screaming saying 'Stephen get to the phone something has happened to your dad.' He got to the phone picked it up and the line was dead so he placed the phone back down onto its receiver.

About five minutes later the phone rang again so he answered it and it was his Uncle Thomas Kelly who told him that his Dad had just been shot. Stephen asked how serious it was and his Uncle Thomas told him that he had been shot in the face but had driven himself to hospital. Stephen thanked his Uncle and hung up. He ran back down to the cellar to get his cousins and told them the news. They got straight into Edward's Mercedes and drove directly over to Newcastle General hospital which was just over a mile away.

John Brian had arrived at the meeting place on time. Stokoe was very agitated. He told John that he had something in his hotel, the Copthorne, and had to go and get it. He then came out and had a gun in his hand and told John that the police had put him up to it and that he had no choice but to kill him. He then shot John once but the gun then jammed. If it had not been for the bullet hitting his teeth and ricashaying down his throat he would have been dead. Stokoe fled the scene whilst John drove to a phone box and rang his solicitor Richard Haswell and told him that he had been shot and that he was going to go home to defend his family. Richard, always calm under duress told John in no uncertain terms that he must get straight to the hospital. John Brian, not for the first time, took his solicitors advice. (Michael Sayers and another man obtained the CCTV of the shooting from the Copthorne Hotel but this was confiscated by the police and was subsequently lost).

Stephen and his cousins arrived at the accident and emergency department where they came across John Brian's BMW with the driver's door wide open and the keys in with the engine still running. Stephen quickly took a look inside. All he could see was broken glass and blood. His heart was beating and the adrenaline was flowing and it hit him that someone had tried to kill his Dad. He went running into the hospital searching for his Dad and was pointed towards the operating theatre. Within seconds he was there and he burst through the doors to find him lying on the hospital trolly bed waiting to be pushed in for an emergency operation. The bullet had entered into one side of his face and lodged inside the opposite side of his lower jaw so he had difficulty speaking. Stephen could see it was not life threatening which was a massive relief.

As they spoke Stephen held his Dad and he looked at him and asked him two questions the first being 'are you okay?' Followed by the second question which was just as important as the first. 'Who did this to you?' Even though he was having difficulty speaking Stephen knew who he meant. His Dad had kept a mobile phone which he was lying on and he passed Stephen the phone and no sooner had he done this then it started ringing. Stephen answered the phone and he held it between his Dads and his ear. Stephen recognized the voice instantly. It was Stokoe and he was crying down the phone begging for forgiveness. He was repeating the words Special Branch and police and saying that they had made him do it. He also said they had supplied him with the .22 hand gun and it was their instructions to try and get his Dad to go down to Birmingham and Leeds.

These were serious allegations. The question is, did Stephen think there was any truth in these allegations? Was this an attempt by the police to make John's death look like a gangland execution whereas in reality it would have been a judicial killing by the police force under the cover of MI5? I will answer it this way. If he didn't believe anything this man had said in the past then how could he believe him now with his Dad lying in hospital. Was the man a Walter Mitty as many have described him? Nobody will ever know, many said that this was out of character for this man. The conversation carried on between John Brian and Stokoe. As Stephen continued listening in his blood was boiling. There was only one thing in his mind. Revenge.

Stephen let Stokoe know that he was there listening. Stokoe said 'Stephen I still have this paperwork here, what shall I do with it?' He could read him like a cheap newspaper and he replied, 'How much do you want for it?' He asked Stephen to meet him in a public place as soon as possible and he wanted £10k to leave the North East and in return Stephen would receive the paperwork that would release John Henry from prison. Stokoe thought Stephen was stupid but this was the chicken trying to trap the fox. Stokoe carried on doing what he did best which was talking and trying to convince Stephen that meeting him was the only option. Stephen told him he was worried in case he came back and killed his dad. As far as Stephen was concerned this fool needed a little reassurance, a tickle under the chin. All Stephen was wanting to do was to get within eyesight of this man.

As he was talking to him Stokoe increased the amount to £20k saying that was the amount that Stephen would have to give him that night if he wanted him to leave his Dad alone. Stephen could feel the confidence coming over in his voice. Stokoe clearly thought Stephen was frightened of him. They agreed to meet by the lake at Leazes Park. Stokoe told Stephen to come alone. Stephen trusted nobody at this stage but made calls to a couple of very close friends of the family who agreed to accompany him.

As more of the family arrived at the hospital to offer support and protection Stephen said goodbye to his Dad and met up with his two close friends. They had ninety minutes to prepare for battle. After a brief conversation they all came to the same conclusion that if Robert Stokoe was to turn up that night it was for the sole reason to kill Stephen. Most people would be concerned about this type of scenario but whilst writing Stephen's book he told me that deep down the thought of it excited him. Stephen's friends reassured him that they would be there in Leazes Park and they would be prepared. Make no bones about it there was to be no mercy shown to this man and his unknown accomplices. Little did Stokoe realise that Stephen had some of the North East's finest bluggers, psychopaths and dangerous bastards watching over him like guardian angels.

The time arrived and the lads arrived early and were plotted up in the park. They knew the place like the back of their hands. Stephen had changed and was wearing a discreet heavy-duty bullet-proof vest concealed by a baggy hooded jumper over the top. He could see two of his pals with fishing rods at the lake. He approached the meeting place from the opposite side of the mini docking area where people pay to ride on the small boats. As he was walking around the lake, he could see a variety of fishermen night fishing which was a common thing back then. The sun had set, it was 9pm. There was a couple of people sitting on a park bench near the lake who Stephen would have to walk past.

There were only a few feet between the lake and these suspicious people sat wearing hoods, who were 100 yards from Stephen. He started to get a bit concerned. He pulled a walk talky from out of his pocket and as he did it crackled into life with the person on the other end saying "2 suspected bogies 100 yards ahead on bench." Stephen had already seen them. As he got closer and closer his heart rate increased and the adrenalin was pumping. Just then he heard a familiar noise, and once heard that sound can never be forgotten. It was the noise of two shot guns being cocked from the bushes behind the bench. It was Stephen's guardian angels letting him know they were there.

As Stephen approached one of the people turned their heads towards him. He was looking straight at them. The person lit a cigarette. It was just a young girl in her 20's sat with her boyfriend. False alarm. Stephen walked calmly past them and a couple more fishermen to his destination. He looked at his watch and as planned he was exactly five minutes early. In those five minutes he started to look back on his life and what had brought him and his family to this. It made him all the more determined to end it there and then. No matter what happened to Stephen the would-be assassin would not leave Leazes Park alive. The clock ticked away and there was no show from Stokoe or any of his associates. Stephen and the lads waited until quarter past then rang his mobile phone but it went straight to answer machine. Unbeknown to them Stokoe had handed himself into the Police and admitted to the shooting of John Brian Sayers.

Stephen and the lads left the park as discreetly as they had arrived and Stephen made his way back over to Newcastle General hospital. By now there were TV cameras and reporters waiting outside so he dove past them and used a different entrance. He met up with a lot of his family in one of the hospitals waiting rooms. There was now about thirty in total. There was also a heavy police presence at the hospital now with six armed police officers with sub-machine guns outside the ward and guarding his room. A waste of taxpayers' money. They were not requested by the family and were not welcomed. The doctor kept coming back and forth reassuring everyone that John Brian was going to be all right and that it was not life threatening but he was still in the operating theatre. Rumours circulated on Tyneside like wildfire.

The Sayers were still not clear on the reason John had been shot but they knew who had shot him. The police had been mentioned by Stokoe on more than one occasion of course, but all John Brian knew was that someone had tried to take his life and there was a high possibility that they would return with intentions of trying again to kill him.

Stephen and his cousins Joe, Philip and Frankie Riley, Tony Sayers and Edward Lennie remained by John Brian's side throughout the night and over the following three days and night to ensure his safety before he was finally released to go home. Prior to his release the doctor told the family that John Brian had to give permission for the bullet they had taken out of his jaw to be handed over to the police but that he had refused this permission. Later that night someone broke into the office where the bullet was held and the hospital filing cabinet was forced open and the bullet was stolen. What sort of people do things like that? Who is at a level where they can seek out such evidence and be able to steal it from a hospital without suspicion? The plot was indeed thickening. Stephen stayed by his Dad's side for over ten weeks until John Brian felt comfortable enough to fend for himself.

Although Stoker was charged with attempted murder this was reduced to a section 18 (GBH with intent).

The shooting John Brian Sayers made front page news

Hitman shoots armed robber's father

By JAMIE MACASKILL

THE FATHER of a convicted armed robber was last night shot in the head by a suspected hitman.

John Brian Sayers, who runs the Westmorland Road Men's Hostel in Newcastle's West End, was being treated in the city's general hospital for gunshot wounds to the face.

The shooting is believed to have happened at around 7pm. It comes just one day after a London-based newspaper claimed two of Mr Sayers' sons — John Henry, 31, and Stephen, 28, — had close links with the underworld on Tyneside.

The article investigated

► Turn to Page 2 ►

Robber's father shot by suspected hitman

■ Son: Stephen Sayers.

FROM PAGE ONE

claims of a nationally organised drugs and crime cartel with strongholds in Glasgow and Liverpool.

Last night, relatives of Mr Sayers, including Stephen and his third son Michael, gathered at Newcastle General Hospital where their father was in a comfortable condition.

It is believed Mr Sayers snr, who is in his 50s, was shot once in the face and received a neck wound. The family's solicitor, Clive McKeag, issued a statement outside the hospital claiming Mr Sayers had been targeted by a hitman.

"Mr Sayers has been shot in the face. It has obviously been an attempt on his life.

"He is comfortable but he will be staying in hospital for the meantime.

"I would stress that Mr Sayers is the victim. There is no suggestion at all that he has done anything wrong."

Last year, Michael Sayers survived an attempt on his life when he was shot six times by an unknown gunman.

A Northumbria Police spokesman said: "I can confirm that John Brian Sayers is in Newcastle General Hospital with shotgun wounds. The wounds are not critical.

"He is not talking to us at all at this moment. He is making no allegations about his injuries, and no complaint as to what has occurred."

In July 1990, Stephen Sayers, then of Bothal Street, Byker, was among four men each given a two-and-a-half year prison sentence for wounding a doorman.

The case was seen as another instance of a tide of violence dominating Newcastle's pubs and clubs scene as rival gangs battled to control a lucrative market.

Hardman Viv Graham, 34, who ran a protection racket in Newcastle's East End, was gunned down in a drive-by shooting on New Year's Eve 1993. His killers have never been found.

Last night's shooting has renewed fears that Tyneside could be on the brink of a fresh outbreak of violence following Viv Graham's death.

After his murder, prominent underworld figures are believed to have vowed to take revenge against those they believe are responsible.

Son in fight to clear his name

By CHRIS HASTINGS

CONVICTED armed robber John Henry Sayers launched a bid to clear his name yesterday - at a special court hearing held in jail.

Mr Sayers, 31, from Newcastle, was thought to have been refused permission to mount his legal challenge in an ordinary court.

Instead a judge presided over the civil proceedings at Frankland high security prison in Durham.

Sayers, who is serving 15 years for armed robbery, started the proceedings in a bid to get his hands on evidence which he claims will prove his innocence. He says the document were kept back from his original trial five years ago by police.

Sayers, who has been swotting up on law books in his cell, represented himself at the hearing but his attempt to get access to the files was thrown out.

His father John said yesterday afternoon he was disappointed with the outcome.

He said: "We have always maintained that John is totally innocent of this charge. We will fight on."

A spokeswoman for the Prison Service said: "I can confirm a case was heard at Frankland jail."

Chapter Thirty Three: Operation Rockstar

In 1995 there was a lot of illegal activity going on throughout Newcastle and the outlying districts. Stephen Sayers was an active criminal at the time and had his fingers in plenty of pies. He used to look after a lot of people whether they liked it or not. Some call it protection but he called it a living. His reputation was well and truly established by this stage and he would go as far as saying that there was not a business man on Tyneside who did not know the fierce reputation of the name Sayers which he took full advantage of. He used to get approached all the time with problems, debts and people would approach him and his associates to assist in these matters and stop whatever illegal activity was going on against them. There was a big boom in drugs in the city too with 'E' the new party drug of choice and it would be naïve to think that families on Tyneside were not profiting from this industry as well. With older brother John being in prison it was Stephen's job to look after the family and he did just that, John Henry even had his own fridge outside his cell in prison which was always full.

The life of a career criminal is like riding a rollercoaster, it brings adrenalin rushes and highs, but it also brings horrendous lows. Although the money was coming in from all angles the brothers were spending it just as quickly and living like rock stars. Michael was struggling with his own demons after the shooting and was by his own admission drinking heavily and taking a serious amount of class A drugs. The police, with John Henry behind bars, were keen to get his younger brothers behind bars and a chain of events would do just that.

Stephen got a call from Peter Donnelly. He wanted to meet him at 'Rick's Public House' in Newcastle. Donnelly was a distant cousin of the family. Stephen had fallen out with him a few weeks earlier and they had a straightener where Stephen had broken Donnelly's hand and spirit. Stephen was hoping that he wanted to pick up where they left off.

As Stephen entered the bar, he saw Donnelly at the bar and told him to get outside. Donnelly certainly did not fancy a rematch in anyway shape or form. Seeing his time was being wasted Stephen walked out of the pub. He wasn't interested in anything this man had to say. Donnelly's business partner was a man called Joe Hunt. At the time he was on remand for discharging a firearm on a security van robbery in Birmingham with another criminal Tony Weldon. Rumours in the Underworld suggested Hunt was a registered informant.

Donnelly had a habit of boasting about his activities and he had been heard telling people that he and Hunt and another man called 'Balmer' were 'minding' a local pub business man who I will call 'Mr X,' but that the arrangement had come to an end because Hunt was on remand and 'Mr X' had not put up the bail surety that he had agreed to. This was music to Stephen's ears. With the brothers' outgoings surpassing their income leading up to Christmas a job like this would come in handy for all concerned.

On the 8th November Newcastle United were playing at home against Blackburn Rovers and 'Mr X' was entertaining guests in his executive box at St James' Park. After the match he went out for drinks with friends to 'Julies' nightclub before heading to his secretary's house for a 'meeting' before she dropped him home in the early hours of the next morning.

On the 9th November 'Mr X' and his wife noticed something was not right in their home. The damage to the window according to forensics was caused by the discharge of a cartridge loaded with lead shot, approximating in size to No.7 shot, in a 12 gauge shotgun. At the moment of discharge the muzzle of the gun was probably some 3-5 yards from the window and the firer was standing to the right of the hole. The height above the ground of the hole in the window together with the pattern of the shot damage within the lounge indicate that the shot was fired upwards into the lounge with the intention of causing damage to the house rather than injury to any person within the room. 'Mr X' had friends in high places and he contacted the police immediately to inform them what had happened.

A few days earlier Stephen Sayers had approached Malcolm Balmer who was a straight working man not a criminal but had been a tough guy in his time. Stephen asked him if he was still looking after 'Mr X' with Donnelly and Hunt. He said he was and that he was also a good friend. Stephen asked Malcolm to go and have a word with him on his behalf. This move became counterproductive as he immediately told his friend Donnelly instead of 'Mr X'. Malcolm didn't do this to cause trouble he was just naive to the situation but Donnelly wasn't. Donnelly had his own agenda.

The police had taken the incident at 'Mr X's' home very seriously and had arrived to fit surveillance equipment and set up phone tapping devices. According to the police audio tapes Donnelly arrived at 'Mr X's' house after Balmer had spoken to him. Despite heavy police presence the two men made themselves at home and began implying that the 'brothers' were responsible for shooting his house up and that they were going to demand money from him over the next few days.

A phone call transcript on 9th November between 'Mr X' and Detective Inspector Hepworth shows that there was only 1 name in the frame and they were going to lay a trap:

Hepworth: Hello

'Mr X': Aye Dave how you doing son? Well it's all go today lad. We've got the lad been and installed the UHF thing. I've got two lads here at the moment… the little mobile one for my pocket and the phone one. I've got two of them. I'm going to take that to work in the morning. Them two lads are still here. I've had Tracy on the phone who is coming within the hour. Is she from Yorkshire or somewhere? She's got a bit of an accent? Well I'll try for her myself. (laughter)

Hepworth: I'll have to try as well.

'Mr X': Well I'll tell you what you're too good looking. You're like that Bob Morton. We've had… Peter Donnelly has been. He wanted to see what the crack was. Well he reckons that it's definitely the Sayers because it ties up with them two mentioning to Malcolm that they were going to put the bite on for a few quid.

Hepworth: He thinks the same as us does he? That it's the forerunner to the bite.

'Mr X': Yes, he also mentioned the other kid who has come out of the nick. Is it Panda or somebody and he's going round demanding money with menaces? Apparently, he was after Keith Kennedy an ice cream lad in the West End. Apparently he put the bite into him a few weeks ago. Peter's more or less saying that they're just ponces. You know what our Peter is like. He says I've never seen ought like this. He says I might have been in bother myself but I've never been to anybody's house and put a gun through the window.

Hepworth: He got a fucking bomb sent to his house.

'Mr X': Ah what the letter bomb. I heard about that. That was a long time ago. How as like. I've tried to find out whether he seems genuine or not. To me he seems genuine.

Hepworth: …Thinking about it

'Mr X': Do you? You think it's all linked?

Hepworth: I think there's the approach from Joe. Two separate things.

'Mr X': Well he reckons that Joe's apparently. He spoke to Joe on the phone and he mentioned that someone was going to come and see me and Joe was doing his nut saying this that and the other. Well the kids locked up isn't he. He says the next step. You'll get a visit at work. He says that'll be the next step and if they come, he says just ring us straight away and I'll come down and sort it out. So, well you know what to do. Well I've got my little tape recorder.

Hepworth: You're just going to start a feud.

'Mr X': I know I know. Which he didn't want to do. You know the kid. I tried to stop him coming but he was already on his way and we had the crime prevention lad – Fred – in one room and Peter was in the other room and I *showed him the mess you know.*

Hepworth then assures 'Mr X' that he is well protected.
Hepworth: Well I've got all sorts of warning signs in the control room here so if there's any messages at all coming from your house the fucking SAS and the cavalry will be there.

'Mr X': Oh tremendous. I'll sleep a bit better tonight anyway. Does that go to Clifford Street – Dave?

Hepworth: All over the fucking place. Everyone will turn up.
'Mr X': Great.

Hepworth: And I've got armed cars coming up.

'Mr X': Champion, Champion. Well I'll tell you what you might need them and all fucking shotguns going off.

They then talk about security at his premises. Or rather lack of it.
Hepworth: What security have you got on the site? Have you got cameras or ought like that.

'Mr X': Nah I've got bugger all. To be honest I've got the lad on foot. He's not even linked with the radio. All he's got to do if there's any problems is he goes into the cabin and rings for assistance. So, I haven't got a great deal of cover. I mean if they come to work it's not a question of well, I mean I want to try and get something on tape obviously, I don't want to be in the position where I press a panic switch in work do I?

Hepworth: Ah no. Get them to make the demand. Just say what's the score. If he was to say look you've had a problem with protection, we want two gran a week whatever well fuck just let them talk.

'Mr X': Just let them say that. And then what do I say what let them get away and let us have a think about it.

Hepworth: Let them get away and have a think about it.
'Mr X': And then I ring you?

Hepworth: Aye.

On the same day 'Mr X' took a call from another friend in the force Bob Morton who he would see regularly at his gym in Jesmond and informed him of

'Mr X': *How you doing Robert?*

Bob: *Ok*

'Mr X': *Aye, oh aye. Busy day today. I've had a lass here from South Shields.*

Bob: *South Shields is it?*

'Mr X': *Aye Undercover. So…*

Bob: *So, are they still there?*

'Mr X': *No everybody's gone now. Davy's got them involved to try and shine a bit of light. They were telling us about the Sayers and all that. One's a coke-head. Completely aye. Not Stephen the other one.*

Bob: *Michael?*

'Mr X': *Aye he'll kill himself with coke. That's what they was saying.*

Bob: *So, they've got cameras set up now?*

'Mr X': *Oh, aye cameras everything.*

Bob: *Outside can you see them?*

'Mr X': *No there's cameras there.*

Bob: *Peter Donnelly doesn't know you're going to the law does he?*

'Mr X': *Peter knew I was going to the law aye. I says there here at the minute. He says I'm not bothered about that I want to come and have a look. He doesn't know about any cameras. I mean this conversation now is being taped.*

Bob: *Is it?*

'Mr X': *Aye as we speak. As soon as I pick up the phone or dial out or an incoming call is automatically taped. I've got the same at work. They want something on tape if they can. They've even given us between you and I, one of them wires for the body.*

Nigel 'Snowy' Abadom was released from prison after serving an 8-year sentence for supplying heroin. Stephen was good friends with Nigel and his brother also called Stephen. The Abadom brothers Philip, Nigel and Stephen made a name for themselves in the seventies. Their father was Nigerian and their mother was English. At the time they were the only black family living in Birtley in Gateshead.

Nigel was hooked on heroin but was trying to clean himself up. He met Stephen after visiting his wife's grave who had died through her heroin habit and he broke down and asked for help. Stephen felt obliged so loaned him £50 and ran around to get him some methadone tablets. Nigel knew 'Mr X' and as a way of repaying Stephen offered to introduce him to 'Mr X'.

It was on the morning of 21st November that Nigel Abadom tried to unsuccessfully contact 'Mr X'. They did however speak briefly on the 23rd November. In the second conversation Adadom said they needed to meet, he said that it was about the 'carry on' at his home. They agreed to meet at the Copthorne Hotel on the Quayside. Abadom said that he was answerable to other people but didn't at that stage name them.

The next day 'Mr X' turned up for the meeting at 11:00am but Abadom failed to show. They did not have contact again until the 28th November at 9:40am when they had a twenty-minute conversation. He called again a bit later and told 'Mr X' that he was merely a pawn of the Sayers brothers. He told 'Mr X' that pressure was coming from Michael and Stephen Sayers. He said he was the 'go between' because he knew 'Mr X'. He also said that the Sayers brothers were responsible for shooting his window out – not themselves personally but others on their behalf and he then went on to describe acts of extreme violence for which he said the Sayers were responsible and he suggested that Michael Sayers had mentioned a shooting in the leg 'so that will teach others when we make a demand we mean it.'

There was another conversation at 12:16pm that same day in which an amount of £50,000 was discussed and that it was to be paid in cash in £20 notes. He then went onto say how the Sayers brothers had discussed the possibility of attacking his business and shooting a driver. They had also discussed shooting a night watchman. He said again that they wouldn't have done it themselves but would get 'a young kid' to do it on their behalf.

In another taped phone conversation on the 28th which lasted just under five minutes Abadom said the Sayers would not come back for more if they got the £50,000. He, Abadom, said he'd 'go to war' for 'Mr X' if they tried to extort more money out of him. In response to that 'Mr X' said he wasn't prepared to hand over the money to Stephen until he got a personal guarantee that that would be the end of the matter.

Because of the connection with Donnelly and Hunt, Stephen wasn't sure if he should make a move but he went against his better judgement. A meeting was arranged in a brief phone conversation for lunchtime on the 29th November. It lasted about 45 minutes with Stephen, Nigel and 'Mr X' all present. They got on well discussing football, 'Mr X' had an executive box and

Stephen was a season ticket holder. All was friendly and calm. A police video camera filmed the meeting but there was a fault with the equipment and there was no audio.

'Mr X' alleged that Stephen told him he wanted the £50,000 quickly as he was out of pocket as a result of Joe Hunt's activities. It was alleged that prior to being locked up Hunt and Donnelly had flooded Newcastle with a batch of drugs and undercut the Sayers on their turf. 'Mr X' then claimed that Stephen said that the protection he would offer him in return for the £50,000 could include arson attacks on rival's business premises. 'Mr X' then mentioned that he was a bit concerned about some of the 'things' Nigel had mentioned on the phone prior to their meeting. Stephen told him to disregard Nigel as he was coming off Heroin. 'Mr X' then said that Nigel had claimed that it was Stephen who had his windows shot out. Stephen told him not to be stupid and explained that he had heard about it and had come to offer him his services to prevent this happening again.

As he was talking to 'Mr X', he could see Nigel sweating profusely. Stephen pointed this out to 'Mr X' confirming that he was in his own personal hell since his release from prison, and was going though "cold turkey "

Stephen explained what he thought of Donnelly and another man Malcolm Balmer 'They aren't worth a chow of baccy.' 'Mr X'asked Stephen how he rated his chances in a straightener with Balmer. Stephen pointed over to 'Mr X's' warehouse and told him to get him down to face him and he would 'address his lip.' Intrigued by Stephen, 'Mr X' asked him if he was prepared to use violence on people. Stephen told him that he would but only against other criminals. 'Mr X' alleged that he had been threatened by a haulage operator whose lorries are quite prominent today on our motorways. He said that he was prepared to pay a substantial amount of money to have him beaten up and would Stephen consider that? Stephen said yes but only for the right money. They then discussed money. Stephen said that he would be happy with £1000 a week and for that he would go wherever and whenever for 'Mr X'. He also said that he wanted payment each week up front as he believed that 'Mr X's' main income came from drugs and not his main business which is what Donnelly had told anyone who would care to listen to him. There was always the risk that 'Mr X' could be arrested leaving him out of pocket.

'Mr X' smirked, there was no denial. He offered Stephen £35,000 a year. That only worked out at £100 a day and Stephen had heard that Hunt and Donnelly had been getting £300 a day. After a bit of negotiation, they shook hands on £50,000 plus bonuses. 'Mr X' was keen he said to meet Michael Sayers which Stephen said he would arrange, 'Mr X' thought that Michael had a personal issue with him and wanted reassurances that the younger brother was not going to hurt him. He also wanted Stephen to 'sort out' Hunt, Donnelly and Balmer and make sure that they kept their mouths shut about his alleged lucrative side business. Stephen was only too happy to oblige with those minor teething problems and would happily do that for free. They went their separate ways. Two satisfied customers. Or so Stephen thought.

Over the next few hours 'Mr X' was quite erratic and making calls to Stephen. He kept looking for assurances and wanted a guarantee that he could call on him 24 hours a day. Stephen found it all bizarre I mean he was simply a fighter for the firm he wasn't a counsellor. He then started asking him to prove his ability in his profession of violence. Stephen said he was happy to oblige but nothing was ever forthcoming. Strange behaviour indeed. His insistence on seeing Michael began to arouse suspicion with Stephen and he had an uneasy feeling in his gut but he finally relented to the request and arranged a meet which can be heard quite clearly on one of the recorded calls I have listened to:

'Mr X': The only thing that bothers us still a little bit is obviously I've met yourself – Michael

Stephen: Don't worry I've just been speaking to our young'un.

'Mr X': Nigel said when he rang us at work yesterday that if I diven't pay up the fifty grand he says the kid's ganna shoot you – you know well I'm like a fucking bundle of nerves.

Stephen: Right I've seen our young'un – right I'm in charge of the brother – right, everything's ok.

'Mr X': Right so as far as that threat.
Stephen: As far as I'm concerned me an' ye are pals.

'Mr X': Right.

Stephen: Me ye and wor young'un are pals.

'Mr X': So, you take care of Michael.

Stephen: Aye no problem at all.

'Mr X': At the end of the day.

Stephen: You'll see him on Friday, I'll bring him to see you on Friday or something …we'll shake hands.

Michael was struggling with his mental health after the attempt on his life and was living in the demonic world of drink and drugs, rarely sleeping, and sinking in and out of paranoia and rarely sleeping at the same address each night. Stephen explained to his younger brother that he needed to reassure 'Mr X' that he had no trouble with him personally and that it would only take him two minutes of his time to do so. The meeting was arranged but when the time came Stephen had to get Michael out of a bar as he had been drinking all night and on a big booze binge.

Stephen should have gone with his gut instinct on 'Mr X'. As they travelled to meet the businessman the police were making final checks on their surveillance equipment. The meeting took place. On the footage the two Sayers brothers seem reluctant to leave 'Mr X's' carpark. They are reluctant to go into his office and are clearly being wary. Abadom goes first as he is the messenger and spokesman for the brothers. He explains that they'd prefer him to go outside. 'Mr X' says he won't as he fears being kidnapped. Finally, and reluctantly the brothers enter 'Mr X's' office. It is clear that the trio are not very relaxed. Michael was said to be hungover and barely uttered two words as the two parties shook hands. Abadom is clearly nervous and switches off a stereo unit thinking that he is turning off the power to any possible recording devices. The police had already got that covered.

Michael is obstructed by Stephen on the footage. It is quite clear that it is Stephen doing the talking. Michael then chips in and assures 'Mr X' that "It'll not happen anymore right." In response to 'Mr X' saying "As long as there's no more threatening." Michael goes onto explain that Hunt had started the issue off between them and asks 'Mr X' what he ever saw in Hunt. 'Mr X' denies any involvement with Hunt but Michael insists that Hunt put him in the belief that he did and that justified him having the hump with him. With all of that settled 'Mr X' seemed happy and Stephen was looking forward to earning some 'straight' money. They arranged to meet later that day to pick up the £50,000 so that Stephen could start work. Stephen then dropped Michael back off at the bar to continue where he had left off. The surveillance tapes had recorded the meeting but the audio had failed which would mean the meeting could be interpreted however the police wanted it to be.

After dropping Nigel off Stephen grabbed something to eat before picking him up again to go to meet 'Mr X' to pick up the money. Nigel wasn't in great form. He seemed very nervous and jumpy as they approached Whitley road near 'Mr X's' warehouse. Stephen was aware of a police cruiser which looked very suspicious so he headed straight past and decided to go to 'Pearson's Garage', to look at some jeeps. Whilst he was driving there, he saw a further three police vehicles pass. There was something not right here and that feeling in his gut was back and it wasn't hunger pains. He drove past 'Pearsons' and did a U turn and a police vehicle followed him and then stopped behind him. Stephen unperturbed got out and went into the garage and asked about a second hand jeep. He then jumped back in the car and headed to the 'Wheatsheaf Pub' further along Whitley Road away from 'Mr X's' business. Nigel was sweating heavily now and Stephen could not get any sense out of him.

He asked him outright if he had been set up? He didn't answer the question instead insisting that he make a call to 'Mr X' from the pay phone in the pub. He called 'Mr X' and asked him why his place was surrounded by police and that he would tell Stephen to pull out of it. Nigel came off the phone and said "You're going to get nicked Stephen." Stephen did not understand why and asked Nigel what he had said to him to cause an issue. Nigel was by now beyond himself. Stephen told him to get back in the car with him as he was going to see 'Mr X' and sort things out face to face. Nigel said he was going nowhere near 'Mr X', so Stephen changed tact and assured him that they would head home. This seemed to calm Nigel down and they both headed back to Stephen's car.

Stephen then U turned again and headed back to 'Mr X's' yard at speed with the police on his tail. He had nothing to hide. He had been employed by 'Mr X'and he was going to pick up his money. It wasn't a crime. As he pulled into the yard the police and armed response swarmed on the vehicle and Stephen and Nigel were told to get out of the car slowly with their hands above their heads. Stephen looked at Nigel and wondered what mess he had got them into. Stephen and Nigel were arrested and charged with the blackmail of 'Mr X' to the tune of £50,000. Michael was oblivious to what had happened. He rang 'Mr X's' factory asking for Stephen but hung up when he was told that he wasn't there. He then phoned a taxi and travelled to South Shields to continue drinking with a female friend. It was here that he heard the news about his brother's arrest and decided to go on his toes.

John Brian Sayers baths his sons,
Stephen, John and Michael

John, Michael and Stephen
at home in York Street

Yvonne (left) with John,
Michael and Stephen

Yvonne Sayers

Left: Peter Sayers,
John Sayers, Tony
Sayers and Stephen
in the late sixties

Right: John Brian
Sayers with Eddie
Lennie

A young Michael Sayers on a 'trap'

John Henry Sayers
served in the Paras

Stephen Sayers
clubbing aged 20

Stephen, Jackie, Davey,
Terry and Franky, Greece 1986

Stephen and John Henry Sayers
in Zoots 1988

The boys with mam Yvonne 1980s

Stephen, Tony Legs Lennie and
Davey Lancaster on the run in Tenerife

Left: Mario, Stephen,
HarryMarsden and
Alan Day

Right: Stephen on
the run in Tenerife

Michael, John Brian, John Henry
and Stephen Sayers

Stephen with Jimmy Slater
and Joe Donnelly

Stephen Sayers leads the march
for his brother's freedom

Tommy Sayers visting his
Dad Stephen in prison

Neil Booth. and 'The Duffer; Lee Duffy

Frankland running the joint

Viv Graham and Billy Robinson

The Night of the Hobo's incident: John Henry, Stephen, Viv, Fish, Rob Armstrong, and others

John Henry is released, 2000

A rare photo of Michael, Stephen and John together on the Bigg Market in the eatly noughties

Stephen and John with Mike Tyson and Evander Holyfield

Stephen Sayers and Roger Daltrey

Stephen with Katie Price

John Henry Sayers on Panorama

Above: Stephen and Tommy
Sayers with Paul Gasgoigne
in Dunston 2017

Left: Albert Sayers and
John Henry Sayers 2020

Christian Simpson, Godson of Freddie Foreman,
Stephen Sayers, Steve Baxter, Albert Sayers
and Steve Wraith

Tony Sayers Snr with
twin sons Tony and Jack

Police raid the home of john Henry Sayers

Mr Nice' Howard Marks with
Steve Wraith, Stephen Sayers
and Alan 'Fish' Tams

Steve Wraith, Tony Sayers, Jayne Mackenzie, Stephen Sayers
and director Garry Fraser at York Street for some film publicity

Chapter Thirty Four: A Sordid Trio

With Michael on the run Stephen was placed on remand in Durham with Nigel Abadom. The police were still looking for Michael and had a feeling that he had fled to Spain. He was a lot closer to home living in his Aunties caravan in Bedlington and was living in plain sight under the police's noses still drinking in all of his usual haunts.

Stephen and Nigel were placed on B wing. There were droves of people putting bags of goods at their door, tobacco, dozens of phone cards, shower gel, pretty much anything of use that you are allowed in prison. When the screw came to the door Stephen could hear him making a lot of noise asking a couple of inmate cleaners what they were doing at Stephen's door. They explained that another screw had let them through. Rules don't always apply when you're the biggest name in jail and a lot of the screws knew Stephen from old, of course some had left, but not all of them. The screw looked at the names outside the door then came in and shook the lad's hands and he started telling them that his nephew had been getting threatened by an idiot off another wing and he was very concerned about his wellbeing. When this inmate was to be released, he asked if Stephen could have a word with him. Stephen smiled and told him it was possible and that he would see what he could do. It was a two second job. Stephen sent Nigel to take care of it and gave the kid the heads up and a warning about the allegations. The young lad was very impressed by it all and wanted to return the favour saying if there was anything he could do inside or outside jail he would.

The lads went downstairs to the servery to collect their food and got a couple of newspapers and went back to cell with a couple of joints to help them get some sleep that night. Stephen woke up the following morning with the sound of screws screaming on the landings. He instantly knew he was back in jail. He got up, washed and was ready for breakfast. Next up exercise. He heard a screw scream at the bottom of the wing, 'Ring ya bells for exercise' which he did. As he was led along the landing inmates were reaching out to shake his hand. He lost count how many. As he went on exercise he was greeted by a group of familiar and unfamiliar smiling faces. Peter Beaumont Gowling, Richy Hall, Michael Alsop, and others. The lads were all full of questions and wanting to know how he was feeling about his case. He told them, "Always remember lads It always seems bad at the beginning but if there was a way to get you in then there is a way to get you out."

Michael Alsop and Peter Beaumont Gowling were serving time for their involvement in a big drugs case. Gowling opened up about their involvement with 'Mr X'. They had been on private jets with him to Newcastle football matches including a trip to the European match in Antwerp with a senior Superintendent in the police. Gowling alleged that 'Mr X' was allowing the use of his vans for the transportation of class A drugs. Gowling also informed Stephen that the reason he had been arrested in a hotel in Heathrow was because a week earlier he had sex with Hunt's girlfriend. She asked him what he was up to and when he would be coming back and he told her quite foolishly that he would be back at the same hotel in 7 days' time. From that careless pillow talk he was arrested.

Gowling alleged that the information was passed to Hunt who then informed a Detective Inspector and the entire observation was set up. Gowling also suggested that 'Mr X' himself was already under investigation by the police for the transportation of drugs. It would make sense. He had protection from the police and in return he would hand them the Sayers on a plate.

Many believed that he had been a major drug dealer for a number of years hence his enormous wealth. He was a very young man; his father had a very poor business and yet his business seemed to expand very rapidly in a short period of time. For a man who claimed he was in debt on one of the many police tapes he had all the attributes of a millionaire. He had a yacht, a house worth £500k with £120k worth of Koi Carp in the pond, the furnishings for the house were over £200k, he had a privately plated Rolls Royce and a £17k Rolex. He was a habitual cocaine user and was regularly seen using cocaine in 'Julies Nightclub', with the son of a prominent football club owner at the time. He played the high life in Newcastle and was well known to the police for that but was clearly left alone because of his high-ranking connections.

With a couple of days until Christmas Stephen received some devastating news. Frankie Kelly his cousin had been on a night out in Newcastle city Centre. He had been in Macey's bar in the Groat Market when he was blasted in the chest at close range during a shootout. He had managed to stagger out onto the street in front of revellers and collapsed. He died at the Royal Victoria Infirmary. Six days later gunman Stephen Rice handed himself him in.

The Evening Chronicle reported the following:

Rice denied murdering Mr Kelly, from Lemington, but admitted manslaughter at Durham Crown Court. The judge heard how Rice ran into his rival by chance during a night out, on December 23.

The killer was already in the packed bar with three pals when Mr Kelly and two friends walked in. Moments later one of the three pulled out a crude homemade pistol and fired at their rivals and as stunned revellers dived for cover Rice pulled a handgun from his waistband and began shooting back. One of the shots hit Mr Kelly in the chest as he attempted to retreat, and the bullet passed straight through his body and hit one of his friends, who was wounded.

Rice said he had been carrying the gun for protection as he celebrated his birthday on the Bigg Market, saying he feared he would be targeted by the Harrison family from Newcastle's West End. Rice was jailed for eight years for his role in the killing after the judge, Mr Justice Morland, accepted Rice, 30, had feared for his life and pulled the trigger to frighten his rivals who fired first.

Michael Sayers luck finally ran out when he was arrested on the 2nd February 1996. He had been drinking in the Ridge Farm Public House in Bedlington and was spotted by the police. He was so drunk that he made no attempt to resist and was placed in a cell to sleep the affects off before he was interviewed in which he replied no comment throughout.

With the court case approaching Stephen's solicitor was then contacted by Leonard Conroy who told him that Hunt had called him from prison and said that he had set Stephen and Co. up. Stephen passed this onto his solicitor. It is also clear from telephone records that Hunt was keeping in regular contact with 'Mr X' throughout his time in prison. It appeared that he was keeping 'in' to ensure everything was alright when he was released so he could pick up where he had left off. Hunt's aim was to do a deal with the prosecution service and get out of prison and go back to work on the streets with some pretty serious approval.

This is not fanciful or farfetched. There have been cases in Newcastle where drug dealers who should have been handed sentences of 18 years have been given 12 months because they were prepared to turn Queen's Evidence. If the Sayers brothers had cooperated like so many around them then the same would have happened for them but they never did and that is what really annoyed the authorities.

One Thursday Stephen was sitting in his cell gathering his thoughts, it was just after dinner. The prison was on bang up until 1.30pm when they would get opened up for work. A screw opened Stephen's door right on time and said "Stephen your solicitors visit has been cancelled. You need to phone your solicitor up" so he went downstairs to phone his solicitor. He told Stephen that there were rumours circulating that 'Mr X' was going to drop the charges over the weekend and if he did then that meant he would be released Tuesday. He advised him not to build his hopes up as it was simply hearsay but it sounded promising to Stephen.

So, the following Tuesday Stephen arrived at North Shields magistrates court for an old-style committal. They were sitting in the cells below the court when they shouted Nigel's name out and they took him to see his legal team. Nigel went up and came back five minutes later. That was not a good sign. He never had a chance to talk to Stephen but he quickly shouted from the passage that the charges were not getting dropped.

In fact, the police were now looking to charge Stephen for a fire which had burned down the Crown Prosecution office and the shooting of a retired police sergeant Bob Morton who was a close friend of 'Mr X's'. It seemed to Stephen that the police were up to their old tactics. Unsolved crime? Blame the Sayers brothers. It turned out that 'Mr X' had now had a change of heart too. It appeared that there was someone working flat out in the background against the Sayers.

I mentioned earlier that Hunt was a double category A prisoner and who was on remand in Winson Green Prison in Birmingham. He had been arrested with another man called Tony Weldon who had nothing to do with this situation.

With 'Mr X's' phone bugged all calls were logged and recorded after the shooting at his house and there were numerous calls between Hunt and 'Mr X' and other members of Hunt's family. When Hunt found out that 'Mr X' was intending to drop the charges against Stephen, he wasted no time in ringing 'Mr X'.

'Mr X' received a call from Hunt on 8th April 1996 where he was clearly heard saying:

Hunt: Divn't weaken son, divn't weaken.

'Mr X': I'm not.

Hunt: I'm with you all the way.

In another call Hunt can be heard mocking the police as he opens with *"Just for the benefit of the tape it's 5:59pm"* before telling 'Mr X' that *"I hope they fuckin' die me man"* in reference to the Sayers brothers.

'Mr X' is clearly under the Hunt's spell and tells his brother in a call on 30th July 1996, *"If there's anything I can do as I say to help 'em even you know Joe's case that's coming up or whatever I will do."* He then goes on to say *"And they can fuck off because they are just toe-rags,"* in reference to the Sayers.

In a call between 'Mr X' and one of Hunt's brothers on Friday 2nd August 1996 at 6:30pm 'Mr X' informs him that the Sayers solicitor has requested records of all conversations between him and the Hunt's which appears to have freaked him out. Hunt's brother then tells him that he has been notified that he is going to be targeted and *"Going to get seriously hurt and that it's definitely from the Sayers, that's the Sayers."* Clearly emphasising the name for the tape.

Then another twist in the plot. 'Mr X's' solicitor contacted the Sayers solicitor stating that he wanted to be *'out of the case'*. There was an exchange of letters between the two parties with 'Mr X's' solicitor suggesting that John Brian Sayers telephone 'Mr X' to discuss the matter. This was a clear attempt to have the Sayers Dad arrested and charged with perverting the course of justice which would have been viewed very seriously by the courts. John didn't take the bait. Hunt was pulling 'Mr X's' strings the question is was he doing the bidding of a handling officer?

Tony Weldon who as I mentioned earlier had been arrested with Hunt did not want to get embroiled in the ongoing situation between Hunt and the Sayers but in a prison letter, he spelled it out in layman terms what had gone on.

In the letter he insists that he 'hasn't turned against the Hunt family for nothing' and then he begins to set the scene:

So, we have been nicked for this. I have admitted to doing everything on this robbery, just to give Hunt a chance to walk. That shithouse promised me the world! In Jan. Hunt got some additional forensic evidence fibre lifts from the getaway cars etc. Because I was going guilty, I wasn't that interested in the forensic. Hunt told me that there was fibres from his jacket in the coats the robbers wore and nowt else. (Which was a lie!)

So, Hunt come to my damper (cell) and said "The Wobbley – Bots (Sayers) have threatened 'Mr X'." A couple of days later he gets a police visit (one of many). So, he's got the bizz coming down from N/cle. I asked him what they wanted and he said "They wanted to know if I had any AK 47's to hand in." Now I always had Hunt down as staunch so I took his word for it. Next thing I know is he's come to my door and says "The wobbley-bots are nicked, cameraed up, taped up bang to rights."

So, I'm immediately thinking that there's a rabbit off. 'Mr X' puts bail up for Hunt, 'Mr X' gets threatened, Hunt gets a police visit, the Bros. get nicked! But cos I thought Hunt was staunch I just kept it in mind, as I had no proof!

Then we go up for committal and Hunt's now totally convinced he's getting bail. Totally! But he's worried incase the bizz slip witnesses into court to I.D. him. So, this bloke keeps coming in and out of the courtroom and I pointed him out to Hunt I said "I know his face, I think he's a brief from N/cle." Shithouse Hunt says, "I've never seen him before, face the front and listen to what's being said."

So, I've come back to the jail and Hunt has stayed behind for his bail app. As I was leaving the building, I noticed that the courtroom was emptied for his bail app. I asked him why and he said "Plan B." I said "So what the fuck is Plan B?" He said, "I've handed 2 kilos of Semtex and some firearms in." I've gone fuckin' crackers. But dickhead isn't bothered one bit.

Next thing I know he's gone to Armley. I was told from a reliable source that the police Regional Crime Squad (R.C.S.) were taking him out of the jail. While he was away, I've had time to collect my thoughts. When he come back, I asked him if he'd got the Sayers nicked. He said "I told 'Mr X' he was a straight kid and to go to the bizz." So, I'm starting to get a bit worried cos as well as all this happening Hunt is going on ridiculous on the landing. He's best pal with all the screws and the nonces. Respected villains are wanting nothing to do with him and are saying to me they think he's dodgy. He's on the phone all day every day and we can get no more than 10 mins a day.

So, I've pulled him in front of the lads (Bud Armstrong a Sayers friend included) and the shitbag has run onto the numbers. I've also realised that the bloke at court he said he didn't know was D.I. Hepworth. I recognised him from

the Brandling at Jesmond when I was red-eyed one night!
He's now on the numbers and refusing exercise. (He's still behind his door now and refusing exercise now, 15 weeks later!!!) Now what am I supposed to think? Are these the actions of a man who's done no wrong? After he's gone on the numbers, I've got this mad fucking letter off his brief.

Weldon then goes on to explain that he has had a letter from Hunt's brief Hindle suggesting that the Sayers have been setting people up, blaming them for things they had not done and then claiming the reward. An out and out lie. Weldon continues.

M and S should have Hunt's brief nicked for slander. I am a staunch kid, always have been, always will be. that is why I have told everybody about Hunt's antics. He's not only set M and S up but he's up to fuckin' all kinds of mad skulduggery, just to get out. I've fucked Hunt off cos he's dealing with the bizz. I'd have fucked my own brother off if he'd done what Hunt has done.
So now I find out that the forensic against Hunt is that the fibres from his suit are on the coats the robbers wore, in all three getaway cars and that he has gunshot residue on the gloves he had on him!!! And seeing as though he was nicked 20 yards from me and that he had his filo-fax on him with my name in it, it looks like it's an uphill struggle for him to get a not guilty. But there's all kinds of evidence missing from the deps!!! Regarding Hunt!
So, what's happened in a nutshell is this. Hunts got his forensic and he's known he's been fucked. But he's said fuck all about it to me. So, he's handing in Semtex and guns and is dealing with Hepworth (no ordinary policeman!).
I mean how could Hunt ever say that he wasn't up to no good? How can he when he's had the commander of the R.C.S. coming to court to shout in favour of bail for Hunt behind closed doors?! I am not prepared to take the chance that he hasn't gone copper. And after he trots onto the numbers, he refuses exercise and hasn't been out of his damper for 15 weeks!!! Believe me, the block isn't a pretty sight here at the Green.

He signs off the letter like this:

Hunt got himself into this so he can get himself out of it. Take care, Tony.

The Sayers were looking at a good stint in prison through all of this. There was no way out for Stephen and Nigel with all of the evidence against them and 'Mr X's' testimony so they plead guilty which gave Michael a fighting chance of walking free from all charges, but after a two week trial at Doncaster Crown Court Michael was found guilty on December 19th 1996 of all charges by a majority verdict of 10 to 2. Sentencing took place early 1997 and the Sayers brothers weren't expecting any favours and they didn't get any from Judge Harkins who sentenced them to 10 years in prison.

Assistant Chief Constable Alan Oliver was delighted with the result. "We have made strenuous efforts to reduce not only the volume of crime in the force area but target organized crime and the insidious nature of the offences which affect not only individuals but the business community in the form of drugs, violence, extortion and protection rackets. We will continue to target those who are trading on fear and violence to enhance their criminal reputations. The Northumbria force is committed, with the co-operation of others including the Regional Crime Squad, Customs and Excise officers and other agencies, to target organized crime and those who carry it out.'

The local newspaper the Evening Chronicle pulled no punches in their editorial either in a piece entitled *'Sordid Trio Finally Jailed.'*

The story we carry today about the convictions of Michael and Stephen Sayers and their accomplice Nigel Abadom, can carry only one description – and that is sordid. Nobody but those who have suffered from their actions will ever know just how much misery they have caused to others in the course of their crimes. The Sayers and people like them probably won't care, and maybe even feel hard done by when the cell door closes on them. The fact remains that some good police work has finally slammed those cell doors on the leaders of one of the North East's most infamous gangland families.

The Sayers and people like them, believe that they are beyond the law most of us look to for protection. Now they've found how wrong they were. Over the last two years the Northumbria Police have cracked down on so called hard men like the Sayers, going for the prime targets on the criminal scene. It was a situation which couldn't be tolerated almost a re-run of Chicago-style gangland warfare in which the innocent, as well as the guilty, were in the firing line. It is the way of the world that something nasty will creep out of the woodwork to take their places but at least they now have good warning that they too, could be in the firing line.

When they got back to the prison Stephen saw his friend heading back from a visit and he told him that he had a nice little bit of draw. He invited Stephen and Michael over that night for a smoke in his cell during association. Association is time given to the inmates to shower, get a haircut or use the phone. As Stephen was walking along the landing to pick up his tea, he bumped into an old pal Mickey Lang who told Stephen that a few lads had the hump with Hunt. Stephen understood why.

Stephen and Michael managed to get 3 bottles of hooch for the night and after tea joined good friend Stuie Henderson from Durham in his cell. As they were getting settled and having their first glass of hooch, they heard a disturbance coming from the landing below. It was two people having a fight or so it seemed. Stephen had a feeling he knew what was going on. All the actions said it was a fight but these lads were not hurting each other. They were just rolling about the floor shouting and balling creating a scene which was their objective as they were there to create a diversion. About 20 screws headed over to break them up leaving only 2 or 3 screws to handle about 180 inmates. The noise of the radios started getting louder as inmates were turning them up in the cells this was to silence any screams. These actions were clearly coordinated by a large group of people. People who were prepared to suffer the consequences.

Stephen was not brand new in this department and he knew what was going down and he had a good guess of who the intended victim was going to be as a lot of people had the hump with the outspoken man. Whatever other people were up to on the wing wasn't Stephen's concern. He headed back into Stuie's cell where Eddie had arrived with the draw he had mentioned earlier. Stephen, Michael and the lads continued getting drunk and stoned until the riot bells went off then refilled their cups and made their way to their own cells. Walking down the stairs Stephen saw a man come from the direction of the shower, his face was beaten to a pulp and there was blood coming out of every orifice then he just collapsed to the ground. Stephen looked across the landing and saw Mickey Lang who gave him a nod. A nod is as good as a wink so they say.

Even though Stephen had not asked for this to happen, he had no doubt that Mickey took it upon himself to put right what he saw was wrong. This beating was a little too much for the prison warders in HMP Durham jail. The screws were shitting themselves. They had just seen a bit of work take place. After that the days were numbered for Stephen and Michael. One of the screws went to see both of them and said he had worked in prisons across the country for over 25 years and he had never seen such professional violence behind bars. There was a slight pause for ten seconds then Stephen asked him what he wanted. The screw produced a quarter ounce of cannabis from his pocket and threw it on the bed next to Stephen and proceeded to tell him he that he had found it when searching someone else's cell who he believed was a friend of Stephens. He told him he was not going to nick him and he most certainly did not want any trouble with Stephen, Michael or their associates. Stephen was quite happy with this. This tough screw was now shitting himself. That screw might have taken it lightly but the governor didn't and he was as good as his word.

Durham jail is always on edge. There were slashings and stabbings almost every day. One day Stephen and Nigel were sitting in the cell when a screw came to get them. Something strange was happening as there was another screw with him an S.O. (Senior officer) who Stephen recognised from old. He said "Stephen I don't know what you have done but there are 2 or 3 governors downstairs and they all want to see you." They were taken down and Stephen entered the room with Nigel who was a little worse for wear on the prison hooch. There was three Prison Officers, three Principal officers and three Senior Officers it was like the who's who of the prison. Nigel seemed to think he was in the Bigg market and not the big house. The Governor came forward and told Stephen he had just come off the phone to the home office and he had to explain why Durham jail had become the most violent jail in the country. He continued, "We know it's not you Stephen, but these young inmates are so impressed by the Sayers reputation that they are doing this to impress you and your brothers John and Michael." Realising that his speech was falling on deaf ears another screw piped up "We should just bend him up and take him down the block Sir". Stephen looked at him and told him to come forward and give it a try. Needless to say, this was a man of words not action. Stephen then told him if he was not going to put forward a constructive opinion then he should shut his big mouth, which he did not like.

The Governor made it quite simple, unless these slashing and stabbings were stopped then Stephen and Michael would be made double category AA prisoners and moved to another prison. This would be a massive inconvenience for them and make it more difficult for their family and friends to visit. Stephen however was standing his ground. He was not being bullied by anyone regardless of what they did for a living. The Governors final advice was to get the situation sorted. Stephen's advice to him was not to make things personal. He asked what Stephen meant by that. He did not answer at first. Then he explained that he could defuse the situation but not from behind his prison door. The Governor asked what he meant, so he told him if there was trouble in the gym or the education block then he could not defuse it if he was sat in his cell. The Governor nodded. He could see where Stephen was coming from.

It just so happened there had been a slashing that morning in the education block on the cookery class which at the time was very difficult to get on. Stephen explained that he needed access to all the wings and the gym in case a situation arose. He knew he could defuse the situations so he was going to use this situation to his advantage and he did. There wasn't a stabbing or a slashing for nearly four months. The Governor was happy and so was Stephen. You could never trust the system though.

Stephen and Michael were woken up the one morning with 20 screws outside their door and the Governor. This was 7am and it wasn't a spin. The Governor walked into their cell and told them that their security categorisation had been changed and increased from a category B prisoner to double category A of which there were only 30 or so out of 60,000 prisoners. John Henry Sayers was also being upgraded from double category A to triple category A and there was only three of these in the country. Being on the book as they call it is no advantage if your hoping to be set free. It does give you an ego boost in prison however. You have screws watching your every move. Waking you up with a touch every hour to see if your there. They play games with you. They have a psychologist listening to every call you make, looking through your history, childhood application forms, they look through everything to find out what your state of mind is and they look for a weakness to try and break you. Let's not forget here the majority of double category A prisoners are terrorists that have stood against this country. So, the lads found themselves walking along the landing carrying their belongings accompanied by 20 or so screws and they were taking them down the segregation unit also known as the block. They separated them from each other and put them in single cells.

It didn't take long for them to adapt to segregation life. Rough food was the norm, there were dog screws that were always barking at someone and who would try and belittle the lads by calling them their second name. These were the ones who felt pleasure from being sadistic. There was one in particular Stephen had come across before who would turn into superman when he put that uniform on and went to the segregation unit. Although this man was not having a go at Stephen or Michael, he was most certainly having a go at everyone else that was in the block, he was nothing but a bully.

The segregation unit was used as a dual purpose for the screws. One purpose was to house people who had been put on punishment for misbehaving on the wings, where they would be served with a piece of paper which was classed as a nicking sheet. The other purpose of the segregation unit was to house double category A prisoners. So, the cells were in very bad condition with windows smashed, bodily fluids all over the walls. They would smell disgusting. There was many a time that Stephen would get woken up by some smack head screaming in the middle of the night because he was going cold turkey for smack. These people will not stop until they get their drugs and it can take the screws hours to finally make the decision to place them elsewhere. Sometimes there is nowhere to put them as the block units would be full. These people would lie on their backs and kick their cell doors for hours on end all night and they would repeat the process the next day over and over again. It can batter other inmates' heads especially when they would have a trial coming up and were trying to concentrate on deposition papers. Stephen and Michael were made of sterner stuff and adjusted well to their environment and like there brother John they got their heads down and did their time without complaint.

In July 1996 at a flat in Croydon the police had booted in the doors and arrested 70-year-old Charlie Kray for his part in a £39m drugs plot. He had been targeted by police over a dozen time since his release from jail in the seventies so I guess it was 13th time unlucky for the twins' older brother who had fallen for a 'sting'. A year later he was given a 12-year sentence for his involvement, meaning he would likely die in prison. He was shipped to HMP Frankland in Durham for the first part of his sentence and he added me to his visitors list.

Stephen and Michael were on the same wing as Charlie along with the 'Wee Man' Paul Ferris.

'If a devil could cast his net' a screw had said one night as he passed the four of them sitting in a cell having some food together. Charlie was thankful of the hospitality the Sayers had shown him since his arrival but something was troubling him and, on a visit, he explained to me that he had brought it to Stephen's attention that in his trial the Sayers family had been mentioned on numerous occasions. The undercover officers that had set up Charlie were in fact from the North East and it seemed that they were trying to link the two families together. My name had also surfaced in the depositions through my connections with the Kray family which I found quite disturbing. Stephen was pleased that Charlie had divulged the information and, on his release, told me that Charlie had said to him 'Not to make the same mistakes as me and my brothers. You can't beat the system. They will lock you up and throw away the keys." This message hit home with Stephen. He was determined to turn his life around on his release from prison.

COMMENT

WE SAY
••••••••••••••••••
Sordid trio finally jailed

THE story we carry today about the convictions of Michael and Stephen Sayers, and their accomplice Nigel Abadom, can carry only one description – and that is sordid.

Nobody but those who have suffered from their actions will ever know just how much misery they have caused to others in the course of their crimes.

The Sayers and people like them probably won't care, and maybe even feel hard done by when the cell door closes on them.

The fact remains that some good police work has finally slammed those cell doors on the leaders of one of the North East's most infamous gangland families.

The Sayers and people like them, believe that they are beyond the law most of us look to for protection. Now they've found how very wrong they were.

Over the last two years Northumbria Police have cracked down on so-called hard men like the Sayers, going for the prime targets on the criminal scene.

It was a situation which couldn't be tolerated, almost a re-run of Chicago-style gangland warfare in which the innocent, as well as the guilty, were in the firing line.

It is the way of the world that something nasty will creep out of the woodwork to take their places but at least they now have good warning that they, too, could be in the legal firing line.

Clearing up the streets of fear

TYNESIDE is a safer place today as members of the North East's most notorious crime families prepare to face lengthy jail sentences

The Chronicle revealed yesterday how Michael and Stephen Sayers, and accomplice Nigel Abadom, were convicted at Doncaster Crown Court of the blackmail of a prominent businessman.

Justice

The three, who will remain in custody awaiting sentence in the New Year, are the latest in a line of Tyneside hardmen to be brought to justice.

Their convictions were the culmination of sustained police efforts to rid the streets of the tyrannical rule of a dynasty of criminal families.

Over the last two years, police chiefs have targeted Tyneside's crime lords and have now helped to put away some of the key villains.

Northumbria Police Assistant today.

"We have made strenuous efforts to reduce not only the volume of crime in the force area but target organised crime and the insidious nature of the offences which affect not only individuals but the business community in the form of drugs, violence, extortion and protection rackets.

"We will continue to target those who are trading on fear and violence to enhance their criminal reputations.

"The Northumbria force is committed, with the co-operation of others including the Regional Crime Squad, Customs and Excise officers and other agencies, to target organised crime and those who carry it out."

Last year, three of the Harrison brothers – James, 25, Joseph 23 and Andrew, 21 – were each sentenced to 10 years for their part in a terrifying shoot-out and firebomb attack on the Happy House hostel.

Conroy himself, together with side-kick David Glover, 27, were jailed last Christmas for a total of 22 years.

tenced to eleven-and-a-half years for masterminding the kidnap and torture of Billy Collier, during which one of his front teeth was snapped with a pair of pliers. Glover was given ten-and-a-half years for his part.

During the seven-week trial, shocked jurors were given an insight into gangland violence in Newcastle's West End involving street shootings and petrol bomb attacks.

Vicious

John Henry Sayers, 32, is already serving a 15-year sentence as the brains behind a vicious £400,000 armed robbery firm in Gateshead seven years ago – a crime he has always strenuously denied.

Dad, John Bryan, 55, was shot at point-blank range in the throat on Newcastle's Quayside in January. He managed to drive to hospital where surgeons removed a .22 bullet.

His two other sons, Stephen, 30, was jailed for 30 months in 1990 for a vicious attack on a club bouncer – and Michael was shot in a

How the Evening Chronicle reported the convictions of Michael and Stephen Sayers and Nigel Abadom

▶ Top North businessman at centre of plot by notorious mob of villains

BLACKMAILED BY GANGSTERS

● **GUILTY** – heavy drinker and cocaine user Michael Sayers

● **GUILTY** – heroin addict Nigel Abadom

● **GUILTY** – Stephen Sayers controlled the drug scene in Newcastle

THE reign of one of the North East's most notorious gangland families came to an end today after three men were convicted of blackmailing a leading Tyneside businessman.

The Sayers brothers, Michael and Stephen, and their accomplice Nigel Abadom face long prison sentences after their bid to net £50,000 failed.

Michael Sayers 29, of no fixed address, was convicted of conspiracy to blackmail by a jury at Doncaster Crown Court. He had denied the charge.

His brother Stephen, 31, of Grange Road, Fenham, Newcastle, and go-between Nigel Abadom, 44, of Coventry Gardens, Benwell, Newcastle earlier admitted conspiracy to blackmail when they appeared at the same court.

Shots

All three will be sentenced in Newcastle in the New Year.

The trio tried to extort £50,000 from a managing director, who cannot be named for legal reasons, by threatening to shoot him if he failed to pay.

The court was told shots were fired through the window of the businessman's New-castle home into a room where his two young sons usually played.

Abadom then made several calls to the man's office saying the brothers would blast him or his nightwatchman if he did not stump up the cash.

In a series of taped conversations the jury heard Abadom claim the Sayers brothers believed the businessman was

EXCLUSIVE
By SUSAN ALLISON

an accomplice of a rival criminal who undercut their Tyneside drug trade by selling at a cheaper price. All three then went to the man's office to clinch the blackmail deal.

Paul Batty QC, prosecuting, told the court Stephen Sayers and Abadom were snared by police officers lying in wait when they returned to the man's office to collect the cash.

Michael Sayers was arrested a month later at a Bedlington pub. The heavy drinker and cocaine-abuser claimed he was dominated by his elder brother who used his hardman reputation as a "dark satanic figure" to frighten, but played no part in the conspiracy.

Michael Topolski, mitigating, said: "His name as a coke-filled assassin was bandied about. Because he was shot and survived his brother was able to use him for his own purposes."

Heroin addict Abadom has served time for a drug conviction and a stabbing.

The jury heard Michael and Stephen were heavily involved in the control of Newcastle's drugs scene, controlling sub-dealers in the city's pubs and clubs. Doormen were paid to allow dealers to operate.

Cocaine addict Michael had a reputation as an aggressive and violent thug who operated a protection racket.

He survived an assassination attempt in 1993 when he was blasted by a gunman who fired through the window of a Newcastle pub. When they were threatening the businessman they claimed Sayers tracked down the gunman and threw him to his death from a seven-storey building.

▶ **COMMENT – Page 12**

TOP SECURITY TRIAL

THE trial was moved from Newcastle to Doncaster because of the Sayers reputation.

In a high security operation Sayers was flanked by five officers as he sat in the dock and driven to court in a high security van led by a police convoy. Armed officers wearing bullet-proof vests stood guard outside court searching everyone who went in.

Van mildert

MEN AND WOMEN
AUTUMN WINTER COLLECTIONS

PAUL SMITH
DRIES VAN NOTEN
DOLCE & GABBANA
VICTOR VICTORIA
NICOLE FARHI
HELMUT LANG
COSTUME HOMME
UNITY
MASSIMO OSTI
CP COMPANY
ARMANI JEANS
HUGO BOSS
CALVIN KLEIN
KATHARINE HAMNETT
PATRICK COX
JEFFERY WEST
NICHOLAS DEAKINS

How the Evening Chronicle reported the convictions of Michael and Stephen Sayers and Nigel Abadom

Chapter Thirty Five: Peter Beaumont-Gowling

Peter Beaumont Gowling who I mentioned previously was a former restauranteur who had amassed a large fortune over the years and who led a champagne lifestyle. Over the years he had become addicted to cocaine and fallen in with drug dealers and would act as a courier for their cash laundering. He had laundered £2.5m in five trips to Ireland making £125,000 in the process but was caught by police boarding a flight in 1996 with £540K in cash. He was jailed for 11 years for the offence a year later.

On release from prison Stephen's involvement with Peter consisted of taking care of much of his debt related problems which were not drug related. Peter Gowling was a wealthy man he sold property in Darlington and was worth over a couple of million pound at the time. He felt secure having Stephen around him. He had chased a couple of people who were trying to shake him down and also one or two who were trying to bully him. After a nights drinking there would always be a party at his house and he loved the Champagne Charlie lifestyle.

Peter could quite easily spend £10K on cocaine put it on the table for everybody until it was gone, he was very generous. One day he called Stephen and explained that he had taken a call from a man who said he was going to kidnap him and tie him up unless he paid him. He just wanted Stephen to meet the man and give him 20k to end his worries. Stephen made some enquiries. It turned out that the man putting the squeeze on was a cousin of his. So, he told Peter he would simply have a word this man to tell him to back off, but as he had been kidnapped in the past he insisted on paying Stephen's cousin to put his mind at rest. Stephen was sat in Peter's front room as the businessman counted the final bundles into the case. He closed it and handed it to Stephen. "There's 30k in there." Stephen nodded, took the case, and headed off to meet his cousin.

They met up in town where Stephen explained that he was looking after Peter. His cousin understood and told him that he had made the threat in a bar one night when he was pissed and that he hadn't meant it and that he should let Peter know that. He then went onto explain that he was finding things hard and his car had been stolen with no insurance which he had given £4500 for. With 30k in the case Stephen told his cousin that he was going to help him out. He handed him 10k to help with the car and for him to take his family on a holiday. His cousin could not believe his luck. Stephen then headed back to Peter's and told him that his cousin had agreed to take £10k. Stephen then explained that he would take 10k as his fee as he returned the remaining 10k back to Peter. He was delighted with the outcome. He just wanted Stephen on board with him. He knew his reputation went before him and that he was loyal. That was all that mattered. Stephen was more than happy to oblige and over the course of time they became good friends.

Peter literally had more money than he could spend at times but hated keeping it in the house after raiders had broken in, tied him up, and robbed him. Peter had a sky-blue Bentley which was only six months old. They couldn't get a taxi one Saturday night so he told Stephen to take his car which he did. He told Stephen he would call him when he needed the car back. Stephen was up sharp on the Sunday morning. He got Donna and the kids in the car and off they went for a day out to Edinburgh. When they came back Peter was at his door with a big smile on his face. He asked Stephen for the keys and immediately went to the boot where he proceeded to remove a sports bag with £100k inside which he had left in the car. Stephen had been driving around in this car but had no knowledge of what was in the boot. When he saw the cash he said to Peter, "It's a good job I'm a careful driver because if the police had pulled me over imagine me trying to explain why I'm driving around in somebody's motor with that kind of wedge in the boot." Peter just laughed it off.

On the afternoon of 14th February 2001 Peter Beaumont-Gowling answered the doorbell at his plush home on Osbourne Road and was shot in the head and body four times at point blank range. He died instantly. He was 52. His body was found by his girlfriend Teresa Holmes at midnight when she returned home. Nobody has ever been convicted of his murder and the case remains open.

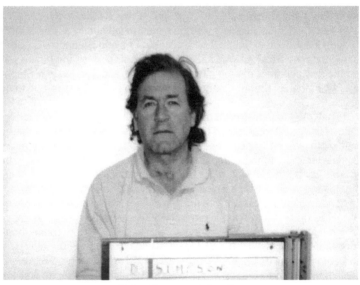

Peter Beaumont Gowling

Chapter Thirty Six: The Murder Of Freddie Knights

Freddie Knights was a family man, a Newcastle United fan and a part time DJ. There were rumours of a darker side to his life but many of his friends and family were not privy to it.

Freddie Knights attended the North Tyneside General Hospital on 1st July 2000. He was seen by a senior house officer in accident and emergency and a doctor who was a locum senior house officer in general medicine. Knights admitted to having a three-year cocaine addiction taking 5-7 grams a night on 2 occasions per week. From this he had developed the following problems:

1. Perforation of his nasal septum. The thin bone plate which divides one nostril from the other. It was painful and associated with pains in his head and left ear.
2. Pain to left side of his chest especially after using cocaine.

In order to control these pains, he took a variety of painkillers including aspirin, paracetamol and co-proxamol. He admitted to using three to four boxes per week of painkillers for last 2-3 weeks. It is clear from this that Freddie was mixing in the wrong circles and his habit was clearly out of control.

For the first time, using court depositions, newspaper reports and interviews I have carried out, I can now give you an insight into the full case.

On the 4th September Lee Watson committed an act of aggravated burglary at 42 Hardman Gardens in Ryton at home of Catherine Madine. At the time she was going out with a known drugs dealer. At approximately 2pm Lee Watson along with Edward Stewart and Dale Miller ransacked and damaged the house. Watson discharged a 410 shotgun into various parts of the premises, twice into the headboard of the bed, once into the mirror and once into the window. The toilet and hand basin were ripped from their positions causing considerable damage. The Renault they were using to get away was seen leaving area. Police attended at 2:30pm and within half an hour they spotted the car at Millers address on Ten Street.

Miller and Stewart were arrested but Watson evaded capture however it did not take police long to track the suspect down. On the 15th September 2000 he was arrested after being seen driving a Cavalier erratically. He was chased and stopped and arrested for driving whilst unfit through drugs. When arrested he had £800 in his possession. He was interviewed the following day but gave no reply as had Miller and Stewart and they were released on bail pending further enquiries. Stewart headed to Birmingham.

Two days later on the 18th September Eddie Stewart travelled back from Birmingham by train and arrived at Central Station. He headed to 77 Deerbush to stay with Stephen Carlton who had picked him up on the instruction of Dale Miller. The following day the 19th September police officer Bob Pallas claims to see John Henry Sayers Millar and Stewart in a layby at Peter Barratts Garden Centre.

On the same day John Paul Hunter and Terrence Mann took the metro to South Shields and they weren't planning on paddling in the sea or building a sandcastle. They arrived and made their way to a café for a cuppa. As the staff were distracted, they went into the staff quarters of café and stole a set of car keys. The plan had gone well so far but with one major flaw. They could not identify the car that the keys belonged to so they dumped them and travelled back to Newcastle City Centre and met up with Tony Leach in Waterloo Street. He was the man who had sent them on the daytrip to 'Shields' for the 'screeve' (stolen car). They tell him what had happened and that they had dumped the keys. Leach was far from impressed so they travel back to South Shields with Leach in a dark red coloured Renault 19 with Mickey Dixon (Mickey Muggins) driving and passenger Billy Harriot.

Dixon was known as Mickey 'Muggins' after stealing a couple of chickens from a van once and missing some cash that was next to them. Leach got them to find the keys and then together they located the car which was a silver Golf. Leach told them to drive the car back to Newcastle and to meet at the Silverlink Industrial Estate just outside of North Shields. The cars drove in convoy, with Hunter driving the Golf, through the Tyne Tunnel to Newcastle. (The police would later obtain CCTV of both cars and phone records between all parties).

The hapless duo were not the best at following orders. Hunter lost the Renault and they got lost. As he did not have Leach's number, he remembered he had John Henry Sayers number on a piece of paper so he headed into Newcastle City Centre and parked up at Central Station and called him from a public phone box. The call was brief and they arranged to meet in Waterloo Street. They headed to the taxi office there where they met John Henry. Leach arrived soon after and bollocked Hunter for getting lost. He then gave Hunter a tenner for petrol and told him to follow him to Shieldfield Service Station, the Jet garage at the bottom of Stoddart Street where he filled his tank up. By this time Hunter was the only one in the Golf. In the Renault Dixon was driving with passengers Leach, and Mann. Harriot was now gone. Once the car was filled up Hunter drove it to a pub in Four Lane Ends where he handed keys and car over to Leach and he then got the Metro home with Mann.

That evening there was a surveillance operation in relation to other matters following Sayers and Leach. They claimed the following:

7:37pm John picked up Tony Leach at home in Forest Hall in his Landrover Discovery.

7:45pm John seen in his Landrover Discovery close to the DSS Building in Longbenton.

7:50pm John seen on Haddricks Mill Road South Gosforth.

7:56pm John seen in Longbenton.

8:04pm Vehicle seen in Peter Barratts layby meeting with occupants of a smaller car. Police claim this meeting was to fully brief the troops and tell them exactly what they needed to do with Freddie Knights.

8:30pm Sayers and Leach arrive at King Neptune Restaurant on Stowell Street. Police claim they attended venue so that they had a perfect alibi. Surveillance officers confirm they are there as does venue manager Chun Yen Mak. Leach makes 9 calls from venue. Police suggest they are to Dixon and Harriot and Stewart. Phone records back this up.

9:01pm According to the police it becomes obvious the plan to kill Knights has failed.

9:11pm Sayers and Leach leave The King Neptune and head along Percy Street. John is pulled over by a Panda car who is oblivious to the undercover officers tailing him. PC Quinney 1198 checks the ownership of the vehicle and makes sure the documentation is in order. He reports that he does not know the passenger (Leach) but that he is agitated and behaving aggressively. John gets a HORT/1 commonly known as a producer which required him to produce certain driving documentation at a preferred Police station. John selects Pilgrim Street.

9:30pm Surveillance team follow John to a layby in Longbenton on Rushall Place. A red Renault pulls alongside the car. There is conversation between the two windows for approximately 4 minutes.

9:38pm John Henry Sayers arrives home alone leaving Leach with occupants of Renault. His car is seen at his address by covert officers DC Goss and DC Heathcote.

At 10pm Ella Hall Freddie's mother was at her home address on Lutterworth Road and there was a very loud bang on her window. It was suggested this was Eddie Stewart. (This came out in the confession he made to Carlton later.) There was also a witness called Donna who lived nearby who said she saw a silver car parked near the house with two males acting suspiciously. Ella was very scared. She had previously had trouble with kids banging on her windows and would always call Freddie to sort them out. Tony Leach who knew Ella and Freddie was aware of this. This night she rang her daughter Shirley who lived across the road. She came over reassured her and told her to lock her doors then left.

Phone evidence sees numerous calls between Leach and Stewarts phones and Leach travelling around Newcastle which the Police suggested he was looking for Knights as he had not fallen into their trap.

The next day September 20th 2000 Police claim:

12 noon to 2:25pm Flurry of calls between John Henry, Watson, Dixon, Leach and Miller.

2:30pm Police find out that Hunter stole the VW Golf but are unaware what it is going to be used for.

3:40pm Surveillance team note a sighting of John Henry, Dixon and Leach together on Chillingham Road at the junction of Tossan Terrace by DC Trotter and DC McCormack.

6:05pm Surveillance Officers DC Perkins and DS Smith and then DS Goss, DS Mitsides and DC Winn see Leach and Dixon together at the Save Garage on Shields Road and then at Leaches home in a Blue Vauxhall Calibra.

6:40pm Watson leaves an address on Deerbush in a taxi to go to Newbiggen Hall according to Stephen Tallen.

6:50pm Hunter calls Leach with regards to some stolen property he wants to fence from a burglary.

6:55pm Phone records place Watson at his bail address Trevelyan Drive in Newbiggin Hall where he is supposed to be staying with a friend called Sandy Jones.

7:20pm Phone records place Dixon in Longbenton and Tony Leach is spotted by surveillance officers in the company of his partner Janet Blayney in a blue Ford sierra approximately an hour before Freddie is shot.

7:29pm Dixon, Miller and Stewart's phones all showing in Longbenton area and calls made between them.

7:33pm Leach calls Dixon then speaks to Hunter then Dixon again

7:40pm Leach and Blayney arrive at King Neptune for a meal spotted by DS Goss and DC Heathcote and DC Mitsides. Hunter and Mann arrive to discuss the disposal of some stolen property. This meeting is confirmed by surveillance officers. They also confirm that Leach gives him some of the money for property but arranges to meet them later for the outstanding monies. This was videoed by police by DC Winn and DC Burton.

7:50pm Leach calls Dixon

7:52pm Police allege Watson now with Dixon in the Renault 19. Phone records show John Henry in taxi office in Waterloo Street.

At 8pm Shirley, Freddie's sister who lives opposite her Mam Ella sees a man walking around from the side of her flat to the front window and he causes the security light to go on. She sees him thump on the window so she runs out and shouts 'What the…" but the man runs off. This is also witnessed by Shelley Wray. Shirley hears her phone ringing, obviously her Mam calling to tell her what has happened. She goes back and answers and Ella is hysterical saying, "He's back, he's brayed on me window again. Who is it? Who is it?" Once again, she has not rung Freddie but Shirley instead.

A witness standing at the Arndale shopping centre which overlooks the area where Ella lives spots a silver VW Golf parked at Whitefriars Way and Lutterworth Drive area. The witness also sees Freddie who recognises him and beeps and waves at him on way to his Mams house. There is a flurry of phone activity then at 8:15pm John Henry is seen by surveillance officers at Waterloo Street.

At 8:24pm a white transit van pulled into Lutterworth Road in Longbenton. Freddie Knights and his partner Grace Wilson were inside and they were travelling back to his mothers' house to pick up his son's school bag which he needed to complete his homework. He had his music on loud and was singing loudly and was happy as his son Alan had just called him to tell him Newcastle United had scored. He then spoke to his mate James McIver who was at the match so he could describe the goal. That call was timed at 20:20pm. The family had just been out for a meal to celebrate son Alans 14th birthday. They drove into the square at the front of Ella's house and got out of the car and started walking to the doorway of Ella's house. Grace looked across the road and saw Shirley her sister-in-law at the kitchen window and gave her a wave. Everything was calm and relaxed. They walked around the van towards the front doorstep, walked up the garden path, through the gate up the garden path to the front door. Freddie was facing the house, and they could still see Shirley at the kitchen window and Shirley's light was still on.

Within seconds there was a rustle in the bushes just a few yards away and a person appeared in front of them masked wearing a black balaclava with eye and mouth holes in it and fired a shot from a sawn-off shotgun which missed them both as they stood on his mothers' doorstep. Grace then saw everything in slow motion as Freddie, clearly in shock, crouched down and put his hands up to his head and shouted 'Wo' as the second shot was fired into his head at close range, the one cartridge spraying at least 8 ball bearing size shots into his head. He stood no chance.

As neighbours poured out onto the street to see what the commotion was all about the gunman made his getaway leaving Grace cradling her dying husband in her arms. His sister Shirley tried to stem the blood flow with towels but it was all in vain. He was bleeding profusely from multiple head injuries. His eyes were closed. He was gone. This had been a coldblooded assassination on the streets of Newcastle.

The police quickly closed off the surrounding area and began taking witness statements and combing the area for clues. Witness statements were taken from residents who were clearly in shock at what they had just witnessed. Carol and Lisa who were walking through Langdale Close, saw the van park and walked past Knights. After she had passed Carol heard two shots and turned and saw a male figure wearing a black balaclava and holding a gun, who ran off. She later produced a sketch and plans which can be seen in this book. Lisa turned after the first shot and saw the second fired, before the gunman ran off. Another witness was a 13-year-old boy given the pseudonym 'George Best'. He saw Knights van drive in and heard the shots. He had seen a silver car on the estate at that time and later identified it from photographs. He also drew a plan of where it had been. Another witness called Frank saw a dark blue Renault drive from Lutterworth Drive onto Whitefriars Way. Witness named Craig had seen two figures at two different houses in Langdale Close. He saw the transit drive in and then heard loud noises. He gave descriptions of the figures that he had seen and produced composite pictures with the assistance of Inspector Kirtlan again which are found in this book.

Andrew another witness simply heard bangs and then looked out and saw a figure with a gun discharge it and then run off. There were other witness statements too. Margaret said she heard the bangs and saw a figure run off carrying an object. John also heard the bangs and saw a figure running off carrying something. Daniel had heard the earlier banging on the window and then heard the shots and saw a figure running off. Margaret likewise heard the gunshots and saw a running figure. Joe heard the bangs and saw a figure running across the grassed area carrying an object wearing a mask. He saw the figure duck behind a fence and re-emerge with the mask rolled up.

The police claim the next set of calls were significant:

8:23pm and 8:25pm Calls from Dixon and Watson to Stewart and Miller to say job done.

8:25pm Dixon and Watson ring Leach.

At 8:30pm John Henry Sayers presented himself at Pilgrim Street police station front counter to produce his documents to PC Thompson in relation to his producer that he received the night before. His documents were in order. PC Thompson spoke to PC Quinney. This conversation was recorded at 20:31pm.

There are then various calls between 8:33pm and 8:40pm between Dixon and Watson and Miller and Stewart with cellular data clearly showing both cars on the move. Miller and Stewarts' phone is tracked to the safe house in Deerbush. Dixon and Watson traced to Coast road then they disappear. Leach is still in the city centre at this time.

At 8:40pm Leach spoke to Hunter then Watson straight after whose phone registered in Walker. He was potentially at Dixons home in Blackwell Avenue. In the case the Prosecution suggested that they changed cars here from the Renault to the Calibra.

Leach called Watson at 8:52pm who was now on Shields road.

At 8:53pm Dixon called Stewart and Miller from his phone and was now in City Centre. This was the last time this phone was used.

9:14pm Dixon was observed on Bath Lane going towards Westgate Road by DS Mitsides.

9:20pm Leach is seen leaving The King Neptune and meeting Dixon who is now driving the Vauxhall Calibra. This suggests that Dixon dropped Watson at safe house before swapping cars. Surveillance officers say that Leach handed Dixon what is described as 'paperwork'. They suggested it was Leach paying Dixon for his work. This meeting was videoed by DC Winn. Dixon departed at 21:26pm Leach re-joined Janet Blayney in restaurant.

21:30pm Leach and Blayney then leave in a Sierra. They travel home via Barclays Bank, Four Lane Ends and the Wine Cellar arriving at East Forest Hall Road at 21:52pm. Leach is still under surveillance by DC Winn, DC Burton, DS Goss.

23:08pm – 23:23pm DC Perkins and DS Smith report seeing the Renault and Calibra parked outside Dixons home 81 Blackwell Avenue Walker.

At midnight the VW Golf had been dumped close to Deerbush in Earsdon Close. Just after midnight a local resident called Barry heard a bang and on looking out of his window saw flames. He called the fire brigade. The call was timed at 00:05am on 21st September. Kevin Marley was one of the officers who attended and found the VW Golf on fire, having been deliberately set alight. The fire was extinguished. A tin of thinners was found nearby. The police attended and recovered the vehicle and photographed it. No significant evidence was found in relation to the Golf.

On the 22nd September 10:44am Leach arrived at Dixons home in the Sierra. He left at 10:49am. This was witnessed by DC McCormack. At 11:04am

Dixon was seen by DC Scott leaving his house and climbing over his wall at rear of his home. He took the Renault to Quick Start Garage in Westfield Court in Walker and was seen by DC Weatherspoon and DC Scott. The garage owner Kevin was told by Dixon that the vehicle had been overheating. When questioned he explained he knew Dixon as 'Micky Muggins'. When the car was examined by a mechanic, he confirmed that there were issues with car. This had caused issues on night of the murder for Dixon and Watson.

Ian the manager of the Coach and Horses pub made a statement saying that he allowed the use of his hose pipe to two men who needed to fill the radiator of their Renault with water on the 20th. After dropping car off Dixon headed home as witnessed by DC Scott.

2 days later Dixon was seen by officers, PC Reade and Hindle driving the Sierra. He was stopped and asked to attend Byker Police station in respect of an outstanding fine default warrant. Dixon then called John Henry Sayers who attended and paid off the £120 necessary to discharge the warrant. PC Douglas made a statement about this.

On the 26th September the police turned up at Johns' home. John was not in but his wife at the time Yvonne was. The police explained that they wished to speak to John about the shooting of Freddie Knights but that they did not intend to arrest him.

The Renault was seized from the garage and was taken away for examination by police. DC Cayzer was in charge of this. Inside they find a diet coke bottle and papers. Fingerprint tests also found Dixons prints on the papers. There was also cellular material on the coke bottle which matched the DNA of Dixon.

The Renault was an enigma as it had not been reported missing. The registered keeper was another man who had part exchanged it on 2nd September at the Palmersville Motor company. The vehicle was not sold by the company and Susan the company sales manageress said that the keys were missing and must have been taken without authority or knowledge of the staff. Tony Leach had an influence at the company and was an associate of David Rankin who part owned the company. Alan of New City Cars confirmed in a statement that he had security provided for his company New City Cars by Palmersville Motor Company and that he had made payments to Janet Blayney Leaches partner. His accounts manager Julie confirmed the last cheque for payment for £1410 was made out to A. Leach.

At 6.35pm John arrived at Market Street Police Station with Richard Haswell. He refused to speak directly to the police. Haswell explained that he would speak for his client. John Henry Sayers was interviewed as a voluntary attender by DS Brown and DC Cooper in the presence of his solicitor Richard Haswell. In interview he declined to answer any questions but his solicitor spoke on his behalf. He would not outline his movements on 19th and 20th September but his solicitor said that he had an alibi for the time of the shooting involving police officers. He refused to say what that was.

The following day Tony Leach attended Clifford Street Police Station as a voluntary attender with Mr Hegarty his solicitor. He gave no comment to questions with regards to Knights murder. He was interviewed by DC Mather and DC Foggin. Towards the end of the interview he pointed to the tape machine indicating that it should be switched off. He said that he would walk up the street with the officer and give his views on the murder. Outside of the police station, in the presence of his solicitor, he told DC Foggin that Freddie Knights had a bad drug habit and indicated that Paddy Conroy hated John Sayers and would be behind it.

On the 13th October Dale Miller and Lee Watson were arrested for failing to stop at a red light in Gateshead after high speed chase in a Ford Orion. They abandoned the vehicle and were arrested by PC Dowson and PC Carr after being chased on foot. Watson dropped a 9oz package of heroin during the chase. Watson also threatened officers with a knife before being sprayed with CS gas. He was charged with possession with intent to supply. (He was imprisoned for 3 years at later date). Miller denied all knowledge of the heroin but was remanded in custody for trial. He was to eventually receive a term of 12 months imprisonment.

The next day PC 956 Wilson attends a report of a burglary at Novocastrian Club, Stanhope Street, Newcastle West. The stewardess is Yvonne Sayers, the mother of John Henry Sayers.

Without drugs Watson began to cold turkey and at Gateshead Magistrates he claimed that he shot Viv Graham and is part of a 'firm' so he was put under pressure by police with regards to the Knights case. Through mobile phone tracking they could place Watson near Ella Knights home on the night of murder so he decided to co-operate off the record and claimed the execution was ordered by John Henry Sayers and Tony Leach.

On the 24th November 2000 Ella Hall was alone at home watching Coronation Street at 7:30pm when she becomes aware of security light coming on. She hears three taps on window identical to those that she heard on the night Freddie was shot. She ran out of the house to her daughters Shirley. Her grandson Alan comes to sit with her to calm her nerves. Nobody else saw this take place. Were her nerves getting the better of her or was somebody who knew she was vulnerable putting the frighteners on her?

PRESS RELEASES + PRESS CUTTINGS.

NORTHUMBRIA POLICE
PRESS INFORMATION
Date: 21st September 2000   Time: 11:15

Subject: Murders
Headline **Longbenton murder release 1**

Details
At about 8.25 last night in the vicinity of Lutterworth Road and Langdale Close,
Longbenton, police attended a firearms incident in which a man in his late 30s
received injuries from which he subsequently died.

The man has not yet been formally identified and police are treating his death
as murder. A man in dark clothing, believed to have been responsible for the
shooting, was seen running out of the cul-de-sac at Langdale Close into the
estate. Police are currently awaiting the results of a post mortem examination
on the victim by a Home Office pathologist.

Det Supt Trevor Fordy, who is heading the investigation, has issued an appeal
for anyone who was in the area at around the time of the shooting, particularly
if they were near Langdale Close, to come forward. They want particularly to
contact anyone who saw a man loitering in the area before the shooting or
running away after the shooting. They can contact the incident room which has
been set up at Clifford Street police station on 0191-2146555. Because of the
present stage of the enquiry there will be no press conference or interviews
today.

Guidance

Update

Authorising Press Officer: Ian Kerr
Information From: DCI Alan Stewart, mobile 07771-980-299 or hash 6793.
Release Method: Voicebank

Above:
Northumbria Police press release about the murder of Freddie Knights

Overleaf:
Police photofit images of the two men wanted in connection with the murder
and a map of the scene

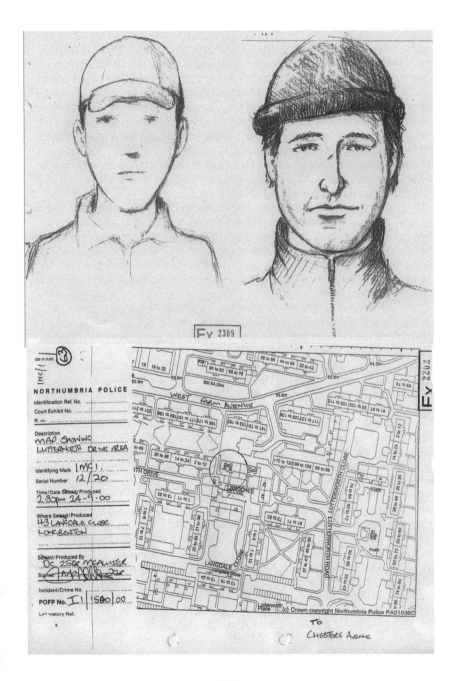

Chapter Thirty Seven: The Net Closes In

On 15th January 2001 Terrence Paul Mann was convicted in respect of the VW golf and John Paul Hunter suffered the same fate on 8th February after both confessed. Later that month on the 28th January 2001 heroin addict Stephen Carlton was arrested for a botched Post Office in Chopwell, Gateshead. After a few hours without his 'fix' he claimed he was in fear for his life and that he had evidence about Freddie Knights shooting. Carlton claimed that on the evening before the shooting Miller and Stewart were at his address at Deerbush with a shotgun and left before returning later on with the weapon. He claims they had a conversation about a Golf car which was parked outside of the flat. They also talked about the weapon (referred to as a 'piece') not having been used and something having gone wrong.

Within about half an hour of their arriving back he claimed John Henry Sayers arrived and gave them both a 'bollocking' in relation to something. He then left shortly afterwards. He also claimed that on 20th September the day of the murder that Miller, Stewart and Watson were at Deerbush smoking heroin which had been obtained from a hollowed-out tree on Black Callerton Lane by Carlton and Miller. This was the area from which the murder weapon would be subsequently recovered.

On the same day John Henry Sayers visited Watson in Durham jail unaware that Watson had turned supergrass. Watsons girlfriend Vania had told Watson that members of the Conroy family had put a gun to her head. Watson had supposedly wanted to speak to John about protecting her on the visit but he simply made small talk and looked nervous according to prison officers.

As the months passed by Watson began to see the error of his ways and asked John Henry Sayers to visit him again in HMP Acklington. This time it was a closed visit. Again, the meeting was rather awkward but it was assumed that he intended to inform John that he had set him up with the police. He did not do this possibly fearing a backlash from his handlers.

On the 29th and 30th March 2001 there was an appeal hearing for an application for taxi Operators license heard at Newcastle Crown Court. The application lodged on 16th May 2000 was rejected on 19th June due to John Henry's involvement. John Henry Sayers along with his Dad, John Brian Sayers and Alan Maughan attended Crown Court but their appeal was dismissed and Maughan was stripped of his private hire and hackney licenses. The Evening Chronicle were there to cover the case and gave it a front page lead the following day.

The next significant date is the 19th April 2001 when Vania Allen visited Lee Watson in Durham prison and there was an interesting conversation recorded between the pair:

LW "Has Dale Been on The Phone to John do you know?"

VA "I think so"

LW "When?"

LW "Come here I'm not going to hit you, you daft cunt. I want to tell you
something man, come here. Tell Dale he's going to have to go and get that
gun moved, because it's got my DNA all over the fucking towel right. Tell him I
want it moved this weekend , I want the fucking towel off, he put the fucking tool
down there, I telt him not to, I telt him to bring the fucking towel back up, he's
left it, I want it fucking moved."

The details are passed onto the police and the decision is made to
arrest Watson and others.

On the 7th May John Henry Sayers had received a call at 11pm to say
the police were coming to fit him up from a trusted friend. So, John packed a
bag and left his home. He stayed at a friend's house in Newcastle for 1 night
before heading to Birmingham.

On 8th May the police swooped to arrest Dale Miller of Cromwell
Avenue Gateshead and Edward Stewart 37 of no fixed abode. They were
charged in connection with the alleged plot to murder Freddie Knights. Two
days later a coordinated operation was mounted in an attempt to arrest the rest
of the accused. John Henry Sayers, Michael Dixon and Tony Leaches
addresses were raided but there was no sign of any of them and they evaded
arrest. Stephen Paul Kingston was arrested on suspicion of the murder. He
denied the charge but claimed to have been involved in committing criminal
damage and is bailed on the 11th May but then is immediately arrested on
suspicion of criminal damage and arson. On the 12th May he was charged with
conspiracy to commit arson following which he made admissions to a number
of criminal offences including arson, criminal damage, burglary and theft. He
claims that he did these at the behest of Anthony Leach with others in exchange
for cash or drugs. The majority of offences were committed for either the
purposes of protection or debt collecting. He provided evidence for 28 offences.
He also stated that he had carried out offences with Michael Dixon again for
Leach and that John and Leach instructed him and an associate William Harriot
to burgle a dwelling house. In total property in excess of £800,000 had either
been damaged or stolen on the instruction of Leach. He claimed another man
Terence O'Donnell had committed the arson attacks with him.

Kingston had originally been arrested for the offence of conspiracy to
murder but was sent a letter explaining no further action would be taken. He
then agreed to make a statement which allegedly throws light on how 'Knights'
made his money. He says:

"I was new, Freddie Knights and I used to buy cannabis off him. I knew him about a year before he died and I met him through Tony Leach. The first time I met him was in Tony's house in Forest Hall when William Harriot and I had been there. I had been buying cannabis off Freddie every couple of days between an ounce and a half a 9 bar at a time paying £40 for an ounce. I am aware that Freddie also supplied cocaine but not to me. I knew that Tony Leach was getting cocaine off Freddie and I saw him getting this on at least 3 occasions.

William Harriot was also there and used to buy E's of Freddie. Tony was getting 3 or 4 packets of cocaine from Freddie and he was paying £25 for the half gram. Terry O'Donnell or someone might also be there. I have had cocaine which came from Freddie off Tony as wages. Billy would buy 10 or 20 e's at a time from Freddie when they were going to the Ikon nightclub in Newcastle for himself. When I first heard that Freddie Knights had been murdered, I spoke to Billy about it. We both knew that Tony owed Freddie £1500 for drugs. A conversation took place in Freddie's house in Backworth between Tony and Freddie sometime before the shooting. I remember being in Freddie's garden. Also present was a woman called Helen, Freddie and Freddie's wife.

Freddie told me that Tony had pulled up outside his house in the Lexus shouting and balling. Freddie had taken Barry's motorised car as part payment for the money owed to Freddie by Tony for drugs. Tony was really angry at Freddie for taking the car, and I saw the car in Freddie's back garden. I know that Tony was a heavy cocaine user, he used to sniff it. I have seen him do this on numerous occasions in his own house and at my house. Before the murder Tony told me to stop getting my cannabis off Freddie, and I sort of agreed with Tony. However, I continued to get my cannabis off Freddie because it was on 'chuckie'. I would get my cannabis then pay for it when I got my dole cheque.

My initial thought was that the murder had something to do with Tony. Tony is a gangster and is certainly capable of doing this or getting someone else to do it. I have never known Tony to get his hands dirty."

On the 12th May Stewart was interviewed. He began by answering questions in the first six interviews and said that he was in Birmingham at his sisters on the day of the shooting, which he had heard about from the media. He acknowledged Watson as a friend and said that through him he had met John Sayers. He claimed not to know Leach or Dixon. He denied knowledge of any of the phone numbers or cars linked to the case. When officers told him that they were going to put matters to him that demonstrated that he had not been telling the truth he declined to change anything and exercised his right to silence. Stewart became concerned and agitated. He asked DCs Costello and Boon how long they thought he would get for the offence. The officer informed him 'life.' Stewart then asked how long a life sentence was. He was told 15 years or more.

Miller was interviewed on 14 occasions over the next three days by

DCs Swainston and Ball. He denied involvement in the murder throughout. He did however answer questions and accepted that he was a close friend of Watson and had known Stewart for a number of years. Confirmed he knew Stephen Carlton and had been to his flat in West Denton on a number of occasions. He said that he had met Leach on one occasion only when Leach was with John Sayers.

The 13th May 2001 saw Lee Watson arrested and taken from prison to North Shields Police station and interviewed between 5:04pm and 5:46pm and the most significant part of the interview can be seen here:

Officer: Right can you tell us what you want to say.

LW: I was contacted by John Henry Sayers and er I went to speak to him and he asked if I knew anybody who would shoot Freddie Knights in the leg.
Officer: Yeh

LW: And I spoke to Dale Miller and Eddie Stewart and they said they would do it.

Officer: Yeah

LW: So, there was a meeting arranged with John Sayers, Anthony Leach, Michael Dixon, and Dale Miller and Eddie Stewart.

Officer: Yeah.

LW: And on the 19th at a certain time that they would be picked up and taken to the Golf.

Officer: Yeah

LW: Under the seat of the Golf would be a shotgun.

Officer: Ok.

LW: And they would then be taken to where Freddie Knights Mam lives.

Officer: Ok.

LW: But it didn't happen.

Officer: Yeah.

LW: Anthony Leach phoned me the next day.

Officer: Okay.

LW: And said that he was busy.

Officer: Yeah.

LW: And could I take them up so they didn't get lost.

Officer: And what happened then?

LW: On the, on the night time I met Micky Dixon at Westerhope Club and I got in his car.

Officer: Yeah.

LW: And Dale and Eddie followed me in the Golf.

Officer: Yeh

LW: Erm, them drove into the estate.

Officer: Yeah

LW: At Longbenton.

Officer: Yeh.

LW: And as we drove away our car overheated and we went into the pub carpark.

Officer: Okay then what happened.

LW: We filled the car with water and everything like that.

Officer: Yeah.

LW And then we got a phone call saying it had been done.

Officer: Yeah.

LW: And erm, I, I went back to Carlton's house and Dale and Eddie came.

Officer: Yeah.

LW: And I told them to wipe the gun of fingerprints.

Officer: Yeah.

LW: And I went home to Sandy's thinking that he had just been shot in the leg.

Officer: Yeah.

LW: And on the morning it was on the news, like news, I cannot remember if somebody told us that he was dead.

Officer: You heard he was dead?

LW: Uh Hu.

Officer: And what's happened since then?

LW: I went back to see Dale.

Officer: Yeah.

LW: And asked him what the fuck had happened like they were only supposed to shoot him in the leg and he says when he had the meet with John, Leachy and Dixon if he couldn't get him in the leg, get him in the head.

Officer: Yeah.

LW: And I lost me temper with Dale saying that you were dragging is into something that I didn't have anything to do with.

Officer: Yeah.

LW: And erm me and Dale went to a place and Dale went down and buried the gun.

Officer: Ok where was that?

LW: Westerhope.

Watson was interviewed 13 times over 2 days by DC Carr and PS Hipgrave and subsequently took the police to a location in the Westerhope area, country lane near the Jingling Gate and he pointed out a location where he said they buried the gun. PC Mackey dug the location up and recovered the double barreled shotgun and then sent it to the Forensic Science Service. It was 10 inches under the soil behind a hedge in Black Callerton Lane past the Jingling Gate pub near St John's church. The wrappings surrounding the sawn-off shotgun (PM/1) were examined and fibres found there matched fibres from the carpet at Deerbush. Additionally, the lace wrapping the gun was wrapped in was similar to the lace in the left shoe found in Black Callerton Lane. A fibre sample from the left shoe was found to be indistinguishable from the lace tying the sawn-off wrapping.

Watson also stated that he had thrown away a pair of shoes worn by Stewart during the job. The shoes were recovered minus one lace by PC Bainbridge and PC Wild. A pair of shoes were later taken from Stewart at Court by consent (size 7 and a half.) They were found to be the same size as the shoes recovered and also to have similar inside feet impressions. Watson was then charged with conspiracy to murder.

Two un-named sources then came forward and claimed a meeting took place between John Henry Sayers, Peter Donnelly and Knights where Knights produced a firearm and threatened John. Intelligence suggested that on 11th September 2000, 9 days before Freddie was killed that there was an incident involving John and others in a vehicle and Peter Donnelly and Duncan Wilson in another vehicle in the Newcastle area. Two vehicles collided with each other, ramming each other and one party from one of the vehicles produced a handgun.

Another motive allegedly came from 20 different sources which related to the time John spent in prison prior to November 1999. Intelligence is, that at that time, Freddie Knights and Johns' wife Yvonne Hudson had an affair together and that Freddie was the father of young John Henry Sayers. This was later disproved by John Henry Sayers with a DNA test. John and Yvonne had actually managed to have sex whilst she visited him in prison and she had conceived and the story was broken in the local paper the 'Sunday Sun.'

On the 14th May Once charged Miller and Stewart appeared before North Shields magistrates. They were in the dock together and Miller was heard to say to Stewart:

"Ed, Watson pulled the trigger and you done the driving and that's the truth."

Stewart was seen to shake his head in response. Stewart was remanded in custody and detained in Durham Prison.

Dixon was arrested by DS Sharkey along with Craig Shepherd in a photo booth in the passport office in Glasgow on 13th May 2001 with a fake passport and newly dyed hair, and he was charged in connection with Knights' murder and with possession of a firearm with intent to use it. He had a false name, Ian McKay. In the glove compartment of the car were benefit books belonging to Ian Mark McKay.

In interview Shepherd refused to confirm his name or cooperate so was given a special warning under section 36 and 37 of the Criminal Justice and Public Order act from 1994. On arrest he claimed he did not know his passengers name, Micky Dixon, however his phone records showed a succession of calls between the pair between 10th and 11th May. He was then questioned about his relationship with Tony Leach.

On 29th May he attended Janet Blayneys house in West Moor to collect a green Isuzu Trooper. Blayney was Leaches common law wife. The police claimed he sold the car on behest of Leach to raise money for him. He was arrested on suspicion of assisting Leach. Finally, they quizzed him on his relationship with John Henry Sayers. He had attended court appearances where John was present and there had been signal communication between the pair. Police then referred to calls between John and Craig between 10th and 16th May including a text on 15th May 2001 saying to Craig Shepherd 'DAG to go to Slaty Lane 9pm tomorrow for clothes.' He was then arrested for assisting John as a person wanted for conspiracy to murder.

Dixon was interviewed by DS Brown and DS Clark on 8 occasions between 16th and 19th May making no reply throughout his interviews.

Prison Officer William Wheatley carried out a security search of Stewarts cell on 22nd May in Durham prison. A letter was seized in Durham Prison written by Eddie Stewart marked 'For The Attention Of The Police."
At the top it said:

Eddie Stewart new statement to the Police.
DOB 23/5/63
Lee Watson rang me to ask me to knock on someone doors as they were going to do him with bats, all I had to do was drive a car. I went to Stephen Carlton's the next day to see Lee Watson and Dale Miller. There's was talk of shooting him the leg with a 22 bullet gun, I says I did not want anything to do with it, Lee Watson said I know too much now and If I did not do it, I would get a bullet in my leg as well. That night we went to, with someone to a pub car park, a silver Golf was there, we got in it, the key were in on the floor and a sawn off shotgun. I said to Dale you're joking mate, I froze seeing the gun.

We drove to Longbenton my phone was ringing and ringing, I threw it on the floor when Dale was not looking and switched it off I told Dale I could not find the house, we went to the Three Magpies Pub and had a pint. Lee Watson and a man called Tony Leach, I told them I could not find the house and my phone was playing up, he was going mad, the man with Lee Watson I now know to be Leachy, they showed me the house and told me to get on with it. I knocked on the window and ran off, nothing happened that night. We went back to Carlton's, they gave me a new phone and put my chip in it and told me not to ring anyone on it or I would get a bullet in my leg and something worse and not forgetting where my family lived.

The next day I asked Stephen Carlton to use his phone to ring my sister when Dale and Lee Watson went out, but I was too frightened to tell her what was going on. That night a man came for us, I think to be Dixon, we followed to Longbenton again he showed us the house and parked the car three streets away and went and knocked on the window. Dale was hiding in the bushes. Dale had the phone at this time, I went back to the car and waited all the time thinking should I drive off, but frightened for me and my family.

I heard a bang, 10 seconds later bang, 20 seconds later Dale running back to the car. We drove off I froze and I went the wrong way to Whitley Bay. We got back to Stephen Carlton's, we changed our clothes and Lee Watson made us burn the car out that night. The next morning, the next day, they came for Dale, they took him away for two hours, he come back and said they wanted to kill me but Dale talked them out of it. I was to go to Birmingham and not say nothing to anyone, I would get it and receive no money whatsoever in all of this.

When in the police station I was talking to the police in my interviews, too scared to tell the truth, when we went for a police extension at court I was in the dock with Lee Watson, he said ;What you said', I said " I was talking to them , but said nothing.' He said 'When you go back to the police station make no reply , or I would get it.' I said nothing, nothing the police said has Lee told to make no reply, I said nothing as I feared for my life and my family. Now I just want to tell the police everything and hope they can help me and my family safety.'

EDWARD STEWART

PS Even Stephen Carlton heard Dale telling me they were going to kill me but has said nothing to police. I even asked him what I should do, he said nothing.

As a result of this letter being seized Stewart was interviewed again on 24th May by DCs Costello and Boon. He refused to answer questions but provided a prepared statement:

"I've taken legal advice off me solicitor and I'm very frightened and fear for the safety of my family. My solicitor has shown me a two-page copy document which he was given earlier today. I do not want to discuss the document, or who wrote it I have received legal advice, whether or not there is any truth in what is in the document, I am worried that if the contents is known to other persons my life and the lives of my family will be at risk. I ask, I ask for as much protection for me and my family as possible. I do not wish; I now wish to remain silent."

On June 2nd John Henry Sayers was arrested by Sgt Kalli and members of an armed response team in Essex after a car chase near the Gants Hill roundabout on the A12 following an undercover operation. John was a front seat passenger. Two other men were arrested with him and charged with assisting an offender. John was in possession of £3067 in cash. At the end of his arrest he said "I am innocent of this crime." He was interviewed by DC Mather and DC Davison on 13 occasions and made no reply throughout.

Wednesday June 6th 2001 saw John Henry Sayers, Dixon, Watson, Millar and Stewart appear at North Tyneside Magistrates charged with plotting the murder of Freddie Knights. Johns charge sheet read as follows:

On or before Wednesday 20th September 2000 at Longbenton North Tyneside or elsewhere conspired together with Lee Shaun Watson, Michael Dixon, Dale Miller, Edward Stewart and others to murder Frederick John Knights contrary to section 1(1) of the criminal law act 1977.

The security at court was very tight with armed Police transporting John Henry the short distance from North Shields Police station to the Magistrates Court. The 'Evening Chronicle' reported, *"Looking relaxed Sayers dressed in a blue shell suit, grinned at his friends and family in the public gallery and his Mum whispered to him, "How are you doing son?" He shrugged and replied "Good."*

The judge remanded them for a week giving the police more time to question them before their next appearance at Newcastle Crown Court. John Henrys Sayers Defence statement was as follows:

"I John Henry Sayers have been charged with conspiracy to murder with Lee Watson, Edward Stewart, Dale Miller and Michael Dixon – I wish to state that I have never conspired with anyone to kill Frederick Knights. I was not involved in the death of Frederick Knights. I also wish to state that I am innocent of this and intend to prove this at trial."

An interesting statement was taken by the police on 18th July 2001. The statement was by Grace, Freddie's widow.

'We originally lived at Hardwick Road in Scotswood where we had lived for approximately twelve years. Another family living in the same area at the time were the Conroy's. Approximately four or five years ago I became aware that Freddie was having some sort of trouble in particular with Mickey Conroy. I'm not entirely sure what the trouble was or how the trouble started but it really only seemed to involve Mickey. The rest of the Conroy family appeared fine and carried on talking to us on a regular basis. Things gradually appeared to get worse and various incidents occurred at our house. We had windows

broken on two occasions with paint thrown through. Freddie's car was also damaged on numerous occasions so much so he had to park it well away from home. I recall an occasion when Mickey actually chased us whilst we were in Freddie's van. He chased us for a while but Freddie managed to avoid Mickey and escape. The trouble seemed to get worse with other incidents of damage.

This lasted for a period of about two years before I had really had too much.' Grace approached the council for house move which was granted and the trouble stopped. She continued:

'My opinion on the whole thing is that Mickey Conroy was trying to get Freddie to work for him but Freddie wouldn't. Freddie wouldn't work for anyone and because of this Mickey wouldn't leave us alone and things got well out of hand.'

On the 7th August Terence O'Donnell called at the home of a prosecution witness 'Helen' to whom he made a series of threats designed to persuade her and Kingston not to give evidence at any court proceedings. He was subsequently arrested and charged with witness intimidation.

Tony Leach was arrested on the 6th September by PS Warner in a holiday home Fell House, Howgill Lane, Sedburgh,Cumbria and charged. A Mondeo was recovered too, it was a hire vehicle, which was hired by a Mr Akram for his wife and it was swapped at the Metrocentre by Doctor Raj. Doctor Raj handed over the keys for his Jaguar. This vehicle was used by Doctor Raj and Tony Leaches sister Jackie. In the vehicle were bundles of papers and depositions for the case which Tony will have looked at, giving him valuable knowledge to concoct some sort of defence. The papers had been served on other co-accused but not Leach. He was interviewed on the 7th September 2001 North Shields Police Station by interviewing Officers DC2685 Petty DC3470 Richardson and was represented by his Solicitor Brian Hegarty. They quizzed him on his whereabouts on 19th and 20th September 2000. They also acknowledged that he attended Clifford Street as a voluntary attender on 27th September 2000 and spoke off record to DC Foggin and DC 3776 Mather and implicated Patrick Conroy as one of the people responsible for killing Freddie Knights.

He is quizzed about a dispute with Freddie Knights over £1500 which he owed to Ella Hall. Money which she had loaned him. They also mention the dispute over the car and asked him if he wanted to take over drug dealing in Longbenton that Knights was in control of. They finished off by asking him if he was in fear of anybody at that moment in relation to giving information about the murder of Freddie Knights. It was clear that the police despite evidence to the contrary were only interested in nailing one man by any means necessary and that was John Henry Sayers.

Chapter Thirty Eight: On Trial

On the 30th November 2001 at the Combined Court Centre, Lowgate in Hull before the honourable Mr Justice Henriques the prosecution and defence met across the courtroom to decide where the trial would be held. Mr Duff represented the prosecution, whilst Messrs, Dunn, Robson, Finch, Hedworth/ Adams, Goldberg and Adams represented Watson, Stewart, Miller, Dixon, Sayers and Leach respectively. The judge's ruling was as follows:

"This is an application by the crown to move the trial venue in the present case. The reason for the application is that there has been so much local publicity involving in particular the defendant John Henry Sayers that there will be difficulties for Mr. Sayers in receiving a fair trial.
Even if the trial commences with no attempt by anyone to interfere with the integrity of the trial, it is plain from everything that I have seen and read that Mr. Sayers is extremely well known in that locality. Even though he is prepared to stand his trial in Newcastle, nevertheless the obligation is upon me to ensure that there is a fair trial. I have seen and read sufficient to conclude that if this trial remained in Newcastle, there would have to be jury protection. That being so, Mr Goldberg, on behalf of Sayers, agrees that the case must move and the only matter that has exercised us in effect today is as to the most convenient location. Having considered all alternatives and having regard in particular to the very large number of defence witnesses – I am told in one of the skeleton arguments possibly up to seventy – to move the case as far away as London from Newcastle, or indeed across the Pennines, would be to impose consider-able hardship upon all those responsible for the defence of each of these defendants. Leeds accordingly, commends itself to me on grounds of convenience. It is approximately one hour fifteen minutes by rail with a direct rail service. Accordingly, that will be the trial venue and the trial judge will be Mr. Justice Douglas Brown."

The jury was sworn in on the 11th June 2002 at Leeds Crown Court and between 12th to 25th June various witnesses were sworn and recalled. On 26th June 2002 Mr. Batty opened his case on behalf of Prosecution. John was represented by Johnathan Goldberg QC. During the trial John took the stand and was cross examined. In the following pages I have condensed his defence and looked at his answers in court in depth.

Firstly, he denied any involvement in the shooting of Freddie Knights. His evidence was a total denial of the matters alleged against him. His theory was that Watson had shot him and that he was working for the Conroys. John had met Freddie in 1980 and had no problems with him. He had no reason to kill Freddie Knights. He was targeted and framed by the police who had elaborated evidence and invented it. He knew even before his release from his 15-year sentence in November, 1999 that the Northumbria Police and other informant associates of theirs were out to get him, the fabrication of evidence in this case proved his point with Pallas claiming he saw him in the Peter Barratts layby.

He said that he had met Watson in Frankland Prison in 1998. Watson, that is "S. Watson", was one of the names given to him by his Dad, mentioned anonymously in the letter to the Chief Constable, so he was suspicious of Watson. On his release he told Watson how to go about opening up a sandwich bar, which in the end he did not open. He said he would not have Watson working for him, and Watson was lying when he said there was anything called the firm and that Watson had not done anything for him or his brothers, Stephen and Michael. He was an enforcer for the Conroys; if there was something, they could not do they would ask him to do it. He said that it was quite untrue that he gave Watson £2000 when he came out of prison. The reverse was true, Watson gave his mother £1000 which had come indirectly from Steven and Michael Sayers, his brothers. The monies paid to Watson in prison were in part to pay him back for that money.

He confirmed that he had known Leach for some time. On his release from prison he worked for Leach in is debt collecting business. He did not have to use force as his very name was enough to get the debts paid, and it was a lucrative business. Leach, he said, was a womaniser, and his long-term partner, Janet, who was a calming influence on Leach, sometimes asked him to help her and advise her. In fact, two of the calls on Leach's phone on the evening of the murder were from Janet ringing him during their reconciliation attempt at the King Neptune restaurant.

Dixon, he said he knew as Micky Muggins, and met him, he thought, in August, 2000. Dixon was mechanically minded, or so he believed, and had a scrap yard, and he advised him on car purchases. Dixon had been a taxi driver and knew some of his drivers.

Stewart, he had met with Watson in a bar after Watson's release, and Watson introduced Stewart to him, and he knew that Stewart smuggled cigarettes and counterfeit clothes mainly from Thailand, but that was the only time he had seen him before he saw him in court.

Miller, he had never spoken to but for one time on the phone, he had never met Miller, and the phone conversation involved a request by Miller for permission to use Sayer's name to warn off Vania's drug supplier. He had no other dealings with Miller.

Stephen Carlton, he had never seen until he saw him in court, and his evidence was fiction. He had never been to Deerbush.

Dealing with the prosecution case, he said it was absurd for the Prosecution to suggest that he would use his own car, the Land Rover, for anything to do with a murder or that he would speak on the phone in relation to anything criminal. He confirmed that he was paranoid about the police, and he knew they had him under surveillance, and at one stage he found a bug in his car.

He insisted that he was not involved in unlawful activity but that he was debt collecting and was running Newcastle taxis which was as successful a business as Newcastle council would let it be.

Dealing with the disputed parts of the case, he was not at the Peter Barratts layby at 2.00 o'clock on the 19th as Pallas had claimed. He explained that he had a friend Peter May, who was a fruit and vegetable dealer, who had a friend or business colleague who was separated from his wife and child, and was having difficulty having access to the child, and that he (John Henry) was asked by May to use his influence to persuade the man who was stopping the access taking place to see the matter differently, and that was why he was in May's company in May's car in the region of Peter Barratt's layby, but not on it, but passing by on the main road at the roundabout at the top of the layby. They were on their way to Seaton Delaval to discuss how to persuade this man to see the error of his ways, and they were in May's 'V 'registered BMW. So, Pallas was right when he said he saw them in a 'V' registered BMW around that time in that region, but had embroidered the story to put him in the layby with Miller and Stewart.

May confirmed this version of events when he took the stand. He remembered a day in September before learning of the death of Mr. Knights. Sayers came to his business in Newcastle, and they went together in his 'V' registered BMW. They went in that car because it was cheaper to use diesel, and he also wanted to show the car off. They went up the A1, along Sandy Lane onto the Western bypass, and then to Seaton Delaval where the Laidlers' business was. They were there for an hour or two, they had a coffee and a chat, and it was agreed that they would get the matter sorted out. As far as he knew no-one had ever spoken to the young man about access. They then drove back the same way, and they would have passed the roundabout at the top of the layby, but never went in the layby, they never drove into the layby and waited there joining another car, it just never happened. He then took John Henry Sayers back to his business premises where Sayers picked up his jeep. This was the only time he had ever given Sayers a lift in his BMW.

The same applied to the Three Magpies incident, where his vehicle was supposed to be alongside the maroon Renault. He was at that time at the layby dropping off Leach, who wanted to go after women, but there was no other vehicle there, and this was an example of the police using a true factual situation to put an invention around it, and the surveillance evidence was false, and the surveillance records had been doctored to support a lying story.

John Henry agreed with the surveillance evidence as to his movements and to his arriving home at 9:40pm. If Mrs. Ella Knight's window was banged on at 10pm, and that is when the murder is supposed to have taken place, then he had no alibi for that which would satisfy the Northumbria police, because he was at home with his partner and children, and indeed in reality he said he had no real alibi for either evening. For the 20th the production of his documents at 8:30pm at Pilgrim Street police station was no kind of alibi at all, and if the shooting was at 8:23pm or 8:24pm he could, without difficulty, have got to Pilgrim Street at or just after 8:30pm. The journey from the taxi office to Pilgrim Street could take at least 10 minutes.

On specific calls from his number he reiterated that he had never spoken to Stewart despite him having John Henry's number saved in his phone. He suggested that he must have been talking to Leach as people would phone him to speak to Leach. He also suggested that his only communication with Stewart would have been about snide Newcastle United shirts or cigarettes. He claimed that he could not remember speaking to Watson on the day of the shooting. He did not accept that they were genuine calls. He claimed that Watson phoned him the day before or after but that there was no record of those calls. It stank he said. He claimed that he did not believe that all of the phone records were genuine, although some were. He said he knew what they were trying to do.

With regards to the 20th September he said that was a normal Wednesday and he agreed that Leach and Dixon were leaving his house about 6pm. He said there was nothing wrong with that but he could not remember why they were there. He confirmed he was at the Peter Barratt's layby at 8pm with Leach in his Land rover, but no other car came near him, and they were there because Leach wanted to meet a woman who had promised to see him there. They waited about five minutes and then left for the restaurant. There was no question of him planning an alibi by producing his documents at the police station that night. He claimed that if he had wanted to produce an alibi that he would have gone into the directors' box at St James' Park that night.
In court he said, "I won't talk to the police. When I attended voluntarily, I agreed that my solicitor should speak for me and I would say nothing. I don't trust the Northumbria police, and therefore did not give them my alibi."

He confirmed that he did pay Dixon's fine for the motoring offence but that Dixon paid him back. This was not a payment from John for services rendered.

With regards to visits to Watson in prison, the first one was in January with Vania Allen and a girl Leanne who was somebody that Vania wanted him to 'get off' with. The next visit was in March when he went with his cousin Joe on a social visit.
In May he got a phone call that the police were going to come and get him, so he went on the run and went to the Midlands and the south and stayed with friends. He did not confirm where.

When cross examined by Mr. Taylor, he said Leach was in an emotional state over the relationship with his long-term girlfriend breaking up, and he was up and down, in a very bad way emotionally, and he was also abusing cocaine. Cross examined by Mr. Batty, he said there was no gang, there was no firm, and when Mr. Goldberg referred to him being a Godfather, it was not as in the film, a gang leader presiding over various criminal activities. He said he was not going to answer any questions on whether his family was a criminal organisation, he was not bound to answer any questions. He had made money through debt collecting and through the taxi firm. He did collect debts partly through fear, he traded on his reputation. Asked what that reputation was, he said, well, it was for doing whatever they thought it was. He was also asked who was part of the plan to fit him up, and he said the investigating officers, the surveillance officers, Pallas, Stokes and Clark were fitting him up.

Asked about Hunter and the Volkswagen Golf, he denied being in-volved with the theft of the Golf. He knew Hunter vaguely. Hunter used to use the taxi office, and they were on "Hello John" terms. He could not explain calls linked between them. He said he would not use a heroin addict to steal a car, and when asked about 60 or so calls between him and Dixon he said that he had no idea. He had only met him in July or August 2000.

Leach had two misfortunes whilst giving evidence. First of all, the case was adjourned for three days meaning his evidence was fragmented and secondly for a good deal of time he was suffering from a sore neck and had been taking painkillers. His version of events was as follows. His partner of 16 years was Janet Blayney and they had one son. The relationship hit the rocks at the turn of the Millenium and by May 2001 it was over. He had never been to prison although he had minor convictions for dishonesty and violence up to the age of 23. With regards to his co-accused he said that he did not know Miller until the case began and Stewart whom he described as a 'little scruff' he met through Watson not long after Watson was released from prison. Watson, he said gave him Stewart's number as he was a gofer for Watson and was driving Watson's drug supplies around for him.

He confirmed that he had a cocaine addiction which got worse after his matrimonial troubles began and Watson was one of his suppliers. He confirmed that he phoned Stewart frequently to order cocaine. He said in court that he had known John Henry Sayers all of his life and that they were very close friends, like brothers. He earned his living dealing in cars and providing security for garage businesses, and debt collection. He said he was not involved in the supply of drugs nor was he in any Sayers firm because there was no firm. He said that he and Sayers after his release from prison in November 1999 worked together in the debt collecting business. He had a number of contacts, the most important being the Co-operative Milk Department, and the arrangement they had was that if debts up to one year old were recovered he received 25 per cent of the recovery, and if they were over a year old 50 per cent.

He said he had known Dixon for years through the car trade, and that he would take the lower range second hand cars off him and sell them. Dixon was not himself mechanical, but he would take cars to garages to have them fixed. Watson, he met in May or June after he had come out of prison. Sayers introduced them. He had heard of his reputation before he met him. He sold

Watson a car, a blue Renault 19, for £1,400, £800 down and the balance was paid in cocaine. The car needed repairs, and he asked Dixon to help with this. He said he was not involved in Freddie Knights murder or in any conspiracy to murder or injure. He had known him for 10 years and he was a lovely person and they were good friends. They had frequent little arguments but they saw each other regularly until a fallout about six months before he was shot, and the row was something over a quad bike and a small child's car, that he felt his son, Bradley, had been badly treated, and he had very little to do with Freddie Knights after that. There was no bad feeling between him and Ella, he thought she was a lovely woman. He did not accuse her of lying at any time but did say she was mistaken when she mentioned money she owed him. He said that Freddie Knights was a small-time drug dealer who did not earn more than £100 a week. Nothing like the amounts that Watson had suggested in his statements. The Conroys, he said, were bullies, a criminal family in Newcastle, and he always kept away from them. Freddie Knights was petrified of Michael Conroy, and this fear continued long after Freddie Knights had moved to Backworth.

In answer to the prosecution's case he said he had no knowledge or connection with a maroon Renault, and that Palmersville Motors were nothing to do with him. He said it was run by David Rankin, who was his partner at one time in the security business, and they did share offices and he did use the Palmersville invoices for security invoices at one time.

He said he was not involved in stealing the Golf in South Shields, and he could not remember if he was in South Shields on the afternoon of the 19th, although he did go there occasionally to take Billy Harriot home.

On the 'Three Magpies' and Peter Barratt's layby incident, he said he was pulling the wool over Sayers eyes over the reason for him going into the pub. He did do not want Sayers to know that he was trying to buy cocaine. He saw a dealer in the pub who had no cocaine on him, but he said his girlfriend could get some, and he arranged to meet her at the entrance to Gosforth Park, by which he meant Peter Barratt's layby, and he told Sayers he wanted to go there to meet a married woman, he did not tell him the real reason, and on the way back to King Neptune restaurant, after she did not turn up, he stopped off at his house to pick up a small amount of cocaine, which he took before rejoining Sayers.

At the King Neptune he could not remember making the calls he was alleged to have made. He confirmed that Dixon did turn up as recorded on the surveillance video, and he handed over the logbook for the Vauxhall Calibra, which Dixon was trying to sell on his behalf. He then went to a cash machine to get money for cocaine, and then went home.

On the 20th he was with Janet Blayney at the King Neptune trying to patch up their relationship. And he denied any complicity in the attack upon Freddie Knights. He described going on the run. He said he arrived home and he saw a mass of police officers armed and he was frightened so decided to go on his toes. "What would anyone else have done in my position." He had been made aware that the police were trying to arrest him, and he ended up in Sedburgh, where he was joined by his sister, Jackie, who tried to get him to hand himself in, and the case papers in the car had been used by her to try and talk him into coming home.

Under cross examination by Mr. Batty he said he could not confirm or deny whether he had used any of the phones the prosecution associated with him. He said he used many phones and would buy 100 SIM cards at £1 each, sell some of them, and as long as there was any credit left on rest, he would use them and then throw them away when they were finished. When asked about further calls from his mobile to a succession of numbers he said, "I can't follow it, I'm not bright enough for it."

He explained that he had no connection with Hunter and that he was a shoplifter, a drug addict and was horrible. He could not explain why he would have phoned Hunter and he had certainly not stolen a car for him.

Lastly with regards to the 19th he said that Sayers dropped him off at the Three Magpies because he did not want to go home before 10pm, when Janet Blayney would have gone to bed and there would be no confrontation, so he was happy to walk, even though it was raining. On the 19th September he could not remember how he spent the day. He was in and out of bed. He could have been in South Shields but could not recall.

Micky Dixon's Evidence was as follows:

In Micky Dixon's evidence he admitted that he had many different jobs, including selling second hand cars. He had two car breaking businesses, and he bought and sold cars up to £5,000 in value. He had been a licensed taxi driver, a registered doorman, and he was known as Micky Muggins because as a boy he stole some chickens from a van and missed cash lying on the front seat. He had a minor criminal record for dishonesty, had never been to prison, and had no convictions for violence.

He said that he had not met Miller or Stewart until he went to court but he had known Leach for a number of years through the car trade and he bought the odd car from him at the cheaper end of the market and Leach also laid some cars on for him to sell. He had met John Henry Sayers through Leach and he had looked at a few cars for his taxi business. He confirmed that he had met Freddie Knights twice and had sold him a Ford Granada. He had not had any trouble with Knights and held no grudge or grievance against him. He had been to his house once when had dropped the Granada off. He had met Watson three times. Leach had sold him a blue Renault 19 and asked him to have the exhaust fixed for him, which he arranged. He thought Watson was boastful and a braggart but had no trouble with him either.

His recollection of the 19th and 20th September were sketchy. He had little independent recollection and had to be assisted by reading the case papers to work out where he was and what he was doing. On the 19th there was nothing in the case papers that helped him. He was certainly not involved in the theft of the Golf and nor had he been on the Longbenton estate.

On 20th September he confirmed he had this car from Leach, a Calibra, on sale or return. He accepted from the surveillance that he was with Leach on the 20th, and also Sayers, but he could not recall anything of his purpose in meeting or speaking with Sayers. He remembered driving Leach in the Calibra to a petrol station, where Leach bought petrol. He then drove him to Daisy Hill, and then to Wallsend, and then dropped him off at a Chinese takeaway near his home and then he went off to try and hawk the Calibra around dealers. Leach had said he was going to meet Janet in a restaurant in town. Dixon said that he needed the documents for the Calibra, and Leach said, "Well, if you're in town I'll give them to you."
He then said that he had a job to do for a neighbour, Joseph Allen, in the Walker area where he lived. He had taken off a central heating radiator for Allen some weeks before because he wanted to decorate, and on that evening, he went round to refit the radiator. He was there till 8pm. He then tried to sell the Calibra to Mr. Allen who he said was half interested.

After he left there, he picked up his friend Gavin Dunn, and as it was Wednesday their regular habit was to go to the Cornerhouse pub for a drink. He got there at approximately 8:10pm. They stayed for about half an hour before heading home to get changed to go clubbing which they always did on a Wednesday. When he arrived home Watson was there, parked in a burgundy Renault opposite his house, and Watson asked him if he could take a look at it for him. He told Watson he was going out but would get someone to look at it the next day. Watson then asked him if he could drop him off at McDonalds on Westerhope Road. He agreed as he was heading into town anyway and had to pick up the logbook from Leach. After dropping Watson off and meeting Leach he decided not to go clubbing and instead returned home and parked the Calibra there, with the burgundy Renault opposite his front door. He did not go out again. Sometime over the next two days he took Watson's car to the Quickstart garage which was a mile and half away from his house. He said that there were some papers in the footwell, which he moved, so that is why his fingerprints were on them. He had also drank out of a Diet Coke bottle, and that would explain his DNA being on the mouth of the bottle.

On the 24th September he was arrested for non-payment of a fine. He tried to contact Leach at his holiday caravan, without success, and the police said, "Try and find John Henry Sayers", and he said "I did, and he came down and paid the fine, and I paid him back straight away. In the next few months", he said "I was occasionally in the company of Leach and Sayers. On the evening of the 9th of May I had no tip off about being arrested. I went to babysit at Leach's house for about half an hour, and I then went for a drink with Craig Shepherd and stayed out till 4:30am. He came back in a taxi but was not dropped off at his front door as he did not want to wake the baby. As he arrived at his house, he saw some men with guns and panicked. He watched from behind a hedge for a bit and then rang Angela his girlfriend and she told him to hand himself in. A policeman had told her that someone was likely to kill him. He then called John Henry Sayers. He said that they had tried to arrest him and he said if they were going to fit him up they would try to fit up those around him, so he decided to go on the run. He didn't know where he was going or what he was going to do. He was in a state of shock.

Asked by Mr. Batty about this, he said he was still in a state of shock a few days later in Glasgow when he applied for the passport in a false name. He accepted he did that, and that he had dyed his hair, but he did not know what he was going to do. Maybe he was going to go abroad. He agreed that Craig Shepherd was with him in Glasgow, and he agreed that he had lied to the passport officer about his father being seriously ill in Holland, and having a sister in Glasgow whom he wanted to break the news about his father to. He denied having anything to do with the shooting of Freddie Knights.

Cross-examined by Mr. Batty, he denied that he had bought a bottle of drink and drank it in the car with Watson on the 20th. He had drunk from a customer's bottle before when he was driving a car. The image of the man at the Tyne Tunnel video bore no resemblance to him and he did not go to Leach's house when he dropped him off to get the Calibra document, or wait outside while Leach fetched them, because Janet Blayney might have come out and she was a very aggressive person.

Under further cross examination he said he was trying to leave the country; he thought his life was in danger. Asked about the journey to Quickstart, and shown the short distance on the map, he agreed it was a short journey. Asked about the diet coke and his DNA, he said, "I imagine I had a drink; I must have been thirsty." It ended up in the footwell because that was where I had probably hoyed it, or thrown it into the back of the car. He denied being in the vehicle for a considerable period of time. He was not Leach's gofer, even though he had driven him round to various places on the evening of 20th with Leach.

Over the course of the 4th and 5th September 2002 at Leeds Crown Court the Judge summed up the case and he finished at 11:30am on 5th and the jury bailiffs were sworn in and the jury retired.

"Well now, members of the jury, that is all I remind you of, and I am going to shortly ask you to retire to consider your verdicts. Before I do there are two final things I must say to you. The first is fairly obvious, and you may have already put this into place, but you have to have a foreman or forewoman to take the chair at your discussions and give your verdicts when you return, so if you have not already done so would you choose one of your number to act as foreman or forewoman. The second thing is this, that you may have heard of majority verdicts. Majority verdicts can only be accepted by the court after a very long

time. That is all I say to you, members of the jury. I am going to ask you to retire. You will obviously take with you your three files, and any other exhibits that you want will be sent in to you. I mentioned the seven different videos on different topics. You will have a video player and those videos will be sent in to you now. So members of the jury, after the jury bailiffs have been sworn will you please retire and consider your verdicts. You will be under no pressure at the end of today, as you have already been told, there was no question of going to a hotel. You will go home and come back fresh tomorrow if you have not reached verdicts today, and so on, until you do, but you must not be under any kind of pressure at all. Take what time you need."

The Jury was sent out and at 4:05pm the Jury returned and was sent home. On the 6th September 2002 the Jury was brought in at 10:04am and retired for deliberation at 10:05am. The Judge was then presented with a note from jury. The questions were as follows:

1. At any time during Watson's custody did Vania Allen have closed visits without recording?
2. Did Frank Maughan know Lee Watson?
3. If we the jury deem one of the defendants only to have stolen or been involved in the stealing of the VW only can he be convicted of conspiracy to cause grievous bodily harm with intent

At 12:30pm the Jury returned. Justice Brown gave the following answers to the jury's questions:

1. The evidence is that there were a number of visits paid by Vania Allen to Watson. One of them was recorded that you have heard of, but there is no evidence as to whether any of the others were recorded or not, there is simply no evidence.
2. There is no evidence that he knew him one way or the other, the evidence is silent on that.
3. The answer to that is no, he cannot.

12:33pm Jury retired
4:00pm Jury returned and sent home for weekend.
9th September 2002 10:00am Jury returned
10:10am Jury retired
3:07pm Jury returned.

The judge asked the foreman if they had reached verdicts on each of the defendants but they had not. They had reached decisions on some however. They found Dale Miller and Edward Stewart not guilty of murder

but guilty of manslaughter. They also found Micky Dixon not guilty of murder or manslaughter but guilty of conspiracy to cause grievous bodily harm with intent. They had failed to find a verdict on John Sayers or on Anthony Leach.
Justice Brown then said:

"Well now, members of the jury, the time has come in my judgement, when I can give you direction as to majority verdicts. That does not mean that you must now proceed to consider the matter on the basis of majority verdicts. Your duty remains that of trying to find unanimous verdicts that remain, but the time has now been reached when I can accept a majority verdict from you, that is a verdict on which at least ten of you are agreed. Now with that in mind would you please retire again and continue with your deliberations."

The fact that Miller, Stewart, and Dixon were all found not guilty of murder was a significant moment for John Henry. The direction that the Judge had given the jury was that if they found the principal offender not guilty of murder then they would have to find the other defendants not guilty of murder.
Mr Justice Brown then said:

"Members of the jury, I am sorry to have brought you down again, but there is a matter upon which I think I might be able to help you by reminding you of the legal directions which I gave you. I know they are in your room; you have not got them in front of you., but can I just remind you of paragraph 14, and when you get back to your room you can look at it again. If you find the principal offender not guilty of murder or manslaughter, with the exception of Stewart, you must find the other defendants not guilty of murder or manslaughter. In this case you have found the defendant Miller not guilty of murder. Consistent with my direction to you, therefore, you must find Leach and Sayers not guilty of murder, do you follow that? "
The jury were then sent home till the following day.
On the 10th September 2002 There were discussions in chambers before the jury returned to court at 1:00pm. The reason for the delay was spelled out by Judge Brown:

"Well members of the jury, I am sorry that we have been so long reassembling, but as you can imagine from the topic we had to discuss there had been some helpful discussion with counsel, and my decision is that the trial will continue with all 12 of you. Now, I must give you this direction. You know that one of your number received a serious and unpleasant phone call last night, which has been discussed individually with me in my room, and each one of you has assured me that it will not affect your decision making in this case, and that you are still capable of approaching the matter fairly. I must say this to you, that this telephone conversation came from an unknown source, and you must not

speculate as to where it came from or who made it, or whose interest was being promoted by the making of it. All counsel in the case, Prosecution and Defence, condemn it roundly, and you must not draw any inference at all from any of the circumstances that you know about this phone call, and I am sure that is what you will do, put it from your mind. You promised me you will do that, and I am sure that is what you will do."

1:05pm Jury Retired.Mr Batty suggested that the Judge would direct a full police investigation by West Yorkshire Police into the events surrounding the juror. 4:27pm The Jury returned. It was now 15 hours and 25 minutes since they first retired to consider their verdicts.

The Clerk: Will the foreman please stand. Madam Foreman, will you please answer my question either yes or no. Have at least 10 of you agreed on your verdict in relation to each of the defendants.

The Foreman: On one.

The Clerk: Have at least 10 of you agreed upon your verdict in relation to either of the two defendants? Have at least 10 of you agreed upon your verdict in relation to the defendant John Henry Sayers?

The Foreman: Yes.

The Clerk: On count 1, murder, do you find the defendant John Henry Sayers guilty or not guilty?

The Foreman: Not guilty.

The Clerk: You find the defendant not guilty?

The Foreman: Yes.

The Clerk: On the alternative count of manslaughter do you find the defendant John Henry Sayers guilty or not guilty?

The Foreman: Not guilty.

The Clerk: You find the defendant not guilty?

The Foreman: Yes.

The Clerk: On the alternative count of conspiracy to cause grievous bodily harm with intent, do you find the defendant John Henry Sayers guilty or not guilty?

The Foreman: Not guilty.

The Clerk: You find the defendant not guilty?

The Foreman: Yes.

The Clerk: Have at least 10 of you agreed upon your verdict in relation to the defendant Anthony Leach?

The Foreman: No.

Mr Justice Brown: Mr Goldberg.

Mr Goldberg: My Lord may he be discharged?

Mr Justice Brown: Yes.

The Jury were sent home for the day.
      On September 11th 2002 10:07am the Jury returned to court; bailiffs were sworn in then the jury retired at 10:08am.

11:04am Leach was found not guilty on all counts.
Sentencing took place on September 11th:

Mr Justice Brown: *Stand up will you.*
      Dale Miller, I will sentence you first. Despite what your learned council says, it is clear to me on all the evidence that this shooting was a gangland criminal activity. I have little doubt that you were paid by someone to ambush and shoot a defenceless man with a sawn-off shotgun. It was a callous and cruel attack, planned to be carried out on the doorstep of the victim's mother. The gun was loaded with large calibre shot. Whether you knew that or not is immaterial. At close range your victim stood no chance. You shot at him twice. The first shot missed, and with the second you shot him in the head. It may well be that you had no intention to shoot him in the head but merely to shoot him and cause him some injury. There is no basis, in my judgement, even by the jury's verdict, to say that this was just a shooting to frighten. The jury have taken the merciful view that you did not intend to kill or cause grievous bodily harm.
      Nevertheless, this offence of manslaughter lies at the gravest end of the scale and despite your learned counsel's submissions, I can see no mitigation. The circumstances are more serious than that in the reported case of O'Mahoney, which can be found in the Judicial Studies Board, the latest

The sentence of the court upon you is one of 16 years imprisonment.

Edward Stewart I have listened with care to everything your counsel has said, but this remains, as I said to Miller, a callous, cruel and planned attack on a defenceless man on the doorstep of his elderly mother. You were the driver, taking the gunman to shoot Freddie Knights with a sawn-off shotgun, and then drive him away again after the shooting. You also played the part – unnecessary, as it turned out – of banging on the window to lure Mr. Knights to the spot. The jury in your case too have taken the merciful view that you did not know that there was a risk that he might be killed, and I must sentence you accordingly. I have to sentence you on the basis that serious harm would be done to Mr Knights, but you nevertheless went along with that, knowing what was to happen. I take into account that, alone amongst those in the dock, in your defence statement you admitted your role as the driver and, as your leading counsel points out, at an earlier stage after your arrest you were resisting the suggestion that you should join in a false story. It is also mitigation, in my view, that on the evidence, on the first night, the night of the botched attempt, you did your best, on the evidence of Lee Watson, to make sure that the attempt was not carried out, but that is the only mitigation. The offence lies at the gravest end of the scale for manslaughter. But, taking those matters into account, the sentence upon you is one of 13 years imprisonment.

Michael Dixon, you joined in this plan to shoot Freddie Knights with a firearm other than a shotgun. You have been convicted of conspiracy to cause grievous bodily harm with intent to cause grievous bodily harm and you knew that the shooting was to take place on the doorway of the victim's elderly mother; and I repeat what I said to the others, this was a callous and cruel crime. Your part was to assist in the stealing of the getaway car and to supervise and provide back up for the shooting itself. The jury have accepted that you did not intend that he should be killed and that you did not appreciate the risk that he might be killed, but anyone who plans to ambush and attack a defenceless man with a firearm commits a very serious offence. I take into account everything that your counsel has said, in particular the reference to you being unwillingly a Category 'A' prisoner. I take that and the other matters that he has ably submitted into account. The sentence I pass upon you is one of nine years imprisonment.

Controversy surrounded the trial after sentencing when the Judge asked West Yorkshire Police to carry out an investigation into alleged jury intimidation. It was reported that a male jury member had received a menacing phone call as the jury were considering their verdicts. Police were also chasing another line of enquiry as the 'Yorkshire Post Newspaper' had received an alleged letter from a juror claiming that a jury member had received an 'improper' approach. The Judge spoke to each jury member individually about the matter but nobody admitted to writing the letter.

On the 2nd October 2002 Lee Sean Watson was sentenced.

Mr Justice Brown: *Lee Sean Watson, stand up, would you?*
The Defendant: *Yes.*
Mr Justice Brown: *You are a ruthless and violent, professional criminal.
On behalf of others you arranged for Mr. Freddy Knights to be ambushed and
shot outside his mother's house. You chose the gunman and the get-away
driver and you took some part in the planning of this offence. You knew that a
sawn-off shotgun was going to be used. By your evidence at trial and your plea
to manslaughter it is demonstrated that you were at the centre of this brutal
killing. Your plea of guilty, your evidence for the Crown, which I bear fully in
mind having listened to it for nearly four days, the assistance you gave to the
police in respect of other serious matters on Tyneside, and all the other matters
urged on me by your learned counsel, I take into consideration. You are entitled
to a substantial reduction in the sentence that would otherwise be passed upon
you because of your plea and particularly because of your stance in giving
evidence against your fellows and I give you the fullest credit that I can. I also
take into account, in relation to the offence of aggravated burglary at Hardman
Gardens, that the bulk of the evidence, came from your own admission to the
police
Nevertheless, that in itself was a serious offence. Breaking into somebody's
house and discharging a firearm into various parts of the furniture with the
obvious intention of creating terror when the occupiers returned.
Taking all these matters into account, for the offence of manslaughter
the sentence of the Court upon you is one of eleven years imprisonment. I bear
in mind that the gunmen I sentenced to 16 years' imprisonment and you would,
in ordinary circumstances, have received a sentence of at least that length
being one of the organisers.
So far as the aggravated burglary is concerned, the sentence of the
court upon you is one of seven years' imprisonment and, taking into account
all the assistance you have given, the fact that you have provided the evidence
yourself to convict yourself on this count, I order that that sentence run
concurrently with the sentence of eleven years and so the total sentence is one
of eleven years' imprisonment. You can go down.*

The cost of bringing John Henry Sayers and his co-defendants to trial
was estimated to be in the region of £10 million which is still to this day one of
the most expensive cases in Northumbria Police Forces history. Costs included
officers from eight forces across the UK who were involved in the manhunt and
hundreds of hours of overtime claimed by officers who took part in undercover
surveillance operations to catch the gang.
The trial itself ran for 58 days at a cost of £8000 a day which came to
£500k. The transportation of the prisoners from prisons such as Full Sutton,

Doncaster and Wakefield each shadowed by a helicopter, and the accumulative security totalled £5 Million. Each day the court was surrounded by Police carrying sub machine guns and police marksmen placed strategically on rooftops. There was a ring of steel placed around Leeds Crown Court causing disruption to hundreds of members of the public going about their business. Every member of the public was searched as they entered the building to attend the trial in Court number 5 as the case was upgraded to a 'Code Black' which is usually reserved for terrorist trials. Even outside the door leading into the court stood twelve armed police. A senior prison service insider was quoted in the 'Evening Chronicle' at the time saying 'It takes an awful lot of people to stage an operation of this size , a lot of equipment and a great deal of planning. All of that costs money. Security on this scale is not unprecedented but it is very rare. That means it is very expensive.'

On numerous occasions we asked investigator Neil Jackson to put in freedom of information requests to obtain an accurate figure of each case involving members of the 'Sayers' family but they have always been politely declined. At the time a spokesman for Northumbria police admitted that the Knights trial had cost the taxpayers millions of pounds but that the true figure may never be 'accurately calculated.

John Henry, I mentioned earlier, was represented by top QC Jonathan Goldberg who had represented Charlie Kray during his ill feted trial for conspiracy to supply Cocaine in the late nineties. During the trial John would often make notes during exchanges and hand the notes to his barrister. Always alert with his mind ticking over, picking out the many inaccuracies in the prosecution case. Humour played its part during those long days with Goldberg being at the centre of many comical exchanges.

On one occasion reporter Rob Kennedy reported that 'He had the jury in a fit of giggles with his take on heroin addict Stephen Carlton, whose home in Newcastle's West Denton was said to be used by the gang as a safe house. Mr Goldberg said "Carlton is all over the shop and in an opium dream. He admitted he was like a zombie at the time of the murder and was out of his head all of the time. He said he could hear people's thoughts when he took magic mushrooms. Perhaps we should give that to the jury, it may well help them!"

John Henry on being cleared wanted to let the world know that he had been the victim of a Police conspiracy, a point that had been hammered home by his QC Goldberg so eloquently in court:

"There is an extraordinary relationship between Sayers and Northumbria Police it's along the lines of the Wild West and Billy The Kidd. Sayers says he has tried to go straight but the Police won't let him. We allege Police corruption, not in the sense of Police taking bribes but what we would call 'noble cause corruption.' The Police think Sayers is guilty and assume he is guilty and want him badly and have given the system a nudge because they think they can't trust the

justice system to get it right and they think he is a menace to society. Fit ups do happen and this kind of corruption is hard to detect because who is better at covering their tracks than the detectives? Sayers may be paranoid but just because you are paranoid doesn't mean the bastards aren't out to get you."

In a rare exclusive interview with Rob Kennedy of 'The Evening Chronicle' John Henry gave his side of the story:

"I've said since before I came out of prison in 1999 that there was a Police conspiracy and I sent a letter to the Chief Constable telling him that. My defence all along has been that I was not guilty and that I was the victim of a fit-up by the police. Every day I was in court I was sure I was going to get sent down and that I might never come out. This whole thing had a real effect on me, it has put my relationship with my wife Yvonne under real strain. In fact, I've split up with Yvonne and she had to sell the house in Heaton, so I'm just living at a mate's house. Northumbria Police decided I was guilty a day or two after Freddie Knights was shot so it must have been a fit-up for them to target me so early on. I want a totally independent inquiry into the police's handling of the case and my solicitor has already written to David Blunkett, our local MP Stephen Byers, and Amnesty International, demanding there is a full investigation. I also want to know why the Chief Constable is not addressing the issue of the jury verdict and why nothing is being done about it. We aren't interested in trying to sue the police at the moment until the issue of an inquiry is sorted out."

He went on to describe his relationship with Freddie Knights being on 'good terms' and having no reason to order his execution and discussed frankly rumours of as possible motive:

"I did know Freddie Knights, but my relationship with him was more positive than anything. In fact, I was giving him protection and looking after him because he was having bother with another family. There were even rumours going around about me having a motive for getting Freddie shot because they tried to say my son was Freddie's son and he'd had an affair with Yvonne. But we've had the laddie DNA tested and that proved I was his Dad."

John also talked of his future plans:

"I don't know what the future holds at the minute. I'm still on a high after the verdict. I've got an application in for a taxi driver's license and an operator's license and while I think the police will object, I hope they give me a chance to make an honest living. I'm not involved in any kind of debt collecting or security anymore. All I want now is for the police to let me go straight and for them to leave me alone and let me make an honest living. I know things have happened

in the past but I just want to move forward if I'm allowed to."

On his co-defendants he said:

"I had never met Dale Miller before the court case, I'd only spoken to Eddie Stewart once on the phone. I knew Micky Dixon because he was a cab driver and a mechanic."
'Supergrass' Lee Shaun Watson had been given permission to withdraw his guilty plea to a murder charge and instead was found guilty of manslaughter and given 11 years. A deal had been done."

On Watson John was scathing in his interview:

"I think Watson grassed on me because he had been led down the garden path by his lawyers. He is just a heroin addict looking after his own back by dropping me in it, but most of what he said was lies. As it is he is now the only one to be convicted of murdering Freddie Knights."

The police naturally denied all accusations of corruption and deals being done. It had been alleged that one of the key prosecution witness Stephen Carlton had cut a deal with investigating officers after being arrested for the Post Office robbery in Chopwell. Barrister Paul Worsley claimed Carlton was handed a new identity and £23k and all charges against him were dropped in exchange for him giving evidence against the gang. A police spokeswoman said, "It was claimed one prosecution witness was paid £23,000 for informing on people, and that a charge of attempted robbery against him was dropped. In fact, £23,000 was the cost involved in accommodating and protecting a number of prosecution witnesses, some of whom were away from home for up to four months, during a protracted trial taking place outside the region."

Northumbria Police Chief Constable Crispian Strachan threw his weight behind the official statement too. "It can be misleading if allegations are presented as fact, especially when they have been discredited,"

Further investigations by journalist Steve Kennedy proved that Carlton had indeed been given a new identity. The drug addict was now living in the South of the country still in fear and still a regular drug user.

Johnathan Goldberg QC in an interview with the Evening Chronicle gave his views on the use of Supergrasses in high profile cases. "It's often a great mistake for prosecutors to rely on supergrasses and it can be a blessing in disguise to defending counsel such as myself. Invariably, they tell lies to lessen their own involvement and it's easy to catch them out by careful cross examination. The acquittal of John Henry Sayers shows it is a mistake for prosecutors to rely on supergrasses."

After the main trial Dixons partner Angela McKay, Sarah Dillon and

Craig Shepherd were put on trial at Newcastle Crown Court for assisting an offender, where they were accused of obtaining a bogus birth certificate and DSS documents to help Mickey get a new identity and passport so that he could flee the country.

In court McKay admitted that she took the birth certificate and DSS documents from Dillon's house and passed them on to a man in a car. They were eventually passed onto Dixon. She claimed she had no knowledge of him committing the offence and also said that she did not believe he would be involved in anything like that. She later admitted that she had delivered the documents to Dillon's home and had lied to protect him.

She also claimed that the police told her that Mickey was a murderer. An accusation that the prosecution denied. In court Prosecutor Euan Duff said, "At no stage at any of the interviews did the police suggest to you that Michael had pulled the trigger."
She replied, "They did. They kept saying he was a murderer. They might not have said it on tape but they were saying it on the way to the police station in the car."

There was a touch of showbiz with this trial too with Scottish ex-footballer Frank McAvennie called as a witness after being innocently involved in the plot. Craig Shepherd had called Frank who he had befriended in Newcastle, asking if he could help book a hotel room in Glasgow for his friend Dixon. In court he explained, "I have known Craig Shepherd for about three and a half years. We both live in the Newcastle area. On the day in question Craig rang my mobile while I was in Glasgow. He said he was finding it difficult to find a hotel. I said that I would see what I could do. Craig didn't say what he was doing in Glasgow – I didn't ask. I phoned two hotels one in Paisley. One was the Brabloch. They told me they had no vacancies. I told them it was for a friend of mine. I played football for Scotland years ago and I get deals at certain hotels. They put me on to the Glynn Hill Hotel and I booked a twin room for Craig."

Prosecutor Duff discredited his evidence by claiming the former player had 'got his lines wrong' because the room was booked at the Brabloch.

On Shepherd he said, "Michael Dixon was wanted for conspiracy to murder. What should you do if you wanted to get out of the country quickly and who should you call on? You should ask someone you can trust and depend on. Craig Shepherd was that person."

Shepherd's explanation was very simple. "Michael Dixon asked me to take him to Glasgow so he could get a passport to visit his Dad in Holland who was ill. I didn't suspect anything and didn't have a problem with it. I was not aware Michael Dixon was a suspect in the Freddie Knights murder at the time. We were sitting outside the passport office and the next thing I knew was police with truncheons got out of a car and handcuffed us."

Craig Shephard was found guilty of assisting an offender and sentenced to 12 months. He served his sentence but passed away a few years later after a bout of pneumonia.

John Henry Sayers final words in the interview to the Evening Chronicle were nothing short of prophetic:

"I know they will be taping me and watching me and while I hope they won't come back for me there's always a chance they will."

Chapter Thirty Nine: Operation Insight

Away from the Knights murder trial a police operation was in full flow to put away the Sayers family for a long time. With Lee Watson co-operating Operation Insight was launched. Here for the first time you can read the allegations made against the family.

Please note these are Watson's allegations and are not factual.

The Alleged Murder Of Clive 'Kicker' Minnikin

Lee Watson stated that he was told by Stephen Sayers that Minnikin was taken from his house, put in the rear of a car and shot as he said he would inform on John Henry Sayers for his part in the Pritchards Security Robbery. A £25,000 reward had been offered by Pritchards for information. Minnikin was last seen on the 1st October 1986. His brother Alan had been jointly charged with John Henry Sayers on the robbery.

It was not possible to substantiate Watson's account due to paucity of information and although Minnikin had been reported as missing from home, no body has ever been found. The police concluded that Watson's revelations added nothing substantial to the investigation into the disappearance.

In the book *Fog On The Tyne* the author says it was rumoured that he was a member of the robbery team and that not all of the gang's money had been recovered by the police. The police were in no doubt that he was murdered by persons unknown.

The Murder of Viv Graham

Watson stated that during 1993 he was wanted by the police in relation to a series of robberies in Switzerland. During this period he took refuge in the Ord Arms Public House in Cowgate, Newcastle Upon Tyne which was owned by his cousin, Cecil Levy. Watson stated that he was acting as bar manager and had the run of the flats above the premises.

Whilst staying at the Ord Arms he became friendly with Stephen and Michael Sayers who had started to drink there after Michael Sayers had been shot in the Darnell Public House. Watson said that the Sayers disliked Viv Graham and his right-hand man Terry Scott because they were losing face due to the pair's activities. Viv had prevented Stephen and Michael and those dealing drugs on their behalf from entering pubs and clubs controlled by him. Scott had allegedly issued a challenge to fight both Stephen and Michael together.

Michael Sayers needed to do something to restore his reputation after being shot. In addition, it was claimed that Michael had received a beating at the hands of Viv some years earlier. This was strongly denied. As a result of all of this Michael and Stephen decided that Viv would be shot. Watson claimed that as Xmas 1993 approached, Michael Sayers was complaining about Viv. When Watson suggested that he be shot, Sayers replied that he was 'sorting it.'

In relation to the events of 31st December 1993 Watson stated that he was working in the Ord Arms. Stephen and Michael Sayers were sitting outside in a red four door saloon car. Watson had a conversation with Michael Sayers through the front passenger window. Watson then returned to the pub. Michael Sayers later returned in an excited state. He was stripping off his clothes. He said that Viv had been shot and that he now ran the town. Watson claimed that Sayers said, "We've had him shot." Sayers then told Watson to get him a towel as he wanted to be seen in the bar. Sayers then went to the bar where he made an issue of being seen and shouted to his brother to order a taxi. Michael then changed into some of Watson's clothes before leaving.

Watson also stated that he did not know how the Sayers had found out that Viv had been shot but he believed that 'Scotch Rob' (Robert Smith) had been in the Wallsend area and had some involvement. He stated that when confirmation later came through that Viv was dead, Stephen and Michael made 3 ounces of cocaine available for celebration. The celebration continued through the night moving on to the Lemington Hotel and then the Cooper's Forge Public House.

Watson named Harry Cushion, "Coco', Cecil Levy and possibly, David Hindmarsh as being present in the Ord Arms that night, He said that whilst they were in the Cooper's Forge, Michael Sayers told him that John Paul Howe had been paid £10,000 to shoot Graham and that Graham Kelly had driven the getaway vehicle. Kelly had smashed a window in Viv's car activating the alarm. When Viv returned to the car on hearing the alarm sounding, he was shot from the car by Howe leaning across Kelly. Watson says that he was told that the firearm used was a .357 Magnum and that a lad called Jason Down had to bump start the car used in the shooting.

Watson also stated that about two days earlier he had spent all night drinking in the Ord Arms with Michael Sayers. In the morning, Sayers told 'Scotch Rob' to go and get the gun that was under the car seat. Smith returned and produced a 'Magnum' from under his coat. Watson described the gun as heavy revolver, dark metal with a wooden handle and with a total length of about 12 inches.

He also stated that whilst he was on remand in HMP Durham another inmate, William 'Scotty' Carlin, told him that he had destroyed the gun used in the Viv shooting on the instruction of Howe and Kelly who had come to his flat. Stephen Keen (Beaney) was present at the time.

Various parts of Watson's statement were confirmed by police:
- All those mentioned were at liberty at the time.
- Staff and customers confirmed that Watson 'holed up' at the Ord Arms and he was arrested there in relation to the Swiss offences.
- Stephen and Michael Sayers were in the Ord Arms on 31st December 1993.

- There was a record of an incident between Viv Graham and Michael Sayers in Madisons nightclub in Newcastle.
- Police enquiries established that Terry Scott did indeed offer to fight both Sayers brothers together in Circus Circus (now Flares) in Newcastle.
- Police enquiries also established that there were a number of documented incidents where Viv or his associates denied access to public houses to the Sayers together with incidents where dealers on behalf of Sayers were assaulted by Viv and his associates.
- In relation to Robert Smith being at the scene of the shooting, a witness described how an associate of the Sayers was standing on the steps of the Social Security offices prior to the shooting.
- The gun used in the shooting was a .357 calibre or .33 using a Magnum round.
- Jason Down had been interviewed and recalled pushing a blue Ford Escort outside the Ord Arms as it needed bump starting.
- Howe and Kelly were criminal associates.
- Howe made admissions in relation to the killing to his girlfriend.
- The description of the shooting was accurate although there were
- discrepancies.

There were also a lot of discrepancies in Watson's statement:
- There were no witnesses who could recall Michael Sayers in a towel in the Ord Arms on 31st December 1993.
- Watson never performed the role of bar manager at the Ord Arms as he claimed.
- Robert Smith was never identified as being present in Wallsend on the day of the shooting.
- No witnesses admitted to participating in a 'cocaine party' on 31st December 1993.
- The manager of the Lemington Hotel states that the party did not attend his premises that night as claimed.
- The description of the shooting was inaccurate as Viv's car was not alarmed and he did not hurry to his car. He went to the shops to purchase dog food and cigarettes before returning to his car.
- Most of the information given by Watson in his statement was relayed to him by third parties. Much of what he related by way of direct conversation remained unchallenged due to the unwillingness of those incriminated to answer questions from the police. However, there was no forensic or identification evidence to link any of those incriminated to the murder
- Although Watson's interviews provided a credible account of how Graham might have been murdered there was insufficient evidence to support any charge against those named as responsible.

The Shooting In The Star Public House 9th October 1995
Watson claimed that he was in Frankland Prison with Stephen Sayers when he told him about a shooting that he carried out at 'The Star' Public House on Westgate Road, Newcastle. He stated that Sayers told him that the shooting was in revenge for Michael Sayers being shot in a public house across the road from Newcastle Central Station. He said Sayers told him that he had gone through the door of the Star armed with a sawn-off shotgun loaded with heavy gauge ammunition specially filled with ball bearings. He started to fire at three men at the bar firing twice before the shotgun exploded as the barrel had been cut too short to the stock. Shrapnel from the shotgun struck Sayers in the foot causing him to leave the scene to avoid leaving blood. As a result of the attack a man called Somerville lost a leg. Stephen 'Gun' Shotton assisted Sayers in the offence either by going into the public house or standing guard outside on Westgate Road. Watson suggested that another person would have been in the bar prior to Sayers entering to advise Sayers as to when his targets were present.

Police investigations into Watson's statement found the following results:
- A shooting did occur in the Star Public House on 9th October 1995 when Alan Harrison, James Somerville and Robert Aitken received shotgun wounds. Somerville subsequently lost a leg.
- Watson was in Frankland Prison at the same time as Stephen Sayers.
- The shotgun used in the offence suffered catastrophic failure of the barrels.
- Enquiries revealed Charles Harrison had hit Michael Sayers in the Half Moon Public House prior to this incident.
- The Sayers and Shotton were at liberty at this time.

There were too many discrepancies however to take Watson's statement any further and insufficient evidence to support any charge:
- Parts of a shattered shotgun recovered after the incident were from a 12-gauge double barrelled over and under shotgun not a pump action.
- DNA recovered from part of the shattered gun was checked against the Sayers and Shotton with a negative result.
- The Half Moon Public house where the alleged incident with Charles Harrison took place is located in the Bigg Market and is not opposite Newcastle Central Station.
- Although Watson knew the second person involved in the incident, he had to be re-interviewed before he would disclose who it was.
- Shot recovered from the scene was bid shot and very fine.
- There was a record of an incident between Viv Graham and Michael Sayers in Madisons nightclub in Newcastle.
- Police enquiries established that Terry Scott did indeed offer to fight both Sayers brothers together in Circus Circus (now Flares) in Newcastle.

- Police enquiries also established that there were a number of documented incidents where Viv or his associates denied access to public houses to the Sayers together with incidents where dealers on behalf of Sayers were assaulted by Viv and his associates.
- In relation to Robert Smith being at the scene of the shooting, a witness described how an associate of the Sayers was standing on the steps of the Social Security offices prior to the shooting.
- The gun used in the shooting was a .357 calibre or .33 using a Magnum round.
- Jason Down had been interviewed and recalled pushing a blue Ford Escort outside the Ord Arms as it needed bump starting.
- Howe and Kelly were criminal associates.
- Howe made admissions in relation to the killing to his girlfriend.
- The description of the shooting was accurate although there were
- discrepancies.

There were also a lot of discrepancies in Watson's statement:
- There were no witnesses who could recall Michael Sayers in a towel in the Ord Arms on 31st December 1993.
- Watson never performed the role of bar manager at the Ord Arms as he claimed.
- Robert Smith was never identified as being present in Wallsend on the day of the shooting.
- No witnesses admitted to participating in a 'cocaine party' on 31st December 1993.
- The manager of the Lemington Hotel states that the party did not attend his premises that night as claimed.
- The description of the shooting was inaccurate as Viv's car was not alarmed and he did not hurry to his car. He went to the shops to purchase dog food and cigarettes before returning to his car.
- Most of the information given by Watson in his statement was relayed to him by third parties. Much of what he related by way of direct conversation remained unchallenged due to the unwillingness of those incriminated to answer questions from the police. However, there was no forensic or identification evidence to link any of those incriminated to the murder
- Although Watson's interviews provided a credible account of how Graham might have been murdered there was insufficient evidence to support any charge against those named as responsible.

Offences of Arson and Attempted Arson

According to Lee Watson, as part of Sayers' plan to instigate a gang war between Stuart Watson and Robin Armstrong, Lee Watson states that a plan was hatched to cause a fire at Stuart Watson's home address on First

Street Bensham, Gateshead and at Watson's brother's house, on Kyle Road, Bensham. Armstrong would be blamed for these attacks. Watson claimed that the matter was discussed in a café in Marlborough Crescent, Newcastle where Sayers tasked Watson with recruiting a team to carry out the attacks. Watson recruited Edward Stewart and James Robert Teasdale to carry out the arson at Front Street but their first attempt failed.

A second attempt was planned this time supervised by Watson, Leach and Dixon again using Stewart and Teasdale to carry out the offence. According to Watson, the five of them travelled in two separate vehicles, one a white Ford Transit van borrowed for the purpose from a builder. At Front Street, it was alleged that Stewart and Teasdale took two large plastic drums containing petrol from the rear of the van and poured petrol over the garden wall of the house. Whilst this was happening, Watson and Leach drove to a nearby street where Leach pointed out a hot dog trailer. After the offence had been committed at First Street, Watson drove the van to his home address in Blaydon before returning it to the builder next day.

There were the following points of corroboration in Watson's account:
- All persons allegedly involved were at liberty at the time.
- An arson did occur at 1 First Street, Bensham, where petrol was emptied over the garden wall and ignited. Large plastic drums were recovered from the scene.
- The white van was traced to its owner who confirmed having loaned it overnight to Leach and Dixon. The van was returned the next morning.
- An attempted arson did occur at a mobile kitchen trailer belonging to James Watson. A ford Orion motor car was observed at the scene as had been claimed by Lee Watson.
- A café owner in Marlborough Crescent confirmed that Sayers was a regular customer.
- Teasdale had been interviewed under caution and fully admitted his role in the arson at First Street and on the hot dog trailer at Kyle Road. He confirmed meeting with Lee Watson and an unknown male at a café in Marlborough Crescent. He stated that a small white van was used to transport the petrol drums to the scene and confirmed that his understanding was that the offences were intended to trigger a gang war.

The discrepancies in the statement were as follows:
- There was no evidence of the initial failed attempt at First Street and Teasdale denies knowledge of any such attempt.
- Whilst Watson alleged that five people were involved, Teasdale contends that only four people were involved – Watson, Stewart, himself and the unknown male.
- Teasdale stated that he and Stewart were in the van whilst Watson and the unknown male were in a sporty type of car when they carried out the 'recce'

at Kyle Road.
- The owner of the van states that it was Dixon and Leach, not Watson who returned the van to him.
- Watson stated that they filled the petrol canisters at the garage at the South end of the Redheugh Bridge whilst Teasdale stated that they were filled at a garage in Blaydon.
- Watson stated that he had nothing to do with making payment for the job. Teasdale stated that he was paid for both jobs by Watson.

The accounts and allegations made by Lee Watson were corroborated to a large degree and there was no evidence uncovered which would significantly disprove the information given albeit that there are a number of discrepancies. The admissions of Watson and Teasdale may have been sufficient for a successful prosecution.

The Alleged Conspiracy to Murder Robin Armstrong
Watson stated that John Henry Sayers intended instigating a 'gang war' between Robin Armstrong and Stuart Watson with a view to taking over their business interests, legitimate or otherwise. Sayers intended having Armstrong murdered in circumstances which would result in suspicion falling on Stuart Watson. Some 2-3 weeks after incidents of arson at the home of Stuart Watson and his brother Leach, Lee Watson and Michael Dixon drove to Armstrong's business premises. Leach pointed out a white coloured fire door and explained that it led to Armstrong's office which could be viewed from outside the chain link perimeter fence. The three of them then drove to a nearby 'Drive Thru' McDonalds restaurant where they sat in the car discussing their plan. Leach outlined how he and Watson would enter the office area, Leach armed with a shotgun and Watson with a handgun. Leach would seek out and shoot Armstrong whilst Watson would deal with anyone coming from other offices who tried to intervene. If Armstrong's girlfriend was there, she too would be shot. They would then all make off in a vehicle being driven by Dixon. The route would take them via a country lane and then through a gap in the dual carriageway. The plan was never implemented, according to Watson, due to the murder of Knights.
Watson's story again was not enough to prosecute and again there were points of corroboration and just as many discrepancies:
- Leach had been a business associate of Armstrong and as such would know the layout of his offices.
- All persons allegedly involved were at liberty at the time.
- There was a history of bad blood between Armstrong and Stuart Watson.
- The road which lead from Armstrong's business premises was a single track, unmarked road, (Mill Lane) which exited onto the A189 dual carriage-way. There was a gap in the central reservation and crash barrier at that

point.
- Armstrong's girlfriend worked with him at the premises.
- There was a 'Drive Thru' McDonalds adjacent to the Mill Lane exit onto the A189.

As for discrepancies:
- Watson was unable to identify Armstrong's premises when taken out in a car and, when asked to identify the McDonalds, he pointed out the facility at Kingston Park several miles away.
- It would not have been possible for Watson to have seen the door to Armstrong's office from outside the compound.
- The fence surrounding the premises was a posted security railed fence, not chain link.
- The nature of Armstrong's business was such that neither Sayers nor Stuart Watson would have been in a position to take it over.

The Sending of a Letter Bomb To Peter Logan Donnelly
A letter bomb was sent to the home of Peter Donnelly on 18th February 1994. The device exploded causing minor cuts and burns to Donnelly's arm. The matter was investigated by police.
Watson's versions of events were that Donnelly and Sayers had enjoyed a good relationship until a letter bomb was sent to the home of Donnelly. Donnelly blamed the Sayers. Watson claimed that the bomb had been made by John Henry Sayers with the help of members of the IRA who he had met in HMP Parkhurst. The reason it was sent to Donnelly was because of a fallout he had with Stephen and Michael Sayers after Donnelly had refused them entry to Rockies Public House.

The discrepancies in Watson's statement were as follows:
- It was believed at the time that the motive for the offence was a dispute over horses. The only person checked at the time against finger marks found on the device was Philip Berriman.
- The fingerprints of Stephen and Michael Sayers, John Sayers, Watson, Leach and Stephen Shotton were checked against finger-marks found on the device with a negative result.
- It was not possible to trace the alleged incident at Rockies as the Northumbria Police Incident Logging System only dated back to November 1997.
- John Henry Sayers was in prison at the time and although in Parkhurst, it was highly unlikely that he would have been able to make such a device in prison (or to get it out of prison).
- Donnelly refused to speak to police and the investigation revealed nothing further in terms of evidence which would assist in the detection of

the offence. However, there was evidence that the offence actually occurred, although claims that the Sayers family were involved could not be substantiated.

The Shooting of Robert Morton 20th March 1996

Watson claimed that whilst serving a prison sentence for robbery at Frankland Prison he established a friendship with Stephen Sayers. He said that Stephen told him about the circumstances of the offence for which he had been sentenced which was the conspiracy to blackmail a local businessman. He said Sayers told him that whilst he was on remand with his co-accused attempts had been made to intimidate the businessman into dropping the case. They were aware that he was under 24-hour armed police guard so they targeted a friend of his, Robert Morton.

Morton was shot in the leg as he left his gymnasium in Ivy Road, Gosforth on 20th March 1996. Watson also stated that Sayers told him that Anthony Leach carried out the shooting accompanied by Stephen Shotton.

Shortly after the shooting, a meeting took place in a swimming pool attended by representatives of the Sayers family and a representative of the businessman to discuss dropping the charges. The location was chosen to prevent covert recording. Trevor Joseph Hunt subsequently telephoned the businessman to persuade him not to drop the charges and tapes of this conversation fell into the hands of the Sayers family.

Watson further stated that following his release he had met Leach in Newcastle. Leach admitted responsibility for the shooting but told Watson that he was annoyed with the Sayers as they had been talking about the shooting in prison. He had visited the brothers and was congratulated by other inmates in relation to the shooting.

Points of corroboration were as follows:

- Watson was in Frankland Prison at the same time as Stephen Sayers and prison records show that they did associate with each other.
- The local businessman confirmed that Joe Hunt rang him to encourage him to continue with the prosecution.
- Robert Morton a friend of the local businessman was shot in the leg and subsequently lost his leg.
- Transcripts of telephone conversations between the local businessman and Hunt were disclosed to the Sayers as unused material prior to the trial in relation to the blackmail.
- The local businessman confirmed that a meeting did take place at a swimming pool between John Brian Sayers (father of Stephen and Michael) and Peter Farrier, a solicitor, who was acting as a friend to the businessman.
- Both Leach and Shotton were at liberty at the time of the shooting.

As for discrepancies:
* Watson stated that the shooting took place in Jesmond as he knew the Brandling Public House was in Jesmond. The shooting actually occurred in Ivy Road, Jesmond (close to a pub called the Brandling).

His revelations were investigated fully but there was no direct evidence to substantiate any charges against Leach or Shotton. Shotton denied involvement in the offence. At the time of the investigation as part of 'Operation Insight', Leach was still at large and so was not questioned in relation to Watson's revelations.

Alleged Shooting At A Flat In Elswick
Watson claimed that this shooting was a follow up to the shooting at the Star Public House. Michael Sayers did not have the nerve to carry out the shooting himself so Stephen did it. In return, Michael Sayers had to carry out the shooting of a man in a flat in Elswick. The shooting was carried out on the man's doorstep using a 9mm pistol. Watson further stated that reference was made to this incident in tape recorded blackmail conversations between Nigel Abadom and a local businessman.

Abadom was convicted with Stephen and Michael Sayers of conspiracy to blackmail a local businessman who cannot be named for legal reasons. Tapes of the conversation between Abadom and this man were exhibited and contained reference to a shooting in Elswick where the intended victim was not at home so a neighbour was shot to assert Sayers' authority. Although there were a large number of shootings of this nature in the West End of Newcastle around this time, this specific shooting was not identified by police.

Conspiracy To Cause Grievous Bodily Harm To Jonathan Miller
Watson stated that there was a meeting between himself, Sayers, Leach and Dixon where is was said that the cartridges discharged in the Hardman Gardens offence would have to be retrieved as the gun was to be used to shoot the head doorman at Legends nightclub in Newcastle.
Watson describes the gun as a .410 single barrel shotgun with cut down and sawn-off barrel. He says that a member of his family supplied it. He stated that Dixon collected the gun from a 'junkie' pal of Dale Miller. He went on to say that Sayers had a partner in the security business and ran doormen.
Points of Corroboration:
* There was evidence to establish that there had been a number of meetings where business proposals had been made to take over the door security at Legends. These attempts had been made by a firm trading as 'Leisure Security', on whose behalf approaches were made by Anthony Farrell, an associate of Sayers who shared business premises with Abcom security, a firm connected with Leach. A later approach was made to Legends by

Farrell on behalf of a company called 'Feelsafe Security.'

The head doorman at Legends, Jonathan Millar, recalled a number of attempts of intimidation:

1. In July 2000 a man identified by another doorman (Nana Miah) as Sayers sat staring at him from a Land Rover Discovery parked opposite the club.
2. That same summer, Sayers, Farrell and an unknown female drove slowly past the door at the club and Sayers made a shooting gesture with hands before dragging his fingers across his throat.
3. Millar recalls being followed by Sayers in the vicinity of his home on three occasions.
4. Millar received a card depicting a man being shot.

All persons allegedly involved were at liberty at the relevant time.
Discrepancies in the statement were as follows:

- Farrell denied any connection with Sayers stating that he only knew him as a cousin of Joseph Eddington, a co-director of his in the firm 'New Leaf Security.'
- Farrell denied ever having been near Legends in the company of Sayers.
- Nana Miah denies identifying Sayers to Millar.
- When Millar first mentioned the incidents of intimidation to a police officer he knew, he did not mention Farrell being present when the threats were made.
- Further enquiries with potential witnesses failed to further corroborate the accounts of Watson and Millar.

Chapter Forty: Operation Stirling -Time At The Bar For John

The verdict in the Knights trial did not go down well with the police nor did the lack of progress with 'Operation Insight.' The amount of taxpayers' money wasted on the trial alone left a lot of red faces at HQ in Ponteland and they would need to lick their wounds and work out another way of putting John Henry Sayers behind bars. In June 2007 he was mentioned during the trial of George Youness who was snared in 'Operation Banjo' for drug distribution. Reading back through the articles online there is no substance whatsoever to the link and is nothing more than sensationalistic journalism linking him with Columbian Cartel gangsters and premiership footballers such as Tino Asprilla. This type of journalism would only help form a false public perception in the years ahead.

John was arrested on 20th November 2007 in his delivery van after a police fraud probe involving millions of pounds. The investigation centred on John's financial activities along with his mother Yvonne and business associates dating back several years. Around £100,000 in used notes had been seized by police at Sayers' home and his mum Yvonne's house in July 2005. Yvonne stated that the £40,000 removed from her home was part of her life savings and that the rest was takings for the pub supply company 'Pubs For Us' which she was involved with. She explained that she had grown up in a culture where ready cash was kept hidden in the home. She told the court "I do not think there is anything odd or unsafe about having money in the house. It is in my nature. I have been counting money all my life and keeping it in the house there is nothing strange about it."

The cash was held under the Proceeds of Crime Act. It was clear that the police were using provisions of the act to target so-called "dirty money" dealings with a view to confiscating assets from those suspected of living on the earnings of criminal activity. The inquiry, carried out by specialist financial experts, was believed to involve several million pounds in assets and money laundering. Others arrested and charged included his mother, Yvonne Sayers, Steven Colwell, Mehmood Mohammed, and Alan Coe. The accused faced 18 charges in total.

On the 8th October 2008 John pleaded guilty at Woolwich Crown Court to offences of cheating the Public Revenue, Fraudulent Trading and Possession of Criminal Property. He was sentenced to 4 years imprisonment. In his summing up the Judge said, "I give you credit for the fact that you have pleaded guilty. I have to sentence you for your part in this sophisticated and elaborate plan simply to make money out of the state and I have come to the conclusion that on counts 1 to 6 the appropriate sentence is one of four years imprisonment." He received a further 9 months for another charge to run concurrently and the Judge went on to explain that he would only serve half of his sentence and that any time served in custody would be taken into account. He was then led from the dock.

Yvonne Sayers pleaded guilty to an agreed basis of plea to an offence of Concealing Criminal Property. Judge Byers asked Yvonne to stand and said, "Yvonne Sayers you were found with a large amount of stolen money in your home. Anybody who conceals criminal property must realise that they are committing an extremely serious offence even if it is something that is done through family loyalty." She was sentenced following a Goodyear direction to 9 months imprisonment suspended for 2 years and allowed to leave the dock to head home.

At a hearing at Woolwich Crown Court on the 27th October 2008 a Deprivation order in the sum of £49,080,00 relating to the sum subject of the charge she had pleaded guilty to was made against her. Confiscation proceedings against her were discontinued by that finding.

Once again, a Sayers court case was front page news and the Evening Chronicle bizarrely labelled John 'an evil genius' which was a term that had been used in court. Alan Coe despite attempting to play the victim was found guilty too and jailed for two years and nine months.

John Henry Sayers was jailed after admitting being the man behind an empire of pubs running a tax scam across the North East.
Sayers installed front men to run the bars, but pulled the strings from the shadows and kept a grip on all the profits, Woolwich Crown Court was told.
The companies he set up to manage the pubs dodged tax, failed to pay VAT, business rates and council tax.

UNDER the spell of "evil genius" John Henry Sayers, bar boss Alan Coe ran a crooked pub empire that cheated the taxman out of hundreds of thousands.
Coe turned his back on his respectable career as a brewery area manager to help the hardman create a network of up to 30 bars that dodged taxes and business rates for nearly five years. But now the 46-year-old is getting used to life behind bars after he was jailed for two years and nine months for his part in the swindle that saw more than £400,000 evaded.
During a four-week trial at Newcastle Crown Court, jury members were told how detectives smashed the Sayers operation by placing a bug in his Skoda car with personalised number plate. They listened as Sayers, 46, and Coe discussed which pubs they were going to take over and laughed as they tricked the authorities over tax dues.
And investigations by a team of forensic accountants uncovered the true scale of their fraud, which involved two separate pub companies running between October 2000 and April 2005.
The firms had former soldier Coe installed as their frontman and he took instructions from Sayers and his mother Yvonne, who creamed off the taxes due to the Government. And, as their trust in him dwindled, police learned

a plot to have father-of two Coe killed was being hatched which led to him being placed in protection, living in a house covered by covert cameras and recording devices. But Coe couldn't escape from the fact he had worked as Sayers' right-hand man, helping him cheat the revenue by filling out false tax returns and companies accounts and lying about which pubs they were running.

Sayers himself was jailed for four years at Woolwich Crown Court last October and more than a year later it was Coe's turn to stand trial on six charges of tax evasion and fraudulent trading and one of money laundering.

During the trial, the former Scottish and Newcastle employee told how he met Sayers in the mid-1990s and in October 2000 accepted a £15,000 cash loan to take on the tenancies of the John Gilpen and Hillheads pubs, in Newcastle.

Coe gave evidence, claiming he had been ordered into the cellar of the John Gilpen and told to hand over both bars' Christmas takings, as Sayers 'hijacked' them both. But that was dismissed by John Black QC, prosecuting, who said the defendant entered into the relationship "with his eyes wide open" and then went on to help him acquire pubs across the region.
And after a day of deliberations, the jury returned guilty verdicts of six out of the seven charges. Judge Michael Cartlidge sentenced him to two years nine months for each offence, all to run concurrently. He said:

"Between October 2000 and April 2005, he assisted John Henry Sayers and his criminal organisation to evade taxes and rates. Alan Coe was a willing subordinate of Sayers. After becoming bankrupt in March 2005, he became of little use to Sayers or his organisation and was effectively discarded.

The Sayers organisation became convinced, probably wrongly in my view, that the defendant was taking money away from the Sayers organisation. The defendant as a result of all this is now at risk of being killed.

He has lost his family life, he has lost his home, he has lost everything. There has been no benefit from the fraud to the defendant apart from the wages he received from the Sayers organisation and now he has lost his liberty." He added: "The man described as the evil genius behind this operation - John Henry Sayers - pleaded guilty and was sentenced to four years. It is apparent that John Henry Sayers is a ruthless and dangerous criminal."

The two companies fronted by Coe on behalf of Sayers were called Neptune Inns and Pubs 4 Us. During the course of the fraud, they evaded £155,000 in VAT, more than £30,000 in Corporation Tax and £157,000 in business rates, which together with interest, brought the value of the con to £410,000.

The court heard in 2006 that Coe's wife's car was torched, while her mother's car was vandalised. Mitigating for his client, David Robson QC, defending, said:

"Mr Coe asks the court to bear in mind first of all that he is a man of good character hitherto and that both in the merchant navy and more particularly as a member of the army, he served for three operational tours in Northern Ireland, sometimes under cover and was discharged as a soldier of exemplary character. He, according to the Crown's case, received other than by way of his salary, no benefit from the fraud that the Sayers family were participating in. Nor did the prosecution suggest there was any truth in what the Sayers family were saying that he had stolen money from them."

Mr Robson told the court Coe had originally been placed under protection with his wife but she wanted to return to Tyneside and contact had to be made with the Sayers to make sure she would be safe.
He added:

"He has lost his own home, which he had on mortgage, he has lost his mother's home, on mortgage, and he has lost his vehicles, which were on finance. He has lost his wife Paula, because she made the decision to return to Newcastle when assurances had been given that nothing further would happen to her and your honour will recall the damage to her car.

He lost his wife and has been at a distance from his two children and is now completely financially destitute. It is also the case that for nearly four years he has been in protected custody."

Det Supt Dave Byrne who led the investigation, said:
"I'm obviously delighted with this conviction and sentence which is the result of a complex investigation over a number of years. We have worked closely with the HMRC and CPS to bring about this prosecution. I would also like to thank all those who worked with the police during this investigation.

We rely on information that communities provide and we use this to target criminals who seek to profit from crime. Not only will we arrest them for criminal offences but we will also work to remove their criminal assets.

We would ask anyone with information about criminal activity to get in touch so we can take action and keep bringing offenders to justice."

Financial adviser Steven Colwell who was accused of helping John dishonestly obtain a mortgage advance for a business venture walked free from court after the case was dropped against him. The 33-year-old, of Bishop Auckland, was cleared at Newcastle Crown Court part way through his trial after the prosecution offered no evidence against him.

Mr Mohammed who ran an accountancy firm on Cedar Road in Fenham, stood trial later in May 2011 and was accused of 'fiddling' the books for John. Jurors found him not guilty.

A year later the police officer who headed the economic crime unit in the case, Phil Butler, bizarrely chose the Sayers cases he had worked on to promote his bid to become the first police commissioner in the area. He was the Detective Inspector in Wallsend in 2000 when Freddie Knights was murdered. He told the Chronicle:

"We set up the incident room and I ran the intelligence cell on that murder. In that case, Sayers and others were arrested. It was high profile and of course we had to have a trial in Leeds under armed protection. The stance was that in 2002 Sayers was a free man, innocent and back on the streets. But in the court case and the build up to it, there were some lines that said there was an involvement in the pub business. At the time we were looking at murder, we were after something bigger, and yet this little bit of intelligence around his pub chains came to be crucial. After 2002, we started to see that Sayers was involved in other activities.

He came back on the radar and I was asked, given the success of our asset recovery, to play a part in this, to support the criminal investigation with the financial investigation. I trained staff, I had trained the chief, and was asked to give this the 'Al Capone treatment', to look at the money. I ended up going on the raid to his house, to his mother's house, where we found thousands in cash and loan documents whose repayments could realistically not be met through his declared earnings. And we found slips of paper with pubs' names and how much barrelage was going through each one. We knew then we had a classic Al Capone case here. He was avoiding tax. That was the easy bit. What we had to do next was interview him.

What has happened in the past is that a lot of officers didn't use their name when dealing with Sayers, just their collar numbers. In certain cases, organised crime and terrorism for example, officers don't have to identify themselves. In this case, officers were very reluctant to interview him with me. Basically, no one would go into this room with me. There was one brave detective sergeant who put himself forward, and him and I did it. At the end of it, Sayers turns to me and says 'I just want to thank you Mr Butler, you are the only police officer who has ever given me his name."

He continued: *"I, along with a lot of people, spent eight years, on and off, dealing with this individual. When he pleaded guilty, there was such a feeling of relief that we had finally done this. Leaving the court, I felt elated. Just a minute later, my dad called to say my mother had been diagnosed with cancer. It was such a terrible mixture. This professional pride for a very small team, just four or five officers working long hours for a long time, then this. It brought me back to the ground. That was really my ultimate case. It proved the point; it justified the decision to set up the squad. I left in 2009, but there was no surprise when, three weeks after retiring, I received a visit from a superintendent who gave me an 'Osman' warning which is a notice that you are in danger of being killed or seriously injured."*

The legal aid costs of the case were revealed years later in an article on the 25th February 2014 and they totalled almost £500,000. It came days after he had been ordered to pay back £250,000 that he had placed in offshore accounts. The Chronicle stated:

Cash paid from a public pot totalling £473,676.86 was used for the hearing in October 2008 in which he was jailed for four years for the sophisticated £400,000 tax con. But it's claimed that figure is dwarfed by the cost of a number of failed prosecutions against Sayers and the 10-year investigation by police into his finances.

Figures uncovered by the Chronicle also show legal teams acting for Sayers, his brother Stephen and co-accused Mark Rowe were handed a six figure sum during their collapsed jury-nobbling trial in November 2010.

The Legal Services Commission would not release a breakdown of how much legal aid was given to each defendant but confirmed exactly £134,158.62 was given to barristers for their expertise during the trial. That figure does not include the prosecution fees or the costs of holding Sayers on remand for 12 months before the trial collapsed because the Crown Prosecution Service failed to disclose key evidence that undermined their case. A Legal Services Commission spokesman said: "We manage costs carefully and legal aid rates are considerably less than those paid to lawyers in privately-funded cases. Trials can cost a lot of money if they last many weeks, are very complex and have thousands of pages of evidence. The law says that anyone facing a crown court trial for a serious criminal offence can apply for legal aid to ensure they have a lawyer, but funding is subject to a means test which could require them to pay towards their defence. We are committed to information transparency and release legal aid costs wherever possible."

Detectives staged a 10-year investigation into the Sayers family that began in 2004. Despite charging John Henry with a string of offences officers have only successfully convicted him for tax fraud.

John's partner Louise Smith hit the headlines by launching a campaign to free him. At the time she was interviewed by the Chronicle and said "John has been taken away from his family. He has four children and is a grandad. He looks after his grandchild and they have deprived him of that. I want to start a campaign to stop this sort of thing happening. John has not been charged with anything for seven years now. He has made mistakes in his life in the past, but hasn't everyone? He hasn't done anything wrong. I would love to set up a campaign for him to free him. There would be a lot of support for him, I know that."

There was a lot of support from friends and family but not from the authorities who wanted their pound of flesh and they were going to make sure they were going to get it.

Chapter Forty One: Stephen Back Behind Bars

In November 2007 Stephen was back behind bars to as he was charged with attempting to pervert the course of justice. Stephen's Auntie Muriel Donnelly had been left with catastrophic injuries after being knocked down in Newcastle in January 2005. She could not look after herself and was reliant on others. Sadly, as the accident was partly her fault, she only stood to gain £250,000 compensation. So Stephen and Joseph Ramsay, Muriel's partner decided to put pressure on the driver of the car Steven Stobbs to change his statement and admit liability for the crash which would have of course boosted the compensation. Stobbs, knowing Stephen's reputation, was having none of it and went straight to the police.

The trial was covered in the 'Evening Chronicle.'

Geoff Mason, prosecuting, said: "A handwritten note was posted through the door of the property where Mr Stobbs at that time lived with his partner. "It said 'can you ring this number' and gave a phone number. Mr Stobbs phoned that number and the man on the end of the phone was Stephen Sayers, who said he wanted to meet to discuss the case."

Mr Stobbs was then visited by Ramsay and a mystery bespectacled man, who urged him to change his statement and say he took his eyes off the road but Mr Stobbs said no, despite offers of being made 'financially comfortable for the rest of their lives'.

After the initial visit in 2006 no contact was made for more than a year but then on October 18 last year Mrs Donnelly was offered £250,000 in compensation, which was rejected on October 22.

At 4.30pm on October 31 Sayers and the mystery spectacles-wearer again turned up at Mr Stobbs' house, when he was out and his family were at home. Mr Mason said: "Because of the first visit Mr Stobbs partner had made some inquiries and had reason to believe they were at risk in some way. Stephen Sayers started to ask that Mr Stobbs alter his statement. They said they would be back at noon the following day to make sure he had changed his statement and they would take it to their solicitors.

"They said there would be no trouble for Mr Stobbs if he changed his statement and the compensation would change to £5m if he said the accident was his fault.

"Stephen Sayers showed her newspaper cuttings of Muriel Donnelly. After being in the house 25 minutes they got up and left and said 'We'll see you tomorrow'."

But Mr Stobbs' partner, described as feeling 'fearful, anxious and concerned', contacted Mr Stobbs and they decided to report the matter to police.

Sayers and Ramsay were arrested on November 1st 2007 and on November 2 the offer of £250,000 compensation was accepted. Mr Stobbs and his family have, the court heard, had to move away from the area.

Sayers, 42, of Heaton, and Joseph Ramsay, 46, of Lemington, both pleaded *guilty to attempting to pervert the course of justice between July 1, 2006, and November 1, 2007.*

Andy Rutter, for Sayers, said: "This offence was motivated by the deepest sympathy for his auntie Muriel. His eldest daughter emigrated to Tenerife and he was planning to join her with his wife and other three children because he knows children bearing his surname are not going to be able to lead a productive life in this area.

Judge Whitburn said the fact Ramsay is Mrs Donnelly's full-time career meant he was able to take an exceptional course and suspend his 12-month prison sentence for two years as part of a community order.

Stephen and Joseph were jailed on 25th February 2010. This was a blow for Stephen who had turned his life around since his release from the blackmail sentence. His time in jail gave him plenty time to reflect on his life and on a succession of visits to him I floated the idea of him writing a book which had previously been met with disapproval. Stephen and the family weren't keen on publicity and the limelight. It wasn't the way that they were brought up. He said that he would give it some thought and we could discuss it when he was a free man. I was going to keep him to that.

During the build up to the trial Stephen's Dad John Brian Sayers had been arrested in December 2009 and was facing nine counts of fraudulently obtaining cash by falsely declaring his income between 2003 and 2007. He pleaded not guilty.
The Chronicle reported it as follows:

Prosecutors claim John Brian Sayers obtained £550,000 by deception from the Lancashire Mortgage Co-operative between July and August 2004. He denies a similar charge with regard to the Commercial Building Society of obtaining £622,000 by deception between January and March 2006. Sayers also denies obtaining £380,000 by deception from Mortgages Plc between January and March 2006.
He pleaded not guilty to obtaining £255,839 from Northern Rock between September and October 2003. Sayers further denies obtaining £337,435 from HBOS in 2004.

A further charge relates to Harpmanor and said to involve him getting £96,000 by deception between November 2004 and April 2005. He also denies a similar charge relating to Abbey National in 2006 and said to involve £132,410. He faces a similar charge regarding a mortgage advance of £30,000 from Capstone Mortgage Services Ltd in May 2007.

Sayers is also accused of obtaining £206,000 by deception from Birmingham Midshires between November and December 2007.

He denies laundering £400,000 between 2005 and 2007. He pleaded not guilty to money laundering between 2005 and 2006, when he is said to have used £150,000 of criminal property.

Things were just going from bad to worse for the family. They needed a change of fortune and quickly.

Chapter Forty Two: Raoul Moat

Stephen had been locked up for about 10 months in HMP Durham. He was in a lovely deep sleep and there she was, the girl of his dreams, Cheryl Cole Sayers. Then all of a sudden, he was awoken by a riot bell going off ringing outside his door because someone had been caught doing something they shouldn't have. Some foolish smack head had spoilt the best dream a man ever could wish for in jail! The bells were blaring and the screws were screaming for everyone to clear the landings and go behind their doors. The majority of screws from the wing had restrained this lad who was screaming to the high heavens for his mother.

Stephen was shaking his head thinking what could his mother possibly do. They carried him down the block. F-wing fell silent again. He then looked at the gab of his cell door and saw his newspaper. He bent down to pick it up and as he did a stiff came under the door.

In prison there are two kinds of mail delivery. One is legal and by the prison service which is assisted by the royal mail for the price of a stamp and the other kind is illegal and run by the inmates. Someone with a trustee's job, a red band which is a letter passed by an inmate for an inmate on a different wing. The name for this kind of mail is "stiffs". Stephen looked through his spy hole to see who had sent it. The lad showed his face and he recognised him from his previous time in Frankland prison. They briefly spoke and Stephen asked him who the stiff was from and he told him it was from a doorman from Newcastle who claimed to have known him but he wasn't told his name. Stephen thanked him, he wished him luck for his forthcoming trial and off he went.

Stephen would get a lot of these types of letters in jail. He'd receive ten letters or so from inmates in Durham jail a week asking for various things, help or advice in one way or another. Whether they were being bullied or had an incoming family member or friend who they wanted him to look after. The Sayers name was the biggest name in North East jails and if people needed help then they would turn to them.

Stephen sat down and opened the letter and he began to read it. It felt like he was reading the words of a man who was struggling with pain and clearly felt wronged and victimised. This man was asking Stephen for advice. It was clear he was hurting. Stephen read the letter a couple of times that day. The tone and words within the letter concerned Stephen. He hadn't decided what to do and needed a bit of time to consider his reply. He decided to sleep on it.

The following morning was a Friday and Stephen's friend's son young 'Riggers' had arrived on the landing. He was inside for a one punch murder. He had been in Newcastle one night and ended up in some sort of altercation with another reveller. A punch was thrown and the man who got hit fell to the floor and bumped his head and unfortunately passed away, 'Riggers' never intended to do anything like that, it is not in his nature to kill. He liked a fight but he was not a killer. Stephen had managed to pull a few strings to get him on the wing with him and he was being placed on his landing in a cell facing Stephen who grew up with his Dad Michael 'Rig' Ridley in Elswick who like Stephen was an 'Elswick Mafia Boy'. Even though the street gang does not exist anymore the bond between them is still strong.

The screw brought him over and opened the door so he could put his stuff in the cell and Stephen thanked him. He had no problem with showing young 'Riggers' the ropes. They were both called to reception so they dumped his stuff and headed up there.

Reception is a busy place first thing on a morning. It's organized chaos because there are some people being released whilst others are heading out to Court for the day. It's a place for flashpoints too where cons who don't see eye to eye pass each other and can end up kicking off with each other. On this particular morning as they approached reception Stephen could see through the holding room glass window that three men were punching the living daylights out of this other man who was holding his own until he ran out of gas. There were no screws in sight. Stephen and Riggers were still in the passage way and had not been put in the holding rooms yet. The first screw arrived on the scene and saw what was going on and hit the riot bell and started screaming "Staff, staff!" About twenty screws appeared in reception within seconds and they burst into the holding room which was holding about thirty inmates who were on their way to court. Now the rest of the screws had arrived another twenty or thirty if not more were charging in Stephen's direction. Stephen and 'Riggers' were still standing outside the door. You have to be cautious in this type of situation that you are not in the screws vision as a participant as you have fifty screws who all want to get physical.

By now the inmates in the holding room were being severely restrained and carried out one by one to the holding cells. When the brother of a lad who had been beaten up decided to get involved, he had chosen to stand right next to Stephen and started throwing punches at the inmate who he believed had inflicted the injuries. A lot of screws came charging towards him and Stephen. They dived on top of him and in the process fell into Stephen. He had to get out of this situation or he would have been hauled away too.

No sooner had that thought crossed Stephen's mind then a big pair of arms came around him and got him in a bear hug and lifted him up and spun him in the opposite direction. In doing so this person was distancing and shielding Stephen with his body against the screws and keeping Stephen away from all the trouble. At the time Stephen was 16 1/2 stone and this person had lifted him up with the greatest of ease. When he turned round and released Stephen unharmed, there was no aggression in his face and no malice or badness this man was helping Stephen.

It was Raoul Moat. He gave Stephen a friendly cuddle. He was genuinely happy to see him. As the screws restored order, they were ushered into the holding room together and Raoul asked Stephen if he had received his letter. This was the man that had written the emotional 'stiff' that had been placed under his door the previous day. Stephen told him he had but that he'd not had time to reply and as he was aware that he was being released in the next day or two that he wasn't comfortable writing him a letter that he may not get a chance to read. What Stephen had to tell him was better said face to face.

They managed to grab twenty minutes together in that holding room and the words they exchanged between each other remain a secret. The screw shouted for Raoul to leave; he was getting released. He gave Stephen another cuddle and wished him well. Stephen told him that if he couldn't be good be careful. We all know what happened next.

Chapter Forty Three: Supergrass

Friday 25th September 2009 and The Sayers brothers, John and Stephen, found themselves back in the dock but this time together when they were arrested for concocting a jury nobbling plot during the Freddie Knights trial and together with Mark Rowe were charged with perverting the course of justice. The prosecutor was Kingsley Hyland.

As the clerk of the court asked John his date of birth he replied "25th September," the clerk looked up and replied "I don't know if this is appropriate Mr Sayers but Happy Birthday."

They stood trial at Woolwich Crown Court in November 2010 thanks to a 'Supergrass by the name of Errol Hay, Hay was a registered police informant and had been for two decades, and was a self-confessed cocaine addict who came forward and claimed that he had made a late night phone call to a jury member Robert Black during the murder trial. Black's name had been read out in court by mistake.

Hay claimed he used an Irish accent and said, "Do you know you've got to make the right decision tomorrow? Your family will be taken care of and you will receive £10,000." He claimed that he was told to make the call by John.

The following day John was found not guilty on all charges. Jonathon Goldberg QC who was defending John told a very different story which was covered by the Evening Chronicle:

Jonathon Goldberg QC, has claimed Hay confessed to the crime because rival Paddy Conroy plotted to send him back to prison.
Hay, described as a "joke figure" who pined for Sayers' attention, knew Conroy after the pair served time in prison together, the court heard.
And during the hearing at Woolwich Crown Court, Sayers' barrister claimed Hay had rehearsed his story and admitted to the crime to win the "gratitude" of the Conroy family.
It was also claimed during the Knights murder trial at Leeds Crown Court, Sayers had accused his rival Conroy of being behind the slaying.
Mr Goldberg said: "Paddy was there when you were in the gallery at Leeds. You saw him a number of times.
"He was there listening and you know there's no-one greater in the whole world Paddy Conroy hates more than John Henry Sayers. Everyone knows that.
"You knew that anyone who could attack John Henry Sayers would get the gratitude of the Conroys."
He added: "I'm betting you've talked to the person who did make that call and you've been briefed to pretend that you made that call.
"The fact that a juror's name was read out in court was a notorious fact in the gallery.
"The fact it was read out was a well-known fact in that trial and anyone sitting in the gallery could've heard it.

"Mr Conroy was one of those people who was regularly in that gallery as well as the many other supporters for both sides.
"It was the best entertainment in town.
"You've said the reason Mr Mark Rowe was at the trial was as muscle because the Knights had the Conroys on their side.
"But during the murder trial a few weeks earlier, Mr Sayers said Paddy Conroy had been behind the killing of Freddie Knights. That was hot gossip in the Newcastle area."
Mr Goldberg claimed it wasn't Hay who made the call, but that he had been given a "rehearsed" insight into what happened in a bid to topple Sayers and put him back behind bars.

This accusation just did not make sense at all. As you have already read in this book, the trial was going well for John Sayers so why would he choose to sabotage his chance of freedom. It would however make sense for any enemy of Sayers to want the trial collapse. Hays also claimed that he was personally thanked by John at 'The Prince Of Wales' pub at a homecoming party. It was all pure fantasy. During the trial it was mentioned that Hays was not a well man, and had just undergone major surgery which had been touch and go.

The trial collapsed just before Christmas in 2010 when it was revealed that Crown Prosecution solicitor David Kingsley Hyland OBE failed to disclose key evidence which prejudiced the trial. He had clearly supressed evidence that would have blown apart Hay's case and Mr Justice Jeremy Cooke hauled him over the coals at a heavily guarded court:

"In my judgement, there was a deliberate, conscious decision to flout the rules of disclosure with a view to putting forward the least damaging admission possible. That took place over an extended period of time with procrastination and prevarication. Whether this is termed bad faith or serious default of duty does not in the end to my mind matter.
It was a gross failure which has undoubtedly prejudiced the defendant and has resulted in an unfair trial in front of this jury which is not curable.
This in my judgement is one of those rare cases where the abuse is so serious because the prosecution has manipulated the process of the court and derived advantages they should not have achieved."

The Evening Chronicle clearly spelled out Hyland's error:
And after making an initial call, Hay said he travelled to a second telephone box less than two miles away in Hetton-le-Hole to ring a second number.
But it has emerged that police launched an investigation to analyse call records from the second box identified by Hay.
Intelligence gathered by detectives showed the call could not have been made

from any of the 14 telephone boxes in Hetton-le-Hole.
And when 48 boxes were checked in a three-mile radius around the area, they too drew a blank for any calls made to Leeds.
Mr Hyland, the head of complex casework unit for Northumbria CPS, claimed he "took his eye off the ball" and insisted he had intended to pass on the information during the course of the trial.
But Mr Justice Cooke blasted the CPS, claiming they had failed to be "full and frank" in disclosing key evidence that would damage their case.
He said: "I have no doubt that (Mr Hyland) was looking to minimise the damage to Mr Hay's credibility and to the prosecution case by making as limited an admission as possible."
He added: "The material was undoubtedly damaging to the prosecution and assisted the case of the defendants in what is essentially, from the prosecution's perspective, a one witness case.
"The defendants knew that the police had been unable to trace a kiosk from which the second call was made but had not appreciated that the police enquiries revealed that the second call could not have been made from the box identified by Mr Hay nor that the billing information established that the call could not have come from any phone box in the area."
Officers from Northumbria Police were praised for their investigation, but CPS chiefs knew of Hay's foul-up before they took the decision to charge Mr Sayers and his co-accused.
The Chief Crown Prosecutor for Northumbria, Wendy Williams, said: "We are disappointed the jury did not have the opportunity to consider the case in full and reach a verdict.
"We recognise the defence raised an important point but disagreed with their argument that we deliberately withheld material."

So another waste of tax payers money and another indication of the lengths the authorities were prepared to go to obtain a conviction. The Sayers brothers and Rowe were going home for Christmas but there was an aftermath to this particular story.

First John Scott and his mother Rosemary came forward and spoke to the Chronicle about their disgust that Hay had avoided a 12-year jail sentence for pistol whipping John in 2003 causing him serious head injuries. Hay had attacked him whilst he was asleep in a house in Weldon Crescent in Heaton with a replica gun. He dumped the replica gun in the Tyne, paid £800 to have the blood cleaned out of the carpet and then raised £2000 to give to John to buy his silence. He had apparently carried out the cowardly attack in revenge for bullying a teenager.

Hay had clearly agreed to turn Supergrass against John Sayers to reduce his sentence and he was rewarded handsomely with a nine-month suspended sentence for the attack. John Scott was unable to return to work and

Hay, who had undergone surgery during the trial was informed that his cancer was terminal and in April 2011 the Chronicle claimed that he had died in Thailand after fleeing there after the collapse of the trial to spend his dying days with his wife and child. His family on Tyneside had disowned him after the trial. A letter was received by the Sayers legal team from Northumbria Police. The letter read as follows:

"I write to inform you that Errol Malcolm Hay, a witness for the Crown in a recent trial involving your client Mr J Sayers, sadly died this morning, Monday, April 4, of natural causes."
Despite the police statement many on Tyneside still believe Hays is alive and well and in the process of writing a book. People I have spoken to claim they have seen him as recently as Christmas 2019.

Chapter Forty Four: The Brightest Star In The Sky

On his release from prison John was determined to start a new life with his partner Louise Smith and his beloved family. Louise had previously worked as a dance and fitness instructor before meeting John and going into business running 'La Gabbia' restaurant in Ouseburn which was opened by former Newcastle United player Steven Taylor at a star-studded night. She also raised money for the Chronicles Sunshine Fund with numerous fundraising events.

I had visited John over the course of his sentence at a variety of Cat A prisons and we met for lunch at 'Paradiso' in Newcastle on his release and we talked about his plans for the future. It was clear that he just wanted the opportunity to live his life. He had Louise by his side and she soon fell pregnant and the baby was due October 2011. They celebrated the birth of their daughter 9 months later but celebration turned to tragedy as Louise collapsed at home 48 hours later. John tried to resuscitate her as the paramedics arrived.

A spokeswoman for the North East Ambulance Service was interviewed by the Chronicle, said: "We were called to a high alert incident and two vehicles were automatically dispatched. We took the call at 11.27pm and the first vehicle set off 30 seconds later.

"The patient had suffered a cardiac arrest. CPR was administered at the scene and natural heart rhythm was restored.

"It took about 20 minutes to get the heart going and the ambulance then set off for the RVI hospital at around 11.51pm. We arrived seven minutes later at 11.58pm."

Louise was in intensive care for five days but sadly passed away with the cause of death confirmed as a brain haemorrhage.

The Funeral took place at St Mary's Cathedral on Clayton Street West on the 7th November in front of 500 mourners and hundreds locked outside. John asked mourners to wear colourful clothes. He wanted the ceremony to be a celebration of Louise's life. Her coffin arrived in the back of a gleaming white horse-drawn hearse. A silver star was placed on the top of the carriage to signify John's tribute to Louise as 'The brightest star in the sky.' On a wreath saying 'Louise' John wrote:

"You sprinkled love and harmony everywhere you went. I thank God for letting me share you for such a time. I love you more than I can ever say. John."

As part of the service John read out a wonderful tribute:

"For nine years you have made my life complete. I did not know that love could be so beautiful as your love for me and life. You have been stolen away from us in such a horrible way.
"The last three days we had together were blissful, to see you flourishing as a

new mammy was worth the pain and emptiness, I must endure for at least you were able to enjoy it."

John also revealed to the congregation that he had fulfilled Louise's final wish which was to donate her organs. He had received a letter from a man known only as Vince which he shared:

"Last week I underwent an operation at the Freeman Hospital for a new liver. I now know that liver came from Louise. She gave me the greatest gift of all – the gift of life."

Chapter Forty Five: Character Assassination

I have followed the Sayers story for many years and got to know the family very well. If there is one episode that sickens me the most it is the accusation of rape levelled at John Henry Sayers in August 2013.

On an early summer's morning police raided his home and the Evening Chronicle who had been tipped off were there to see it happen and this is what they reported:

In a statement released by Northumbria Police a spokesman said: "A search warrant was carried out at a premises in Fossway, Byker. A man was arrested."

Officers attended Mr Sayers' Euromarket business, which is a cash and carry wholesale company supplying food to restaurants across the North East, at around 8am.

Four police vans and two marked cars were used during the operation. A Golden Labrador search dog was led around the property and into a string of cars parked on the pavement outside the building.

A grey VW people carrier was also searched by officers wearing latex gloves before spades were taken from a police van into the rear of the property.

Two officers wearing forensic suits were seen analysing the bins down the side of the building while officers scaled the walls to gain access to the building. A man, who did not want to be named, witnessed the drama unfold. He said: "A man was brought out in handcuffs really early on. There were police here all morning and they've had dogs and forensic teams going over the house. It's crazy that this sort of thing is going on in broad daylight when people are driving past."

Mr Sayers lives in a flat above his Euromarket food supply company on Fossway, in Byker, Newcastle. The windows to his home are covered in metal mesh and tall steel fencing surrounds the property.

John appeared in court a couple of days later on the 17th August and was charged with three counts of rape and a count of conspiracy to rape alongside Sharon Loftus and Anne-Marie Taylor who were both charged with one count each of conspiracy to rape against one female victim. John entered no official plea and Richard Haswell defending indicated that his client denied all charges.

The Evening Chronicle were in the press gallery to report events:

Emotions ran high in the public gallery as about 20 of Sayers' family and friends, along with relatives of Loftus and Taylor, listened to the lengthy hearing. Loftus, 45, Wallsend, and Taylor, 42, Daisy Hill, Newcastle, also didn't enter official pleas although their solicitors, Kate Matthews and Peter Farrier, respectively indicated they too adamantly denied the charges.

Sayers, wearing a green top, told the court his name, date of birth and address, and occasionally turned to speak to his family in the back of court. Prosecutor Nick Cartmell said the charges could only be dealt with at the Crown Court.

He told the District Judge that the charges related to an alleged attack in Gillies Street, in Byker, on February 20 this year but a report wasn't made to the police until August 8

District Judge Sam Goozee remanded all three in custody until their next appearance at Newcastle Crown Court later this month.

The defence solicitors indicated they would be making an application for the case to be heard at Leeds Crown Court at that appearance.

When the judge told the court of his decision to remand the trio, some of the members of the public gallery burst into tears and Taylor, in the dock, fainted.

As Loftus was cuffed and led out of the dock, Sayers went to the aid of Taylor and was passed a glass of water to give to her.

A distressed, heavily pregnant woman in the gallery also had to be supported as she struggled to stand.

When Taylor came round, she was led away.

As Sayers was led away, he turned and waved to his family and shouted "I love you, bye, bye. I will be home soon, don't worry about me."

John and his co-accused were back in court on 31st August. He appeared by video link from Frankland Prison for a preliminary hearing at Newcastle Crown Court. The prosecution applied for the case to be held outside of Newcastle to 'get Sayers a fair trial'. The defence didn't oppose the application and Judge James Goss QC said he would see if he could get the case moved to Leeds. Journalist Rob Kennedy covering the hearing also announced that John would be applying for bail which he duly did and was rightly awarded at the beginning of October. His application had been originally rejected by prosecutors in September.

The conditions of bail were that he 'must not interfere with prosecution witnesses and must live and sleep at a specified address.' The prosecution had pushed for 'an electronically monitored curfew' but his barrister Andy Rutter objected on the grounds that 'He intended to restart playing rugby, and will not be able to do so with an electronic tag' and the Judge agreed with him. He was released along with Sharon Loftus and given a court date of 8th November for a plea and case management hearing, but John and his co-accused would not have to wait much longer for this farcical case to collapse.

On the 16th October John was a free man after spending more than eight weeks in Category A prisons including Frankland and Wakefield.

Dan Warburton of The Evening Chronicle reported the following:

Officials from the Crown Prosecution Service (CPS) and Northumbria Police said they had carried out an "extensive investigation" but confirmed the case had been discontinued.

They said they were "no longer satisfied there is sufficient evidence for a realistic prospect of conviction".

Mr Sayers said: "This charge was character assassination from the get go. "Anyone who knows me knows I was brought up the right way by my mother; to respect women."

During bail hearings earlier this year his legal team described it as a "hollow case" and said the evidence was "weak".

It emerged Mr Sayers wore a ring "the size of a dinner plate" which contained his late partner's ashes. And during police interview he stripped his shirt in an effort to prove his shoulder was not covered in tattoos, as claimed by witnesses.

Andrew Rutter told Newcastle Crown Court: "This is a man subject to constant surveillance and eavesdropping. He is one individual whose whereabouts will be known to the police 24 hours a day."

During the bail hearing prosecutors read transcripts from the 2002 murder trial of Freddie Knights in which prosecutors quizzed him on his notoriety in the North East.

Prosecutors claimed Mr Sayers "traded" on his reputation. Opposing bail, prosecutor Gavin Doig said: "We say Sayers has a fearful reputation and trades on that reputation and uses it.

"We fear if granted bail he is more likely to be able to use that reputation to interfere with the course of justice than if he were kept in custody."

Mr Sayers always denied conspiracy to rape and three allegations of rape at an address in Byker, Newcastle.

Sharon Loftus, 45, Wallsend, and Ann-Marie Taylor, 42, of Daisy Hill, were also accused of conspiracy to rape but the case against them has also been dropped.

CPS reviewing lawyer Helen Gaunt, from Yorkshire and Humberside's complex casework unit, said: "As part of our ongoing review process, I have carefully considered all the evidence I have received from the police, and consulted at length with leading counsel.

"I have applied the code for Crown Prosecutors and the CPS policy on prosecuting offences of rape.

"I have considered all the evidence in this case in accordance with the code for Crown Prosecutors and I am no longer satisfied that there is sufficient evidence for a realistic prospect of conviction against the defendants. On that basis I have advised discontinuance of the proceedings."

A Northumbria Police spokesman said: "We actively encourage people to report incidents of rape to either us or a third party.

"We treat every report of rape extremely seriously and have a duty to

investigate thoroughly every report we receive.
"An extensive investigation has taken place and a file of evidence was
presented to the CPS. The CPS made a decision to charge but has
subsequently made a decision not to proceed with the prosecution."

     John Henry Sayers was smeared with false rape allegations in order to
take him off the streets for as long as possible, his lawyers have told a court.
Sayers' barrister told the court the conduct of the prosecution had been
"lamentable" and said there had never been any chance of a conviction.
Andrew Rutter said Sayers had suffered the stigma of being accused of rape
only in order to have him locked up on remand as a category A prisoner for as
long as possible. And he claimed prosecutors only halted the case because he
had been released on bail.
Mr Rutter said: "We are dismayed at the conduct of the prosecution throughout
these proceedings.
"The decision to charge in August was based on them saying there was a
reasonable prospect of conviction. We are now told the same test is being
applied and the Crown form the view it no longer passes that test.
"One asks what has changed. The evidence has not changed as far as we know
since the decision to charge. One could say the case has got stronger against
Mr Sayers, who on September 9 was positively identified by the complainant.
"That begs the question what has changed? The one thing that springs to mind
is the bail status of Mr Sayers. The suspicion is this criminal process has been
used to incarcerate him for as long as possible, in the knowledge there was no
realistic prospect of conviction.
"He has then been passed from category A prison to category A prison to
category A prison and the fact of this allegation was plastered all over the local
press, with the stigma that attaches to allegations such as these. That leads to
the conclusion this was an abuse of the system."

     Sayers was granted bail earlier this month after weeks remanded in
high security prisons, including Frankland and Wakefield.
He had been refused bail in September when prosecutors said the police were
still trying to speak to witnesses.
But Mr Rutter said: "It turned out they were looking for further victims, not evi-
dence to link Mr Sayers to the premises. It led to further incarceration when it
was not necessary.
"The conduct of the prosecution throughout has been lamentable and is very
much open to question."

     Prosecutors said the complainant had been re-interviewed and after
reviewing the evidence, a decision was taken to discontinue the case against
Sayers, Sharon Loftus and Ann-Marie Taylor.
The prosecution admitted they then sent two letters to the defendants
containing errors, which further complicated matters.

     In the first they said the trio should plead not guilty and not guilty verdicts would be entered, but they meant to say the case would be discontinued. The difference is a case can be resurrected without leave from the Court of Appeal when it is only discontinued. A second letter referred in error to proceedings taking place in the magistrate's court, rather than the crown court.

In another mistake, no-one from the prosecution turned up at court for a hearing at the end of September.

Robert Adams, for Miss Loftus, said: "It's a concern the way the case has been conducted."

Taylor's barrister said her name had been "dragged through the mud in the city where she lives" on allegations which were without foundation. And he said she had received no explanation or apology for what happened to her.

Sayers always denied conspiracy to rape and three allegations of rape at an address in Byker, Newcastle. Miss Loftus, 45, Wallsend, and Miss Taylor, 42, Daisy Hill, also strenuously denied allegations of conspiracy to rape.

The trio sat in the public gallery at yesterday's hearing as the case was formally halted. Sayers has described the allegations as a "character assassination" by police.

That is exactly what this was, 'character assassination.' As a footnote to the case the prostitute who had made the charges came forward and admitted that she had been 'pressurised' into making the statements against John. This came as no surprise to Sayers or his legal team.

After spending Christmas at home with the family John took the unprecedented step of writing an open letter to the Evening Chronicle in February 2014 to reveal his anguish at losing his mam and wife during a seven-year probe into his finances. Branded a "crime boss" by prosecutors, John Henry Sayers claimed "rats" had been trading on his name in a failed bid to secure their own freedom.

In his letter to the paper, John wrote:

This case has dragged on for seven years and during that time I have lost my two best friends, my mother, Yvonne, and my wife, Louise Smith. Through the love and support of my extended family and friends and the dogged professionalism of my solicitor Richard Haswell, I have remained upstanding.

The case has cost many hundreds of thousands of pounds needlessly. The assets that I had in those days would have paid over £1m back to the taxpayer had they been handled properly.

The previous week he had appeared in court as detectives secured a serious crime prevention order and confiscated £230,000 from his empire that he had stashed in Cyprus and Spain. He was also ordered to pay nearly £30,000 left from his estate after receivers stripped "extraordinary amounts" from his assets which included a string of pubs across the North East. He had admitted staging the £400,000 tax scam in 2008 and was sentenced to four years in prison.

When I arrived at Woolwich Crown Court to contest the Proceeds of Crime Act (POCA) application I was told by my QC, Mr [Nicholas] Valios, and his junior, Mr [Jamie] Carr, that this is the most unfair legislation ever devised and that in essence I could not win any argument because I have to prove that I do not have what the prosecution say I have. I therefore again had to agree this figure.

Rats – who like a lot of other low-lives – [have] decided to tell a pack of lies against me. This was simply so that [they] could avoid the consequences of the trouble that [they] found [themselves] in and would say anything the police wanted.

I pleaded guilty and it has taken seven years for the POCA to finally come to an end. These rats have no morals or scruples or any obligations to family or friends. They are leeches and parasites upon the people that they know for their own selfish greed.

The final insult was when I was falsely arrested for an offence last year, kept in custody for six weeks, only to be released without an apology. I am disappointed that I was not able to have my say in court but I am taking this opportunity to redress the balance.

These are my own personal views and I have waited a long time to say them.

This was not the first time John had spoken out against the Supergrasses. He had appeared on a BBC1 Panorama in October 2012 on an episode entitled 'Return Of The Supergrass' and said;

"It's too easy for anybody to go and tell lies without there being any fear of reprisal by the system. In 1990 I got 15 years for conspiracy to rob. In 2007 I got four years for tax evasion and in between that I've had two to three years on remand for different offences. I knew the police would leave us alone for a short while because they had been embarrassed but I knew they would be coming back."

And how right he was...

A Northumbria Police spokesman used the Chronicle to dismiss his claims. They said:

"We strongly refute any suggestion that we unnecessarily target individuals.
"Northumbria Police has a duty to investigate any reports or allegations of criminal behaviour and acts with the highest level of integrity and professionalism in doing so.
"Mr Sayers was sentenced to four years in prison in 2008 after pleading guilty to

offences involving fraud and tax evasion. It was right that we used confiscation powers following this and are pleased with the decision of the court to return to the public purse."

This financial game of cat and mouse continued into 2015 and John was front page news again regarding a shortfall in payments after a clever legal move by Richard Haswell. The Chronicle reported on the 8th July 2015 that John had paid back a fraction of a suspected £900,000 tax swindle. They claimed that the prosecutors and police faced criticism after a ten-year investigation had netted just £214,224.66 of John's cash. He had been ordered to pay back the cash or face a return to jail. Following the shortfall his lawyers applied for a Certificate of Inadequacy. This was granted which meant John did not have to pay back the remainder of the cash. Police refused to comment on how much the investigation cost.

In the Chronicle article Richard Haswell claimed that receivers had failed to look after tax payers' interests. He said:

"The tax payer has lost a vast amount of money in this case.
"The receivers have just looked after their own costs and not the tax payers' interests. If they had come to us originally for this amount of money it would have been paid, saving time and tax payers' money."
In one transaction it is believed they handed back Sayers' Howlett pub, on Whickham View, Denton Burn, to the mortgage company who then sold it to a national supermarket chain for hundreds of thousands of pounds.
It's now being argued that some that this cash could have been funnelled into the public purse through the Proceeds of Crime Act instead.
A police spokeswoman said: "We would not disclose costs of such investigations."
A spokesperson from the CPS said that Sayers had been granted a Certificate of Inadequacy after the necessary inquiries were made and the file is now closed.
"We only use receivers when it is efficient and effective to do so," the spokesperson added. "Whilst receivers are procured by us, they are approved by the court and work for the court. Their fees and expenses are paid out of the sums that they manage to reclaim from convicted criminals and this must be approved by the court."

The Chronicle went on to explain the chain of events as follows:

Prosecutors originally claimed Sayers had benefited to the tune of £898,956.32 from a four-year tax scam whilst he was in charge of a network of pubs across the North East. Detectives seized £29,938.66 after obtaining a High Court ruling which froze Sayers assets in 2009. It was during an intricate examination of his accounts they discovered evidence he had stashed £220,061.34 in Cyprus and Spain.

Police had originally claimed John had made £1,761,840.73 before he was jailed in 2008 for four years in prison for the tax scam. But following a change in legislation that figure was revised to less than £900,000. It's claimed that much of Sayers' personal fortune went to receivers appointed by the High Court to manage his assets. The Chronicle understands the team of receivers were paid in the region of £400,000 in fees as they staged a fire-sale of Sayers' long list of assets.

Chapter Forty Six: Operation Erebus

The John Brian Sayers case that I mentioned in Chapter 41 finally reached its conclusion in 2013 to when forensic medical consultants ruled him unfit to stand trial diagnosing him with a depressive illness stating he would have "difficulties instructing his legal advisor or following court proceedings".

Prof Don Grubin, a specialist in forensic psychiatry at Newcastle University who also worked with Northumberland Tyne and Wear NHS Foundation Trust, told a court hearing 72-year-old Sayers suffered from "depressive episodes".

He said: "It's right that I have seen the defendant John Brian Sayers and prepared reports on him in relation to whether he is fit to plead or not."

Prosecutors accepted the diagnosis and the judge ruled that his mental illness made him unfit to plead and as a result could not face prison for his crime. He had been allegedly fiddling his VAT forms, claiming that he had made £8,000 over 8 years but he was actually making tens of thousands of pounds from a business portfolio that included rented property, a men's hostel and pubs across Tyneside. This had all come to light during investigations into John Henry's tax affairs and the police launched 'Operation Erebus.' Investigators alleged that he owed in the region of a half a million pounds to HMRC. The Chronicle reported the following:

John Black QC told the jury Sayers – who said he had 30 years' experience as a property tycoon – submitted mortgage applications claiming he earned as much as £180,00-a-year from a pub, a men's hostel, a care home and rented property. But at the same time, he dodged tax totalling more than £460,000 over an eight-year period.

Defending barrister Nicholas Valios QC argued Sayers, of Moorside North, Fenham, Newcastle, should be given an absolute discharge for the swindle. He said his client is already attending appointments voluntarily with psychiatrists.

He told the court: "He has been undergoing psychiatric treatment for some years in any event and will continue to undergo that treatment.

"It is important to consider if a supervision order or attaching a condition is going to serve, in reality, any useful purpose. The probation service just don't understand the law for unfit to plead."

Sayers was also accused of carrying out a mortgage fraud by securing loans and re-mortgaging deals on properties in Moorside North where properties sell for in excess of £500,00.

The allegations also centred on a men's hostel on Westmorland Road, Newcastle, and a re-mortgaging deal on land near Market Street, Hetton-le-Hole, County Durham. Prosecutors claimed he said he was a hotelier and property developer to secure loans from institutions including Northern Rock, Harpmanor Ltd and the Lancashire Mortgage Corporation. But it was claimed this was a lie to dupe lenders into giving him loans so that he could "rob Peter to pay Paul".

The grandad was feeding his own debt and accumulating vast sums of cash totalling around £710,000 in his personal Barclays' bank account. Between 2003 and 2007 six companies granted him mortgages after he claimed to own a 100% share in a property development company on Westgate Hill Terrace, Newcastle, named JB Sayers Properties, it is said.

A defence team denied the accusation and insisted he was not tricking the institutions by lying about his occupation and the purpose of his loans.

Judge Guy Kearl imposed a supervision order on John Brian to undergo treatment. Eight counts of fraud were left on file and whilst the prosecution chose not to seek a retrial on an accusation of mortgage fraud, his solicitor was advised that should his health improve the prosecution had the right to demand a retrial on the other 8 counts and that if he was found guilty he could face a spell in prison. In court the Judge handed him a two-year supervision order and said:

"This is not a conviction; this is a finding of the court that he has done the act. He has not been convicted and this is the most appropriate order. This is a supervision order on mental health provision to take the medication and undergo treatment with a psychiatrist."

It was not only the Sayers family who were put under investigation in the noughties. 'Operation Grapple' was set up to investigate Tony Leach and Mark Rowe and his immediate family. They were alleged to be involved in a cash conspiracy and were originally charged with money laundering, but the case eventually collapsed in March 2011 as prosecutors were unable to prove that the £102.795 that Leach had placed into his partner Paula Rowe's account was 'dirty money.' Mark Rowe admitted tax evasion admitting that he had put £12,000 into the 'Turbinbia Pub' but had not declared it and not paid tax on it. The Chronicle covered the case:

Paula Rowe, Mark's sister and partner of Leach, pleaded guilty to two counts of deception, having lied to a mortgage company about her salary to get advances of £4,000 and £10,000 on the mortgage. She kept up the repayments.

Leach, 45, of High Heaton, got 12 months suspended for 12 months, with supervision and was fined £1,000 and told to pay £1,000 towards prosecution costs.

Mark Rowe, 40, of Walker, was fined £3,000 plus £2,000 costs and £3,390 compensation.

The Police seemed to have Rowe on their radar after he was arrested and questioned alongside Stephen Sayers and Lee Cheetham. Cheetham was arrested on a conspiracy to murder charge after a shooting on December 14th in the 'Wheatsheaf Pub' carpark that left 47 year old Colin Ferry with gunshot wounds in his arm and leg. Three weeks later a 54 year old man was shot in the back on wasteland in Seaton Burn, North Tyneside.

The Chronicle reported that Cheetham had been issued with an 'Osman Warning,' which is a threat to his life. Cheetham, who owned LTT Tyres on Union Road, Byker in the city's East End, and lived with his wife Corrina, 38, said:

"I don't know who carried out these shootings but it's nothing to do with me. They are taking people in for 20 hours and it's a fishing exercise. The police are saying that someone is going to come and shoot me.They want me to implicate someone, but I don't know anything."

Police said the two attacks were a result of a "simmering feud" between gangland rivals and a spokesman previously stated the inquiry was centred on "internal disputes between criminals".

The Chronicle went on to explain that Mr Ferry had been put under armed guard following his shooting and had spoken to investigating officers.

Rowe who was 41 at the time was arrested and held for more than 20 hours as detectives continued to investigate the incidents.Officers had also raided a property on Chillingham Road in Heaton as well as a family business nearby as they stepped up their probe.

Chapter Forty Seven: Tup Tup Shooting: If You Can't Get The Cat Get The Kittens

Saturday June 6th 2015 10:30pm, and doorman Matthew McCauley was expecting a busy night at 'Tup Tup Palace.' The traffic lights had just changed and the roar of passing taxis and buses was broken with a few loud cracks and the roar of a motorbike, followed by a sharp pain. McCauley had been shot in the arm and two other staff were injured as the night air was filled with screams from innocent young Geordie girls looking for good time. The police and medical services were on the scene quickly, the venue was closed and the road outside the venue taped off causing total gridlock for punters on their nights out.

Two weeks prior to the shooting on 23rd May 2015 John Henry Sayers Jnr had attended the venue with his cousins and was ejected from the club by the doormen and had been punched in head by two of the doormen in the process. The incident was recorded on the CCTV system.

On the 28th May 2015 a person not connected to the Sayers in anyway John Gates was refused entry to 'Tup Tup' by McCauley as he was aggressive and threatening towards the staff. This man was well known to door staff in Newcastle, and wore a distinctive necklace with a gun pendant attached to it. He showed McCauley the necklace and said 'This bullet's for you." He then went on to threaten McCauley saying, "I'm going to get my shotgun and come back and shoot you." This incident was also captured on the club's CCTV. Within days of the shooting Northumbria Police took the bizarre step of issuing John Henry Sayers Jnr and his cousins Moe and Tommy Sayers a disruption notice which read as follows:

"Northumbria Police believe that you are involved in a threat to the personal safety of staff employed at Tup Tup Palace, Saint Nicholas Street, Newcastle Upon Tyne. We are concerned that these individuals, their family and/or their properties may be harmed or damaged by yourself and/or your associates. I therefore suggest that you take such remedial action to ensure you or others who you know or believe may be involved in this matter to refrain from any act, which would amount to a threat or use of violence towards another."

This infuriated Stephen Sayers who approached his solicitor Richard Haswell for advice and he decided to raise the issue with reporter Katie Davies at the Evening Chronicle. In a frank interview he said:

"It's relentless persecution by Northumbria Police. It's a case of hate the cat, hate the kittens. "They haven't followed in the footsteps of their father and they are both going into the Marines - one in just four weeks' time. Because I've said I've turned my back on crime I ultimately feel the powers that be are now causing a disruption on a higher level. They will link the Sayers to anything.

I was what I was but not anymore.

Northumbria Police have had more than a pound of flesh from our family and now they want a leg or a head. It was nothing to do with us whatsoever. We didn't know the person that was shot. My sons are going to fight for Queen and country - one next month and the other is in training. My nephew is also a cadet. They haven't followed in the footsteps of my brother and I. They are law abiding people who just want to do their bit for their country. They are quiet lads; they are good lads. They box and they are preparing themselves for the military and are trying to get their fitness levels up."

A 26-year-old man was then arrested on suspicion of attempted murder but released without charge early into the investigation and then it fell silent for a while.

I got a call from Stephen on the 1st November 2016 asking if I could get a hold of Neil Jackson from Media Arts as he wanted him to do some filming. Could I also get a hold of a Chronicle journalist as he wanted some publicity for something, he wanted to do that week.

Stephen along with John and Mark Rowe were going to launch legal action claiming £30,000 against the head of complex casework unit for Northumbria CPS David Kingsley Hyland OBE for supressing evidence to keep them in prison during the Jury nobbling trial. This was the man who had stood up in court stipulating that in the case of the Sayers brothers in this case 'Life should mean life!' Once the deception was outed in court Hyland claimed that he, "took his eye off the ball," and insisted that was always his intention to present this information in the trial. I will leave you the reader to decide whether that would have been the case!

Mr Justice Cooke had been less than impressed with the revelations and said, "The material was undoubtedly damaging to the prosecution and assisted the case of the defendants in what is essentially, from the prosecution's perspective, a one witness case. In my judgement, Mr Hyland was always looking to avoid disclosure by giving an admission in as limited a form as the documents allowed."

Keiran Southern from the Chronicle joined Neil, Stephen and myself in a leafy affluent part of Tyneside on the 3rd November 2016. We had an address for Hyland. Stephen wanted to doorstep him and hand him the papers in front of the media. With Neil and I filming and Keiran taking notes Stephen knocked at the door and after a short while a woman answered. Stephen asked if Kingsley was home as he had something for him. The woman looked confused. She had never heard of him. It turned out that the sat-nav had sent us to the wrong house and Kingsleys house was actually around the next corner of the cul-de-sac.

As we started walking towards the house, I caught a glimpse of a man walking towards us with shopping bags. It was him. We turned the camera on

him as Stephen said 'Kingsley you know who I am. I have something for you."
With that he handed over the papers to the startled man. "See you in court,"
Stephen said as we headed back to the car. Keiran ran the story the following
day. Job done. It would be interesting to see how this one played out.

Meanwhile tragedy struck the Sayers family again in November 2016
with the death of the Sayers brothers' Mam Yvonne. She had suffered a stroke
five years earlier and had never truly recovered. Her funeral was held the
following month at a packed St Mary's with Stephen leading the tributes in the
Chronicle. He said:

*"My mother was a very special woman. She was always there for me and my
brothers as children. We never wanted for anything. She was always working
hard to make sure that we had the best of everything and as we grew older she
was always there for us. Since the stroke our mother has needed round the
clock care and she really had no quality of life. I would like to thank our friends
and family for their support and condolences at this difficult time and give
special thanks to our good friend Ellen who has been caring for our mother
each day over the last five years."*

Early morning raids on Wednesday 8th February 2017 saw 12 men
arrested including John Henry and Stephen Sayers. Two days later Tyne Tees
Television announced that three men had been charged. John Henry Sayers
and Michael Dixon were charged with conspiracy to murder whilst 'Tup Tup'
Doorman Russell Sturman was charged with assisting an offender in the
commission of an offence. The other nine men including Stephen were released
on bail pending further enquiries.

In interview John recognised the officer who had personally
interviewed him and tried to fit him up for rape in his previous case "immediately" but said nothing until four hours into the interview because he knew what
was going on and was not happy about it.
"Honesty doesn't come into Northumbria Police when they are dealing with
me," John said in the transcripts and refers to them as, "the same group of bent
bizzies." He also said: "Last time you sat opposite me in an interview room you
accused me of rape. To me, it's the worst crime going, so I don't trust you."

The transcripts show the officer denying fitting him up but admitting
that it was him which should not have been allowed to happen. John, Mickey,
and Russell were to appear at South East Northumberland Magistrates court in
Bedlington the following day.

I had been working that week with Stephen on his documentary and
he asked me if I would attend the hearing with him. I was happy to and booked
in Neil Jackson from Media Arts to film the day's events. Stephen said he would
pick me up on the day at 9:30pm. I was up and ready but Stephen wasn't
running on time. His daughter Stevie-Lee called me at 9:45am asking if we

had left yet and I told her that I was still waiting for her Dad to pick me up.

As I was on the phone, I could see the police helicopter flying towards my house. This wasn't uncommon, you would usually see it once a week if not more. It seemed to getting closer to my house though which was strange. I then saw Stephen's white van pulling into my street at speed. As he pulled in the helicopter was just hovering over my house. It was like that scene in 'Goodfellas' where Henry Hill played by Ray Liotta is paranoid that he is being followed. Well there was certainly no question here that we had our very own escort to Bedlington.

When we arrived at court we parked up on double yellow lines. Stephen pointing out that he didn't pay the fines so he wasn't concerned. As we got towards the court, I counted at least 8-armed response cars and 14-armed officers. As we approached one of the cars we were told to stop and asked for our names and date of births. This security was completely over the top and clearly for show. The police were fine with us and once the checks came through, we were on our way. Neil was on the other side of the cordon and like me could not believe what we were seeing.

Neil stayed outside as Stephen and I headed into court and joined the rest of the family including Stephen's sons Moe and Tommy, and John's daughters Rachel and Antionette and son John Henry Jnr.

The clerk of the court tried to explain that only a few of us would be allowed into the court but to be fair he was on a hiding to nothing. I took my place in the press gallery as proceedings got underway. John, Mickey and Russell stood together in the dock behind a glass partition. John gave me a wink and acknowledged his family as the charges were read out. Mickey was already serving a sentence in Holme House so he headed back to prison, John was remanded whilst Russell was released on bail with specifications that he had to reside at a particular address. John expected as much and knew that he would be facing another long wait behind bars as a Cat A prisoner.

John appeared by video-link from Wakefield Prison on March 10th 2017 at Newcastle Crown Court. Mickey Dixon did likewise from Frankland and Russell Sturman was in the dock as they all pleaded not guilty to the charges. A provisional date of August 7th was set for trial in Newcastle but as anticipated application was put in by barristers to move the trial to another area and there was once again a push for a trial without jury which was keenly contested and overturned by defence barristers.

I visited John at Wakefield in July 2017 with good friends Karen Seafield and Jason Heels. We went through the check procedures and past the sniffer dog. We were then taken through another couple of doors into another smaller room where we were searched again by screws before finally accessing a special room for Cat A prisoners like John. Another visit was taking place in there too. Colin Gunn a notorious gangster from Nottingham was having a visit from friends as John greeted us all.

John informed us that he had seen his solicitor that week and that there had been an interesting development. Michael McDougall was serving a life sentence for the murder of a takeaway boss in South Shields Tipu Sultan and he had approached John on the exercise yard one day and told him that he had carried out the shooting at 'Tup Tup'.

John wasn't convinced by the 'confession' in fact he thought he was wearing a 'wire' but notified his solicitor and a statement was taken. McDougall claimed that he had been approached at the last minute to act as a gunman in a drive-by shooting and that he was offered £5000 in cash and a substantial quantity of cocaine in payment. Was this the bit of luck he needed or a cunning plan by the authorities? It wasn't clear until both John and McDougall were arrested for perverting the course of justice.

To me it appeared that the evidence on the case was weak and circumstantial against John and to save embarrassment the police and the prosecution needed a 'plan B' to justify the costs of the investigation and this was it.

They say you have never made it in criminal circles until you have a trial at the Old Bailey in London. A court which has seen showcase trials for the Krays, The Richardsons and now the Sayers. John Henry and his co-accused stood trial in the summer of 2018.

The prosecution claimed that John had ordered the shooting of door staff at 'Tup Tup' after the assault of his son at the venue. They claimed that he had recruited Sturman to find out who was responsible and old friend Michael Dixon to send the message that you 'don't mess with the Sayers' by carrying out the shooting.

As I mentioned earlier the case itself was weak. The police had no direct evidence connecting John to the conspiracy case. McDougall was also in the dock to stand trial alongside John for the perverting the course of justice charge, plan B.

CCTV was shown to the jury of John and McDougall looking at a laptop in a holding cell following on from their conversation on the exercise yard. The prosecution claimed that this was the moment that John told McDougall what he needed to say in his statement. The computer in question had actually frozen rendering it useless.

As I have already mentioned Dixon was already serving a sentence. He had been arrested as part of 'Operation Tobago'. This was a conspiracy to murder a man called Christopher Brown. The prosecution alleged that John Beckwith, Wayne Peel and Anthony Peel recruited Mickey Dixon to carry out the shooting. After legal discussions he pleaded guilty to conspiracy to possess a firearm with intent to cause fear of violence, which carries a maximum sentence of 10 years in prison.

The key evidence against Dixon in the 'Tup Tup' case was a piece of wadding found at the scene. Prosecution barrister Mr Dennison insisted that this wadding that was found at the scene by PC Denyer and given the name PD/1 which was 'picked up with his gloved hand and put into a new paper exhibits bag and then he had kept it inside that folded over paper bag until he returned to Forth Banks police station. He clearly knew that it was an important exhibit and he then transferred it into a plastic exhibit bag and sealed it inside that bag. Dennison continued:

"It remained sealed in that bag until it was taken to the forensic laboratory where it was taken out in sterile conditions and examined. A mixed DNA profile of at least five contributors was found. You know that the likelihood of that profile being from Michael Dixon and four others unknown rather than five un-known people is at least one in a billion".

Questions were asked of PC Denyer as to whether the plastic seal could be put on the bag but not pulled tight so the item can be removed - the 'old lag's trick.' Well there's not a shred of evidence to support that."
He went on to say that the gun recovered in Operation Tobago is *"just the sort of sized gun that must have been used in the shooting at Tup Tup Palace".*
All the evidence in that case was that he was a hired gunman. It proves he was willing to carry out a shooting using a sawn off-shotgun and a high-powered motorbike. And it proves he was willing to do it in furtherance of someone else's cause."
Phone evidence also went against Dixon. CCTV shows the gunman coming from the East of Newcastle, Walker. Dixon lived in Walker and was using his phone in that area prior to the shooting. His phone records also show that he had been in Ashington earlier that day. The significance of that being that the guns found during 'Operation Tobago' had been stored in Ashington. His phone records showed him back in Walker by 16:53pm. It had only been a flying visit to Ashington. Just long enough to pick 'something' up.
Dixon refused to make any statement once arrested and charged and refused to take the witness stand. The prosecution suggested that was because he had no explanation and with all this evidence against him that he was the gunman. Ms Wass defending Dixon tried in vain to convince the jury otherwise. She described the exhibit as "a tiny piece of plastic on which was found a minute piece of DNA". She went onto say that "From the moment that wadding was ejected from the shotgun, it was trampled over, breathed on, stored in an unclean jacket and then in circumstances we have no idea about. It was so contaminated I suggest you ignore the scientific findings. In that period of 10 minutes when it must have been on the ground it was trampled by people wanting to get into 'Tup Tup Palace." She also reminded jurors that it had been moved from a paper bag into a plastic bag potentially causing further contamination.
John took the witness stand in the case and the Evening Chronicle

it full coverage: He discussed his early days growing up in Newcastle first:

"It was a game - the police would try and catch my uncles and aunties, and we would try and not get caught.
"My great grandma and her nine daughters were all arrested for selling fruit and veg on the streets of Newcastle."
Sayers said he grew up thinking the police were "bullies" as a result.
He then moved onto how he had been 'fitted up' in previous cases.
The jury heard his first conviction was in 1990 for robbery, for which he still maintains his innocence.
"Northumbria Police employed an informer to say he had spoken to me and we had arranged it. He got a two-year sentence and I got 10."
After being released from prison in 1999 with a "reputation as an ex-robber", he says he went into an "informal debt collecting business".
Sayers said his reputation was helpful because "people were impressed by the fact I had been in prison for so long".

The court heard he was acquitted of another offence after a trial in 2002, and pleaded guilty to tax evasion in 2008.

In 2009 he was arrested on suspicion of approaching a juror in the 2002 trial. In the wake of the judge ruling he could not get a fair trial, Sayers said he made a Panorama programme about the use of informers giving evidence when they are being paid.

Sayers said that case "proved beyond a shadow of a doubt how corrupt they were towards me".

His barrister Michael Holland QC asked about how his reputation had stopped his efforts to go straight.

"I have never been able to do that since I got out in 1999.

"For an example, I work for my mother's business supplying fruit and veg to restaurants.

"If I go to a new restaurant to try and get work, the police come in behind me and say 'do you know who that is?'"

When asked whether he "wanted to give them an excuse to lock him up", he said he had "too much to lose" as the sole parent for two young children.

Sayers also told the court he found out McDougall was going to say he was the gunman on July 13, 2017 in the exercise yard.

"He revealed why he was in that prison.

"He explained what he had done in his offence, that he had just had treatment for cancer.

"I don't know how it came out but he just said he had done that one - the one that I was charged with."

Sayers said at that point he asked McDougall to take his coat off because "I thought he was wired up".

"I said I wanted him to make a statement to my solicitor and he said he would."

He was also asked about prison CCTV footage of him showing McDougall footage of the shooting, saying McDougall *"asked if there was footage of him on the bike".*

Sayers said he showed him the footage because *"it was either upset him and he doesn't make a statement, or show him and get him to tell my solicitor what he had told me".*

Cross-examining Sayers, prosecutor Simon Denison QC asked him about his former debt collecting business, which he admitted was *"unlawful"*. Mr Denison said it was an example of him *"using your reputation as a ruthless criminal"*.

And when asked about his reputation for *"intimidating people"*, Sayers said: *"Reputation is a bit like gossip, people add to it."*

Mr Denison added: *"You say it's always Northumbria Police. It's always them lying, it's never you."*

Sayers was also asked whether *"an attack on your son is an attack on you"* that *"couldn't go unpunished".*

He replied: *"I certainly wouldn't go into the city centre and shoot someone for nothing."*

When Judge Mark Lurcraft QC sent the jury out friends and family were confident that John would be found not guilty of the 'conspiracy' charge. The jury took their time and they were out over the weekend and into the following week. After 6 days they came back at 14:40 on 20th August and John and Mickey were both found not guilty of conspiracy to murder and conspiracy to possess a firearm with intent to endanger life by a majority verdict of 11 to 1.

The Chronicle reported that, *'The pair gave audible sighs of relief in the dock as they were cleared of the offence of conspiracy to murder.'*

John and McDougall were unanimously found guilty of perverting the course of justice over the false confession by McDougall who was unable to provide 'basic' details about the shooting he claimed to have carried out.

Sturman, was acquitted on the charge of assisting an offender by allegedly providing Sayers with CCTV footage of the scuffle at the club and he cheered in the dock before giving a hug to John and Mickey before being released.

Judge Lucraft QC warned the three convicted defendants that they would be looking at custodial sentences as described in the transcripts.

"In your case Michael McDougall, I appreciate you're already serving a life sentence."

"John Henry Sayers, you have been on remand for some time, but you must still expect to receive some custodial sentence."

"Michael Dixon, one of the issues for me is the question of the length of the term you should serve, bearing in mind your previous conviction which occurred at a broadly similar time."

This was another failure for the police and at great expense to the taxpayer. Their statement to the press summed up their disappointment:

"This case was thoroughly investigated by a team of dedicated detectives. The evidence was subjected to careful scrutiny before a decision was taken to charge and it was only right that this evidence was put in front of a jury. We respect the decision the jury has made."

Judge Lurcraft remanded the three men into custody and sentencing took place on Friday 21st September at the Old Bailey. John was jailed for three and a half years; Dixon was jailed for life with a minimum of eight years whilst McDougall was handed 2 years.

The Police's Head of Crime, Detective Chief Superintendent Lisa Orchard, was quoted in the Chronicle:

"Attempted murder is a really difficult charge to prove and obviously the jury didn't think there was enough evidence to prove that charge, but Michael Dixon has been found guilty of possessing a firearm with intent to endanger life. I'm satisfied of the fact that Michael Dixon is the gunman and he's going to be put behind bars."

"Michael Dixon is a dangerous career criminal who showed a complete disregard for the lives of innocent people. This was a drive-by shooting at the heart of Newcastle's night-time economy.
He fired a sawn-off shotgun into a crowded place – we could so easily have been dealing with a fatal incident.

Newcastle is a popular and safe city for both tourists and residents, and thankfully incidents such as these are incredibly rare. We are satisfied that the city is a safer place with Dixon behind bars."

John spent most of his sentence as a Cat A prisoner at HMP Full Sutton in Yorkshire. In November 2018 his step sister Joanne passed away in her sleep and he put in an application to attend the funeral. His application was rejected after a risk assessment was carried out and it was deemed 'too risky' for him to join mourners at West Road Crematorium. Hundreds packed into the church to pay their last respects including Stephen, Michael and their father John Brian.

In December 2018 a month after his 'sister' had been laid to rest the prison authorities decategorized him to Cat B status. This was a step towards freedom. John was finally released on electronic tag in April 2019 and his kids all travelled down to pick him up. Karen Seafield had run a 'Free John Henry Sayers' Facebook page and she wrote the following statement on the page:

"We can now confirm, John Henry will be home today. From John

himself, his family and admin, we would like to thank you all for the support you have shared on a social media level this past 26 months.

Thank you for the cards, letters, emails and messages you have all taken the time to send to John on a personal level, especially during the trial which I know truly did make a difference to him.

His family and friends have waited for this day since February 8 2017 and once again believed that justice will prevail, it did, he's coming home and now hopefully can get on with his life surrounded by his doting family."

Stephen hit out at the police after the trial so I will leave the final word on the case to him:

"We have just recently experienced another abuse of power by Northumbria Police. Me and my brother John Henry Sayers were recently arrested for the Tup Tup shooting. I was given bail which I did not have to attend and my brother was remanded for 20 months for a crime he did not commit.

Northumbria Police charged my brother and placed him in the top court in the country on charges if convicted would have resulted in a life sentence never to be released. The evidence against him was non-existent.

They charged him and ran a case with circumstantial evidence which is a liberty in itself. They tried for a trial with no jury again and fortunately failed. The actions of these people is medieval. I ask the public to pause for a moment and ask a question how many millions has Northumbria police wasted?

Chapter Forty Eight: Stick That In Ya Dockramentary!

Paddy Conroy is a name many of you will know whether you're from Tyneside or not. He appeared on television in 2006 with Donal Macintyre. He was wearing a white vest, making a curry and smoking joints with local 'triads' in his kitchen. He comes from a notorious West End family many of whom I know and get on well with. I have seen it written in some books and articles over the last few years that the Sayers and the Conroys hated each other and were 'at war'…this is simply not true. The war was taking place in one man's head. Paddys.

There is no doubt that Conroy was a handful back in the day. His arrest and subsequent conviction for the kidnap and torture of Billy Collier who had openly boasted that he was going to dig up one of Conroy's relatives' graves and throw the contents through his window, gained him his reputation alongside his violent henchman Davey Glover Jnr. His subsequent escape from a prison van on the felling by pass on the way to court also gave him the title 'Britain's Most Wanted' for a short while but according to Phil Berriman's book 'The Waccy Baccy Boat' things were not quite as they seemed with that escape. I will let him continue the story about a man who he calls 'Newcastle's self proclaimed Godfather…In his own mind.'

'One of my best above-board customers was Delta Taxis. I supplied them with everything to keep their fleet running and growing from their very beginning and knew all of the owners and staff. They supplied taxis and mini buses to the prison service, sometimes to transport 'low risk' prisoners to court, hospital, funerals or between prisons.

My friend John was one of the owners. He said on that particular day, Delta supplied two mini buses, which were booked to go to Newcastle Crown Court. They certainly weren't told that the passengers in one bus were the first division gangsters, Conroy and Glover, who until that day had been transported in high-security prison trucks. Such dangerous passengers were not part of their contract.

Even stranger was the fact that for the first time ever, the civilian drivers were given specific instructions as to the routes each bus had to take. Instead of sticking together, one bus was directed to take the A1. The other, containing the mobsters, was directed onto the A19 and then the bypass towards Newcastle where the ambush was waiting. As if they were expecting to make bail, all of their property and a significant amount of cash was on board with them. Each was cuffed to a female prison officer. Eh? There was no security cage or partition between them and the driver.

Previously, the police wouldn't attempt to arrest either of these men without armed back up. When Conroy was arrested after a car chase, the pursuing bobby was screaming on the radio for an armed response vehicle before attempting to stop him. Now they were being transported in a civilian minibus, like a couple of naughty juvenile delinquents! Alarm bells were ringing. Glover punched the officer and pulled on the handbrake as soon as he saw the two cars at the pre-determined spot on the bypass. A Range Rover and BMW pulled up and out jumped some masked men with nothing more than a couple of baseball bats. Both prisoners were quickly un-cuffed without a struggle and sped off in different cars, along with their cash and personal belongings. The truth about this highly dubious incident was kept from the public for as long as possible.

Without doubt, it was the least dramatic escape in the history of the prison service. When details did come out, there was public outcry. It was blamed on cost-cutting. But anyone who'd been near a court building or used a main road knew fine well that high-security prison vehicles were still in use every day. Let's face it, a town centre police patrol wouldn't transport a drunk to the police station unless safely separated from the driver; there was something very wrong here. For Her Majesty's Prison Service to be involved in the facilitation of such an escape, would need the approval of someone very high up the chain, possibly, even the Home Secretary. Customs have the pull to get someone released, but not by faking an escape.

Something that added to my own suspicion was the fact that no guns were present. Conroy's gang had a reputation for guns and many were found when he was arrested. Just one-gun present, even a replica during the escape, would have been far less obvious and much more effective than waving baseball bats around on a busy road. It simply didn't fit the profile of the gang; it only added fuel to the rumours.

If the Home Secretary or customs had authorised the facilitation of the escape to allow an important registered informant back onto the streets for operational reasons, he would surely insist that minimum force was used. The ruthless Conroy gang trademark was 'gratuitous violence'. Yet just one prison officer got a fat lip. But of course, we're not talking about any old villains! These boys were in the Conroy Gang who, it seemed, were allowed to wreak havoc in Newcastle with impunity. Either the crime squad had them under surveillance for much bigger things, or there are registered informers involved, who despite regulations, are allowed to commit crime in order to gain credibility in the underworld. If any of you out there wonder why some people, including yourself, lead a charmed life; think on'

He finishes the chapter with these words:

'Conroy's intended meteoric rise to the top of the hashish business on the Costa del Sol had resulted in three separate crews and more than six tons of drugs being nicked. Maybe jail was the best place for him.'

I witnessed Conroy's obsession with the Sayers family first hand when I travelled to meet him at his home with Neil Jackson to interview him about his family's alleged run in with the Krays at Newcastle station. Another figment of his imagination.

We arrived on time and were told to meet him at his allotment at the back of his house. We were met by his close friend Bullock at the locked gates and walked down a dirt path to a little shed. A cockerel crowed as Conroy appeared from behind the door saying 'Welcome to my war bunker.' Neil and I looked at each other and stepped into the lion's den. Inside it was dusty with a dirty table in the centre and three wooden chairs. 'Get the kettle on Bull, 'Conroy said as the cockerel crowed again before strutting in to join us.

It wasn't my first meeting with 'Conroy'. We had both attended the wedding of crime writer Bernard O'Mahoney in Alnwick. Conroy was best man and was staring at me throughout the proceedings. At the reception I had my back to the top table. I felt something hit the back of my head. And again. I turned around to see 'Conroy' laughing. He had thrown a couple of peanuts. I chose to ignore him. We never spoke.

As Neil set up the camera Conroy started smiling at me, trying to suss me out. I smiled back and started to look through my notes. Neil hit record and Conroy started talking about the 'Sayers'. I explained that I wasn't here for that but he insisted on talking about 'them' and making a few derogatory comments whilst moving the mugs of hot stewed tea around to make his points. I decided to let him get it all off his chest before I commenced the interview proper. The interview, which can be seen in full on my YouTube channel, wasn't very informative, and didn't help us get to the bottom of why 'the Krays' were visiting Newcastle. We were there an hour or so. We posed for a couple of photos and then left.

Conroy was quick to jump onto social media in the noughties and at one point had no less than four individual Facebook accounts. With both Stephen and John in prison he took to all of his accounts day after day and wrote many slanderous comments about the Sayers family which were collected and stored by the Sayers solicitor for a 'rainy day'.

When Stephen was released from prison, he too joined Facebook and on more than one occasion challenged Conroy to a 'fight for charity.' Stu Armstrong and Joseph Ramsey offered to stage and promote the fight and Frankie Fraser's son David rang Conroy as an intermediary to offer him a fair fight. Conroy was livid and went onto Facebook to say that he would 'Fight Steve Wraith For Charity,' as he believed I was an agent for 'MI5' and was trying to set him up. The post was removed a few hours later.

That 'rainy day' appeared On February 17th, 2016 when a Facebook post by Stephen Sayers annoyed Conroy so much that he reported him to the police and made a five page statement which you can find in this book. I will let an article from 'Vice Website' explain:

'Stephen Sayers accused Conroy of being a paedophile on a post on Facebook after hearing from a 'reputable source' that Conroy's ex-wife had seen an image of naked girl appear on his computer before telling her husband, "She does not look over 16, Paddy." Conroy said he deleted the picture immediately and that it was unwanted spam. He has since taken a lie detector test about this, the result of which backed up his version of events.

That Conroy chose to go to the police about this is mildly surprising, given that during the Macintyre documentary (filmed a few years earlier) he went on an explosive rant in which he accused Sayers of "coppering every cunt" (grassing), said in a manner that implied it was a terrible thing to do. But I suppose being accused of noncery must be enough to justify a bit of coppering?

Despite Sayers originally being accused of sending a barrage of abusive posts, on the day of the court case – the 5th of October – charges were changed so they only related to a single malicious message. The post in question described Conroy as a "jealous grass" who "will shag ya kids give'm [sic] half the chance". The post also claimed that he had "blamed his innocent son for the hard core [sic] child porn" and included the hash-tag #GetThePeadofilesOffFaceBook

Prosecuting on behalf of Conroy, Brian Payne began by outlining the longstanding history of animosity between the Sayers and Conroy families. He said there had been "long running and bitter disputes played out on numerous platforms, and done over a number of years, now being played out on Facebook". He pointed out that Conroy had never been arrested for any offences related to paedophilia or child porn, and mentioned that, now that both Sayers and Conroy are "in middling years", their feud had migrated from the streets to the internet.

Sayers' solicitor claimed that he had merely been responding in kind to similar abuse from Conroy. "The advent of social media has been like manna from heaven for Mr Conroy, and it continues to this day," he said. "He has accused [the Sayers family] of murder, sexual offences and a whole host of gangland activities that are, of course, unfounded and without merit. The more concerning allegation from Mr Conroy, for which there may well have been serious consequences, is that Mr Sayers is an informant for the police, the National Crime Agency and, ridiculously, MI5." He argued that claiming Sayers is a police informant could have placed him at risk of serious violence, and added that "Mr Conroy accusing Mr Sayers of posting offensive material is like someone living in a glass house and throwing a boulder".

Sayers entered a guilty plea for posting an offensive message online, but maintained he had believed his accusations against Conroy to be true. He was ordered to pay a £110 fine, £20 victim surcharge and £350 in court costs. "I personally think this is a waste of taxpayers' money," Sayers said after the case.'

After the court case Conroy disappeared from Facebook and disappeared from Newcastle. He had been furious that Stephen had pleaded guilty and that he had not been able to have his say in court in front of his lone supporter Bullock. The following day he sent Bullock to Stephen's Uncle Alberts fruit and veg pitch on Northumberland Street with a hand written note begging for an 'end to the war'. There was no war to end.

Stephen coined a new phrase from the trial 'Doing a Conroy,' to describe someone turning Queens Evidence. He began using the term on numerous interviews and documentaries in the hope that it would stick. It did.

Word had it that he had set up in a caravan on the roadside near Hexham and was selling 'award winning pies'.

As well as falling out with Stephen he had fallen foul of former friend Bernard O'Mahoney who released a video on YouTube in 2018 of him phoning the police to report him. Hardly the behaviour of an elite criminal.

I will leave the final word on Conroy to Phil Berriman again:

'In Newcastle, he was just a bully with a big stick; far more successful organisations and gangs on Tyneside weren't scared of him and his arch enemies just laughed at him.'

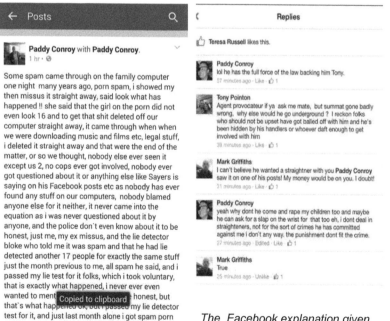

The Facebook explanation given by Conroy

MG4D

Written Charge(s)	URN	10U0/00692/16
Attendance Required	Custody Number	16/006830
	DOB	12/08/1965
	Arrest Summons	16/10EE/01/6830B

STEPHEN MAURICE SAYERS

POSTAL REQUISITION

You are charged with the offence(s) below

On WEDNESDAY 03 AUGUST 2016   at 1000

you must appear at the courthouse at
NEWCASTLE UPON TYNE Magistrates Court
MARKET STREET (EAST) NEWCASTLE UPON TYNE NE991AU
to answer the charge(s).

If you do not attend, the court may issue a warrant for your arrest. If a warrant is issued for your arrest, you may be held in custody until you are brought before the court.

Police Bail
If you are on police bail for the offence(s) you do not have to return to the police station and your police bail has been cancelled.

Advice and help
If you need advice about what to do you should get help from a solicitor or advice agency at once. If you cannot afford a solicitor you may be able to get free advice about your plea, or how to apply to the court for a representation order so that you can have a solicitor at the hearing. Do not wait until you first come to court. If you need any general advice about the court, contact the court office at NEWCASTLE UPON TYNE
01912327326

Page 1 of 3

MG4D

CHARGE (S)

Offence Sequence No. 001 H.O. Class 196/07 MCS Code 58FD CCCJS Code CA03005
ON 17TH FEBRUARY 2016 AT NEWCASTLE SENT BY MEANS OF A PUBLIC ELECTRONIC COMMUNICATIONS
NETWORK MATTER, NAMELY ABUSIVE FACEBOOK MESSAGES, THAT WAS GROSSLY OFFENSIVE OR OF AN
INDECENT, OBSCENE OR MENACING CHARACTER
CONTRARY TO SECTION 127(1)(A) AND (3) OF THE COMMUNICATIONS ACT 2003

Above: The charge sheet

Dear Stephen

Re: Allegation of Malicious Communication

We write further to the hearing at Newcastle Magistrates Court on the 5th October 2016, when you were represented by Mr Rutter of Counsel.

At Court, we advised you that because you had stated you had sent the message, the test was therefore whether a person of reasonable firmness would find the message offensive. You took the sensible advice and decided to plead guilty.

Your case was called into Court and you duly entered a guilty plea. The Prosecution outlined the facts of the case and Mr Rutter was then able to put forward your mitigation with the following facts:

1. You are not a police informant.
2. You suffered years of provocation from Mr Conroy's malicious allegations of rape, murder and other criminal misdemeanours.
3. Mr Conroy had admitted on his own Facebook page that child pornography was on his computer but it appeared as spam. This occurred 15 times and he blamed Northumbria Police or NSIS.

The Magistrates accepted your mitigation and you received a fine of £110, £20 victim surcharge and £350 in costs. This made a total amount of £480 and is to be paid at the rate of £10 per week.

We can also confirm that Northumbria Police have asked you to press charges against Mr Conroy, however, you have declined as you do not want to be put in the same position as him, namely a police informant.

We advise you not to appeal this sentence, however, if you do wish to appeal, you should contact us as a matter of urgency as any appeal must be lodged within 21 days.

Richard Howard Solicitors is a trading name of Richard Howard Ltd.
Richard Howard Ltd is a Limited Company registered in England & Wales (Registration No. 08887273)
VAT Registration No. 598 4596 53

Members of Newcastle upon Tyne Court Duty Solicitor Schemes
Holders of Legal Aid Agency General Criminal Contract
Authorised and Regulated by the Solicitors Regulation Authority

Above: The final outcome in the case with Paddy Conroy.

Overleaf is the five page statement Paddy made, reproduced in full.

RESTRICTED (when complete)

MG11

WITNESS STATEMENT

CJ Act 1967, s.9; MC Act 1980, ss.5A(3) (a) and 5B; Criminal Procedure Rules 2005, Rule 27.1

Statement of: Patrick James Conroy

URN ☐ ☐ ☐ ☐

Age if under 18: ... *18 ...... (if over 18 insert 'over 18')   Occupation: ...unemployed...

This statement (consisting of 5 page(s) each signed by me) is true to the best of my knowledge and belief and I make it knowing that, if it is tendered in evidence, I shall be liable to prosecution if I have wilfully stated in it, anything which I know to be false, or do not believe to be true.

Signature: *PJ Conroy*   Date 17/02/16

Tick if witness evidence is visually recorded ☐   (supply witness details on rear)

I am the above named person and I reside at an address known to the Police.

For years now I have had problems with a local newspaper known as the Sankes. I do not want to talk about the problems with the family in the past, however there has been some incidents over recent weeks which I have to comment on.

I have had numerous Facebook accounts over the years, however some of them have now been closed down. I am currently using 2 accounts both under the name "Paddy Conroy". The 2 accounts I have are the account I use to talk about problems I have had with the Sankes family and other problems I have had with Northumbria Police.

I had an account under my name which was closed down by Facebook approximately 3 weeks ago. This account was opened under the following email address conroy.paddy@yahoo.co.uk. Attached to this account I had on Arts page which I used to promote drawings I had done myself.

Around 5 months ago there were some offensive

Signature: *PJ Conroy*   Signature witnessed by: ....

2006/07(1)

RESTRICTED (when complete)

RESTRICTED (when complete)

MG11(CONT)

Page No. 3 of 5

Continuation of Statement of: Patrick James Conlon

comments placed on the wall of this page. These
comments were written on this page from the
profile of a male I know to be STEPHEN
SAMMES. SAMMES is currently receiving a lot of
publicity in relation to a book he has released.
SAMMES has wrote about me in this book which has
been published.
On this occasion SAMMES placed around 20
messages on my page which were all offensive.
These messages stated that I was a
"PAEDOPHILE" and stated that I had been arrested
for these types of offences. I only read a few
of these messages before deleting them all so that
nobody else could read the lies he had written. I
immediately blocked SAMMES from this page. This
profile has been closed now as I mentioned
earlier.
SAMMES has a few FACEBOOK ACCOUNTS which he is
currently using. He has "STEPHEN SAMMES" which
shows him as living on ELSWICK ROAD and having
attended SAINT MARY'S COMPREHENSIVE. He also has
the "STEPHEN SAMMES" GROUP PAGE along with the
"THE SAMMES GROUP". SAMMES uses these groups to
promote his book and to comment on various things.
Over recent months I have been sent
numerous attachments from friends showing me

Signature: P J Conlon Signature witnessed by: ....

2006/07(1)

RESTRICTED (when complete)

RESTRICTED (when complete)

MG11(CONT)

Continuation of Statement of: Patrick James Coveney

comments that James has made about me.
These comments have been offensive and have even
branded me as a PAEDOPHILE. The comments have
then led to people commenting on this, who have
thinks towards me have been made. The people
have been saying things like " HE WANTS HIS
THROAT SLIT" and " HE SHOULD GET SHOT IN THE
HEAD." which are clearly directed at me.
James has continually placed comments like this
on his profile which will lead to offensive things
being said about me. All these comments are not
true and they are making people think badly
of me. I do not go onto James profile and
look at the comments as they are too offensive.
He has continued to be post these comments
branding me a PAEDOPHILE throughout this time.
On approximately 2nd FEBRUARY 2016 I received a
message from a friend who had seen this on
James FACEBOOK PAGE. This comment said " Ed
since 26 YEARS we have had to listen the ow the
rambelings scandal of anny my jealous goss, will
shut up kids give'm half the chance sadben
this man was arrested Ed Thousands of hard core
graphic images of child pornography on his
personal comp with my image of 2 years".
This comment had been liked by four

Signature: PS [signature]   Signature witnessed by: ....

2006/07(1)

RESTRICTED (when complete)

RESTRICTED (when complete)

MG11(CONT)

Continuation of Statement of: Patrick James Conway

5000 people or was read by lots of others.
This comment and all of the others are not true
and I find them very offensive.
I believe that Sambes is putting these comments
on but he is going unshiydshns between me
and his family.
I am very upset about the comments and I
feel like killing him. He has caused me lots
of trouble between me and my family.
I am concerned about some of the threats that
have been made. People get done over for
false allegations like this. I am concerned as
Sambes does have a lot of influence with a
lot of people.
Sambes does not have the right to say these
things about me.
I am willing to abide by the decision of
Northumbria Police is whatever in this matter.

VICTIM PERSONAL STATEMENT -
This incident has caused me a lot of problems
with my family due to the false allegations. I
have had to stop all of my childrens charity
work in the area. I have been distressed as a
result of his comments. I would like this
statement read out in my behalf at court.
I have told the Police he you can check.

Signature: P S Conway   Signature witnessed by:

2006/07(1)

RESTRICTED (when complete)

RESTRICTED (when complete)

MG11(CONT)

Continuation of Statement of: Patrick James Graham

if I have been arrested for these types of thing. This will prove that I have not ever been questioned for any sexual offence PC

Signature: PS Conroy

Signature witnessed by:

2006/07(1)

RESTRICTED (when complete)

Chapter Forty Nine: A Happy Ending?

Conroy's appearance on 'Macintyre's Underworld' and his unwarranted cyber abuse and slander of the Sayers family was the catalyst for Stephen Sayers to finally write his book. I mentioned earlier that I had asked the question but not been given any encouragement. In spring 2015 we met at his close friend's house Angie Harts with Fish Tams. He asked me to talk through how the book would work. I explained that I would carry out a series of interviews with him and then type up the transcripts and that I would work with my writing partner at the time to create the book. He said that he would prefer to go through the interview process with his daughter Rebecca if that was ok with me and that I could then shape the book from her notes. We shook hands on the deal and I left.

The whole process took time to formulate but we got there in the end. Stephen had to face a lot of demons but found the whole process very therapeutic. We launched the book to a packed house at the Tyneside Irish Centre in Newcastle on St Andrews Street where the Sayers used to have a 'pitch' selling fruit and veg, very apt. The Evening Chronicle serialised the book and it quickly became the best seller over Christmas.

As the first reviews came in, we were blown away with how well it was received. The public loved the emotion and humour and were only too happy to 'let the bad boys into their lives.' A substantial donation was made to two charities from the profits of the book to 'St Oswalds' and 'Cash For Kids,' at Stephen's insistence and we handed over cheques to their representatives in the new year.

Stephen was not media trained, in fact quite the opposite. You only need to read his countless depositions to see he is used to saying 'no comment,' but he took to publicising the book on radio and television like a duck to water. His interview with local legend Alan Robson on 'Nightowls' was excellent.

With the success of the book we enlisted the help of Neil Jackson at 'Media Arts' to film a documentary. I scripted it and presented it and it was launched a year on from the book at the same venue on St Andrews Street. Again, sales went through the roof. The Sayers had become a brand in Newcastle and now we needed to spread the word further afield.

With the success of the book and documentary I was approached by another local author Dave McCaffrey who was keen on working with Stephen on a fictional crime book. So, I got the two of them together and they hit it off. Stephen came up with the characters and storyline and David did the rest. 'By Any Means Necessary' was released in December 2016 and was a big success.

Stephen was delighted with the success of the books and documentary and was keen on taking the next step.....a film. I was too but it's not an easy task pulling a film together. You need a good script first of all, then a director, actors, and most importantly money and lots of it. Out of the blue in

2019 Stephen called me to say that he had a guy that he wanted me to meet and that he was a double Bafta winner and he wanted to make our film.

We met up with Edinburgh based writer and director Garry Fraser at 'Portifinos' in Newcastle and over a bottle of red and discussed the way forward. He had a great CV winning 'Baftas' for his documentary 'Everybody's Child' and for 'Trainspotting 2', and had just had his gritty drama 'The Grey Area' commissioned for the 'BBC' and he wanted his next project to be 'The Sayers.' We got on like a house on fire and over the next 12 months he ran workshops and casting sessions to cast the film and started to develop the script.

As an actor myself I wanted to go through the process and put myself forward for a role in the film and Garry was happy for me to do just that. I was blown away when I got down to the last twenty-five from two hundred and the following week when he asked me if I would accept the role as Stephen, I was speechless but had enough words left in me to say yes! Melly Barnes was cast as Michael, Alfie Dobson John Henry, Tony Sayers as John Brian and Jayne Mackenzie as Yvonne. There were also roles for Gary Firby as Viv Graham, Paul Venis as Lee Duffy and a cameo for Brian Cockerill playing himself. At the time of writing the first draft of the script is almost ready and a budget being drawn up for investors so watch this space.

In July 2020 Albert Sayers finally hung up his apron and the family pitch on Northumberland Street was no more. I spent a lot of time with Albert over his last 7 years on the pitch and having lunch with him at 'Paradiso' and 'Portifinos,' a few times each week. He was a mine of information and would always offer help and advice on the various 'Sayers' related projects and was a good man to run ideas past with regards to my other business activities including the pro-boxing game.

In 2018 I sat down with him and the Sayers cousins Eddie Lennie and Tony Sayers to discuss putting together a book about the origins of the family. After a lot of hard work, research and effort 'A Breed Apart' was released in 2019 by Eddie and Tony to great acclaim. Over 120 years of Sayers history which Eddie described rather aptly 'Catherine Cookson meets Goodfellas.' The launch was once again at the 'Tyneside Irish Centre' and the first print run sold out in no time.

As for the case against Kingsley Hyland that is still ongoing with an end game finally in sight. John Henry Sayers is working hard and is spending quality time with his family. Michael is fit and well and Stephen is contemplating a life abroad in the sun with his partner and his dogs Ronnie and Reggie. So, is this a crime book with a happy ending? I guess we will all just have to wait and see....